Mometrix
TEST PREPARATION

I0883892

# TerraNova® NEXT

## Grade 8 Mathematics Test Prep Guide

Written and edited by the Mometrix Test Preparation Team
Printed in the United States of America

# TABLE OF CONTENTS

# Introduction

**Thank you for purchasing this resource**! You have made the choice to prepare yourself for a test that could have a huge impact on your future, and this guide is designed to help you be fully ready for test day. Obviously, it's important to have a solid understanding of the test material, but you also need to be prepared for the unique environment and stressors of the test, so that you can perform to the best of your abilities.

For this purpose, the first section that appears in this guide is the **Success Strategies**. We've devoted countless hours to meticulously researching what works and what doesn't, and we've boiled down our findings to the most impactful steps you can take to improve your performance on the test. We start at the beginning with study planning and move through the preparation process, all the way to the testing strategies that will help you get the most out of what you know when you're finally sitting in front of the test.

We recommend that you start preparing for your test as far in advance as possible. However, if you've bought this guide as a last-minute study resource and only have a few days before your test, we recommend that you skip over the first two Success Strategies since they address a long-term study plan.

If you struggle with **test anxiety**, we strongly encourage you to check out our recommendations for how you can overcome it. Test anxiety is a formidable foe, but it can be beaten, and we want to make sure you have the tools you need to defeat it.

# Strategy #1 – Plan Big, Study Small

There's a lot riding on your performance. If you want to ace this test, you're going to need to keep your skills sharp and the material fresh in your mind. You need a plan that lets you review everything you need to know while still fitting in your schedule. We'll break this strategy down into three categories.

## Information Organization

Start with the information you already have: the official test outline. From this, you can make a complete list of all the concepts you need to cover before the test. Organize these concepts into groups that can be studied together, and create a list of any related vocabulary you need to learn so you can brush up on any difficult terms. You'll want to keep this vocabulary list handy once you actually start studying since you may need to add to it along the way.

## Time Management

Once you have your set of study concepts, decide how to spread them out over the time you have left before the test. Break your study plan into small, clear goals so you have a manageable task for each day and know exactly what you're doing. Then just focus on one small step at a time. When you manage your time this way, you don't need to spend hours at a time studying. Studying a small block of content for a short period each day helps you retain information better and avoid stressing over how much you have left to do. You can relax knowing that you have a plan to cover everything in time. In order for this strategy to be effective though, you have to start studying early and stick to your schedule. Avoid the exhaustion and futility that comes from last-minute cramming!

## Study Environment

The environment you study in has a big impact on your learning. Studying in a coffee shop, while probably more enjoyable, is not likely to be as fruitful as studying in a quiet room. It's important to keep distractions to a minimum. You're only planning to study for a short block of time, so make the most of it. Don't pause to check your phone or get up to find a snack. It's also important to **avoid multitasking**. Research has consistently shown that multitasking will make your studying dramatically less effective. Your study area should also be comfortable and well-lit so you don't have the distraction of straining your eyes or sitting on an uncomfortable chair.

The time of day you study is also important. You want to be rested and alert. Don't wait until just before bedtime. Study when you'll be most likely to comprehend and remember. Even better, if you know what time of day your test will be, set that time aside for study. That way your brain will be used to working on that subject at that specific time and you'll have a better chance of recalling information.

Finally, it can be helpful to team up with others who are studying for the same test. Your actual studying should be done in as isolated an environment as possible, but the work of organizing the information and setting up the study plan can be divided up. In between study sessions, you can discuss with your teammates the concepts that you're all studying and quiz each other on the details. Just be sure that your teammates are as serious about the test as you are. If you find that your study time is being replaced with social time, you might need to find a new team.

# Strategy #2 – Make Your Studying Count

You're devoting a lot of time and effort to preparing for this test, so you want to be absolutely certain it will pay off. This means doing more than just reading the content and hoping you can remember it on test day. It's important to make every minute of study count. There are two main areas you can focus on to make your studying count.

## Retention

It doesn't matter how much time you study if you can't remember the material. You need to make sure you are retaining the concepts. To check your retention of the information you're learning, try recalling it at later times with minimal prompting. Try carrying around flashcards and glance at one or two from time to time or ask a friend who's also studying for the test to quiz you.

To enhance your retention, look for ways to put the information into practice so that you can apply it rather than simply recalling it. If you're using the information in practical ways, it will be much easier to remember. Similarly, it helps to solidify a concept in your mind if you're not only reading it to yourself but also explaining it to someone else. Ask a friend to let you teach them about a concept you're a little shaky on (or speak aloud to an imaginary audience if necessary). As you try to summarize, define, give examples, and answer your friend's questions, you'll understand the concepts better and they will stay with you longer. Finally, step back for a big picture view and ask yourself how each piece of information fits with the whole subject. When you link the different concepts together and see them working together as a whole, it's easier to remember the individual components.

Finally, practice showing your work on any multi-step problems, even if you're just studying. Writing out each step you take to solve a problem will help solidify the process in your mind, and you'll be more likely to remember it during the test.

## Modality

*Modality* simply refers to the means or method by which you study. Choosing a study modality that fits your own individual learning style is crucial. No two people learn best in exactly the same way, so it's important to know your strengths and use them to your advantage.

For example, if you learn best by visualization, focus on visualizing a concept in your mind and draw an image or a diagram. Try color-coding your notes, illustrating them, or creating symbols that will trigger your mind to recall a learned concept. If you learn best by hearing or discussing information, find a study partner who learns the same way or read aloud to yourself. Think about how to put the information in your own words. Imagine that you are giving a lecture on the topic and record yourself so you can listen to it later.

For any learning style, flashcards can be helpful. Organize the information so you can take advantage of spare moments to review. Underline key words or phrases. Use different colors for different categories. Mnemonic devices (such as creating a short list in which every item starts with the same letter) can also help with retention. Find what works best for you and use it to store the information in your mind most effectively and easily.

# Strategy #3 – Practice the Right Way

Your success on test day depends not only on how many hours you put into preparing, but also on whether you prepared the right way. It's good to check along the way to see if your studying is paying off. One of the most effective ways to do this is by taking practice tests to evaluate your progress. Practice tests are useful because they show exactly where you need to improve. Every time you take a practice test, pay special attention to these three groups of questions:

- The questions you got wrong
- The questions you had to guess on, even if you guessed right
- The questions you found difficult or slow to work through

This will show you exactly what your weak areas are, and where you need to devote more study time. Ask yourself why each of these questions gave you trouble. Was it because you didn't understand the material? Was it because you didn't remember the vocabulary? Do you need more repetitions on this type of question to build speed and confidence? Dig into those questions and figure out how you can strengthen your weak areas as you go back to review the material.

Additionally, many practice tests have a section explaining the answer choices. It can be tempting to read the explanation and think that you now have a good understanding of the concept. However, an explanation likely only covers part of the question's broader context. Even if the explanation makes perfect sense, **go back and investigate** every concept related to the question until you're positive you have a thorough understanding.

As you go along, keep in mind that the practice test is just that: practice. Memorizing these questions and answers will not be very helpful on the actual test because it is unlikely to have any of the same exact questions. If you only know the right answers to the sample questions, you won't be prepared for the real thing. **Study the concepts** until you understand them fully, and then you'll be able to answer any question that shows up on the test.

It's important to wait on the practice tests until you're ready. If you take a test on your first day of study, you may be overwhelmed by the amount of material covered and how much you need to learn. Work up to it gradually.

On test day, you'll need to be prepared for answering questions, managing your time, and using the test-taking strategies you've learned. It's a lot to balance, like a mental marathon that will have a big impact on your future. Like training for a marathon, you'll need to start slowly and work your way up. When test day arrives, you'll be ready.

Start with the strategies you've read in the first two Success Strategies—plan your course and study in the way that works best for you. If you have time, consider using multiple study resources to get different approaches to the same concepts. It can be helpful to see difficult concepts from more than one angle. Then find a good source for practice tests. Many times, the test website will suggest potential study resources or provide sample tests.

## Practice Test Strategy

If you're able to find at least three practice tests, we recommend this strategy:

### Untimed and Open-Book Practice

Take the first test with no time constraints and with your notes and study guide handy. Take your time and focus on applying the strategies you've learned.

### Timed and Open-Book Practice

Take the second practice test open-book as well, but set a timer and practice pacing yourself to finish in time.

### Timed and Closed-Book Practice

Take any other practice tests as if it were test day. Set a timer and put away your study materials. Sit at a table or desk in a quiet room, imagine yourself at the testing center, and answer questions as quickly and accurately as possible.

Keep repeating timed and closed-book tests on a regular basis until you run out of practice tests or it's time for the actual test. Your mind will be ready for the schedule and stress of test day, and you'll be able to focus on recalling the material you've learned.

# Strategy #4 – Pace Yourself

Once you're fully prepared for the material on the test, your biggest challenge on test day will be managing your time. Just knowing that the clock is ticking can make you panic even if you have plenty of time left. Work on pacing yourself so you can build confidence against the time constraints of the exam. Pacing is a difficult skill to master, especially in a high-pressure environment, so **practice is vital**.

Set time expectations for your pace based on how much time is available. For example, if a section has 60 questions and the time limit is 30 minutes, you know you have to average 30 seconds or less per question in order to answer them all. Although 30 seconds is the hard limit, set 25 seconds per question as your goal, so you reserve extra time to spend on harder questions. When you budget extra time for the harder questions, you no longer have any reason to stress when those questions take longer to answer.

Don't let this time expectation distract you from working through the test at a calm, steady pace, but keep it in mind so you don't spend too much time on any one question. Recognize that taking extra time on one question you don't understand may keep you from answering two that you do understand later in the test. If your time limit for a question is up and you're still not sure of the answer, mark it and move on, and come back to it later if the time and the test format allow. If the testing format doesn't allow you to return to earlier questions, just make an educated guess; then put it out of your mind and move on.

On the easier questions, be careful not to rush. It may seem wise to hurry through them so you have more time for the challenging ones, but it's not worth missing one if you know the concept and just didn't take the time to read the question fully. Work efficiently but make sure you understand the question and have looked at all of the answer choices, since more than one may seem right at first.

Even if you're paying attention to the time, you may find yourself a little behind at some point. You should speed up to get back on track, but do so wisely. Don't panic; just take a few seconds less on each question until you're caught up. Don't guess without thinking, but do look through the answer choices and eliminate any you know are wrong. If you can get down to two choices, it is often worthwhile to guess from those. Once you've chosen an answer, move on and don't dwell on any that you skipped or had to hurry through. If a question was taking too long, chances are it was one of the harder ones, so you weren't as likely to get it right anyway.

On the other hand, if you find yourself getting ahead of schedule, it may be beneficial to slow down a little. The more quickly you work, the more likely you are to make a careless mistake that will affect your score. You've budgeted time for each question, so don't be afraid to spend that time. Practice an efficient but careful pace to get the most out of the time you have.

# Test-Taking Strategies

This section contains a list of test-taking strategies that you may find helpful as you work through the test. By taking what you know and applying logical thought, you can maximize your chances of answering any question correctly!

It is very important to realize that every question is different and every person is different: no single strategy will work on every question, and no single strategy will work for every person. That's why we've included all of them here, so you can try them out and determine which ones work best for different types of questions and which ones work best for you.

## Question Strategies

### ✓ Read Carefully

Read the question and the answer choices carefully. Don't miss the question because you misread the terms. You have plenty of time to read each question thoroughly and make sure you understand what is being asked. Yet a happy medium must be attained, so don't waste too much time. You must read carefully and efficiently.

### ✓ Contextual Clues

Look for contextual clues. If the question includes a word you are not familiar with, look at the immediate context for some indication of what the word might mean. Contextual clues can often give you all the information you need to decipher the meaning of an unfamiliar word. Even if you can't determine the meaning, you may be able to narrow down the possibilities enough to make a solid guess at the answer to the question.

### ✓ Prefixes

If you're having trouble with a word in the question or answer choices, try dissecting it. Take advantage of every clue that the word might include. Prefixes can be a huge help. Usually, they allow you to determine a basic meaning. *Pre-* means before, *post-* means after, *pro-* is positive, *de-* is negative. From prefixes, you can get an idea of the general meaning of the word and try to put it into context.

### ✓ Hedge Words

Watch out for critical hedge words, such as *likely, may, can, often, almost, mostly, usually, generally, rarely,* and *sometimes*. Question writers insert these hedge phrases to cover every possibility. Often an answer choice will be wrong simply because it leaves no room for exception. Be on guard for answer choices that have definitive words such as *exactly* and *always*.

### ✓ Switchback Words

Stay alert for *switchbacks*. These are the words and phrases frequently used to alert you to shifts in thought. The most common switchback words are *but, although,* and *however*. Others include *nevertheless, on the other hand, even though, while, in spite of, despite,* and *regardless of*. Switchback words are important to catch because they can change the direction of the question or an answer choice.

### ✓ FACE VALUE

When in doubt, use common sense. Accept the situation in the problem at face value. Don't read too much into it. These problems will not require you to make wild assumptions. If you have to go beyond creativity and warp time or space in order to have an answer choice fit the question, then you should move on and consider the other answer choices. These are normal problems rooted in reality. The applicable relationship or explanation may not be readily apparent, but it is there for you to figure out. Use your common sense to interpret anything that isn't clear.

## Answer Choice Strategies

### ✓ ANSWER SELECTION

The most thorough way to pick an answer choice is to identify and eliminate wrong answers until only one is left, then confirm it is the correct answer. Sometimes an answer choice may immediately seem right, but be careful. The test writers will usually put more than one reasonable answer choice on each question, so take a second to read all of them and make sure that the other choices are not equally obvious. As long as you have time left, it is better to read every answer choice than to pick the first one that looks right without checking the others.

### ✓ ANSWER CHOICE FAMILIES

An answer choice family consists of two (in rare cases, three) answer choices that are very similar in construction and cannot all be true at the same time. If you see two answer choices that are direct opposites or parallels, one of them is usually the correct answer. For instance, if one answer choice says that quantity *x* increases and another either says that quantity *x* decreases (opposite) or says that quantity *y* increases (parallel), then those answer choices would fall into the same family. An answer choice that doesn't match the construction of the answer choice family is more likely to be incorrect. Most questions will not have answer choice families, but when they do appear, you should be prepared to recognize them.

### ✓ ELIMINATE ANSWERS

Eliminate answer choices as soon as you realize they are wrong, but make sure you consider all possibilities. If you are eliminating answer choices and realize that the last one you are left with is also wrong, don't panic. Start over and consider each choice again. There may be something you missed the first time that you will realize on the second pass.

### ✓ AVOID FACT TRAPS

Don't be distracted by an answer choice that is factually true but doesn't answer the question. You are looking for the choice that answers the question. Stay focused on what the question is asking for so you don't accidentally pick an answer that is true but incorrect. Always go back to the question and make sure the answer choice you've selected actually answers the question and is not merely a true statement.

### ✓ EXTREME STATEMENTS

In general, you should avoid answers that put forth extreme actions as standard practice or proclaim controversial ideas as established fact. An answer choice that states the "process should be used in certain situations, if..." is much more likely to be correct than one that states the "process should be discontinued completely." The first is a calm rational statement and doesn't even make a definitive, uncompromising stance, using a hedge word *if* to provide wiggle room, whereas the second choice is far more extreme.

### ⊘ BENCHMARK

As you read through the answer choices and you come across one that seems to answer the question well, mentally select that answer choice. This is not your final answer, but it's the one that will help you evaluate the other answer choices. The one that you selected is your benchmark or standard for judging each of the other answer choices. Every other answer choice must be compared to your benchmark. That choice is correct until proven otherwise by another answer choice beating it. If you find a better answer, then that one becomes your new benchmark. Once you've decided that no other choice answers the question as well as your benchmark, you have your final answer.

### ⊘ PREDICT THE ANSWER

Before you even start looking at the answer choices, it is often best to try to predict the answer. When you come up with the answer on your own, it is easier to avoid distractions and traps because you will know exactly what to look for. The right answer choice is unlikely to be word-for-word what you came up with, but it should be a close match. Even if you are confident that you have the right answer, you should still take the time to read each option before moving on.

## General Strategies

### ⊘ TOUGH QUESTIONS

If you are stumped on a problem or it appears too hard or too difficult, don't waste time. Move on! Remember though, if you can quickly check for obviously incorrect answer choices, your chances of guessing correctly are greatly improved. Before you completely give up, at least try to knock out a couple of possible answers. Eliminate what you can and then guess at the remaining answer choices before moving on.

### ⊘ CHECK YOUR WORK

Since you will probably not know every term listed and the answer to every question, it is important that you get credit for the ones that you do know. Don't miss any questions through careless mistakes. If at all possible, try to take a second to look back over your answer selection and make sure you've selected the correct answer choice and haven't made a costly careless mistake (such as marking an answer choice that you didn't mean to mark). This quick double check should more than pay for itself in caught mistakes for the time it costs.

### ⊘ PACE YOURSELF

It's easy to be overwhelmed when you're looking at a page full of questions; your mind is confused and full of random thoughts, and the clock is ticking down faster than you would like. Calm down and maintain the pace that you have set for yourself. Especially as you get down to the last few minutes of the test, don't let the small numbers on the clock make you panic. As long as you are on track by monitoring your pace, you are guaranteed to have time for each question.

### ⊘ DON'T RUSH

It is very easy to make errors when you are in a hurry. Maintaining a fast pace in answering questions is pointless if it makes you miss questions that you would have gotten right otherwise. Test writers like to include distracting information and wrong answers that seem right. Taking a little extra time to avoid careless mistakes can make all the difference in your test score. Find a pace that allows you to be confident in the answers that you select.

### ✅ KEEP MOVING

Panicking will not help you pass the test, so do your best to stay calm and keep moving. Taking deep breaths and going through the answer elimination steps you practiced can help to break through a stress barrier and keep your pace.

## Final Notes

The combination of a solid foundation of content knowledge and the confidence that comes from practicing your plan for applying that knowledge is the key to maximizing your performance on test day. As your foundation of content knowledge is built up and strengthened, you'll find that the strategies included in this chapter become more and more effective in helping you quickly sift through the distractions and traps of the test to isolate the correct answer.

Now that you're preparing to move forward into the test content chapters of this book, be sure to keep your goal in mind. As you read, think about how you will be able to apply this information on the test. If you've already seen sample questions for the test and you have an idea of the question format and style, try to come up with questions of your own that you can answer based on what you're reading. This will give you valuable practice applying your knowledge in the same ways you can expect to on test day.

**Good luck and good studying!**

# The Number System

## Relationships Between Real Numbers

**Sets** refer to a collection of elements. When some elements of a set are contained in another set, the second set is referred to as a **subset**. For example, 4 is a natural number, and natural numbers are a subset of whole numbers. This means that 4 can be considered a natural number and a whole number. Visual representations such as **Venn diagrams** can be helpful when analyzing sets and subsets. Venn diagrams show the relationship between a collection of elements using overlaps and intersections. Consider the Venn diagram below.

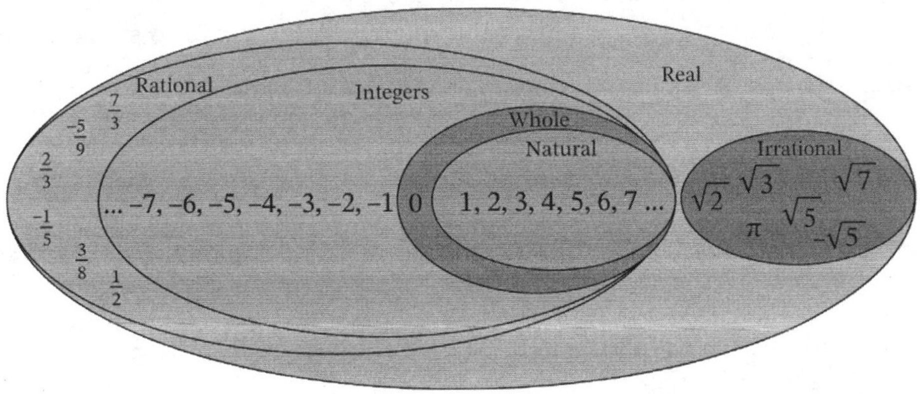


Notice how **natural numbers** are a subset of **whole numbers**, which are a subset of **integers**, which are a subset of **rational numbers**. All these sets and subsets fall into the set of **real numbers**. Nearly every number is considered a real number. Numbers that are not real numbers are considered **imaginary numbers**.

Numbers are considered **irrational** when they cannot be expressed as a ratio of two integers. Essentially, numbers that cannot be expressed as fractions are irrational.

For example, $\pi$ is irrational because when it is expressed as a decimal it never terminates. Decimals that never terminate cannot be expressed as fractions, therefore pi is irrational.

It is important to remember that real numbers can be rational or irrational. However, numbers that are not real are considered imaginary numbers. Imaginary numbers (not seen on the Venn diagram) are numbers that yield a negative result when they are squared. For example, $\sqrt{-1}$ is an imaginary number because $(\sqrt{-1})^2$ is -1.

## Approximating Irrational Numbers

Rational numbers can be expressed as a fraction. For example, 2.0 can be expressed as $\frac{2}{1}$. 0.3333... can be expressed as $\frac{1}{3}$. 0.5 can be expressed as $\frac{1}{2}$. Irrational numbers cannot be expressed in fraction form. If a decimal never terminates and is not repeating, there is no way to determine its fractional denominator. This makes it impossible to express it as the ratio of two integers.

It is often necessary to **estimate** the value of irrational numbers. Reviewing the **perfect squares** can be helpful in estimating irrational numbers. For example, $\sqrt{1} = 1$, $\sqrt{4} = 2$, $\sqrt{9} = 3$, $\sqrt{16} = 4$ and so on.

Estimating the value of square roots of numbers that are not perfect squares can be achieved using estimation. For example, when estimating the value of $\sqrt{5}$, consider this two-step thought process.

Think about a number line with all the perfect squares listed in order.

Ask yourself, "Between which numbers does the new number fall?"

On a number line, $\sqrt{5}$ falls between $\sqrt{4}$ and $\sqrt{9}$. This means that $\sqrt{5}$ fits between the numbers 2 and 3 ($\sqrt{4}$ is 2 and $\sqrt{9}$ is 3). This means that $\sqrt{5}$ is between 2 and 3 on a number line, but closer to the number 2.

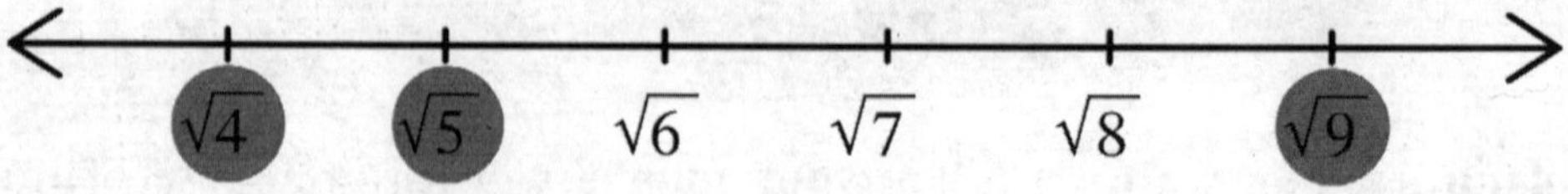


Another irrational number that is often estimated is the value of $\pi$. In decimal form, $\pi$ never terminates. This means the full value of $\pi$ cannot be expressed in fraction form. However, the approximated digits of $\pi$ can be expressed as the fraction $\frac{22}{7}$. This is a value that can be plotted on a number line. $\frac{22}{7}$ falls between 3 and 4 on a number line but closer to 3.

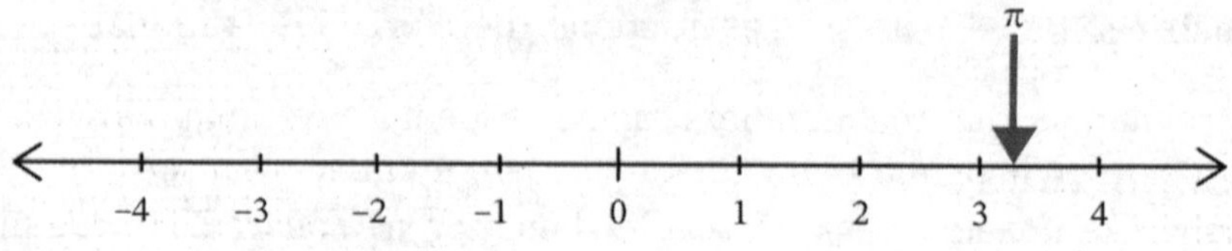

## Order Real Numbers

Real numbers can fall into subsets such as natural numbers, whole numbers, integers, and rational numbers. Real numbers that are not rational are considered to be irrational numbers. Irrational numbers cannot be expressed as the ratio of two integers. In other words, irrational numbers cannot be expressed as a fraction.

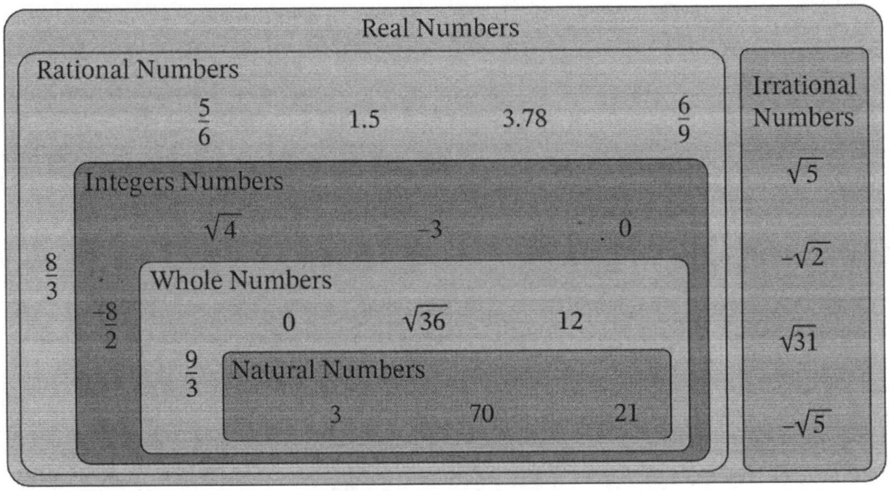


When ordering a set of real numbers, it is important to start by **converting** all the values to the **same form**. In general, it is most convenient to convert all numbers into decimal form rounded to the same place value. For example, consider the set of numbers below.

$$\left\{5\frac{11}{13}, \sqrt{30}, -\frac{8}{5}, \pi\right\}$$

All these values are considered real numbers. Start by converting each value into decimal form expressed to the thousandths place.

$$5\frac{11}{13} = 5.846$$
$$\sqrt{30} = 5.477$$
$$-\frac{8}{5} = -1.600$$
$$\pi = 3.142$$

Now that all the real numbers are in the same form (decimal form), they can efficiently be arranged. The set of real numbers ordered from least to greatest would be $-\frac{8}{5}, \pi, \sqrt{30}, 5\frac{11}{13}$.

Use the same process when ordering real numbers in real-world scenarios. For example, consider the three cylinders below. When ordering the volume of cylinders from least to greatest, start by converting each volume into the same form. Here we use decimal form rounded to the tenths place.

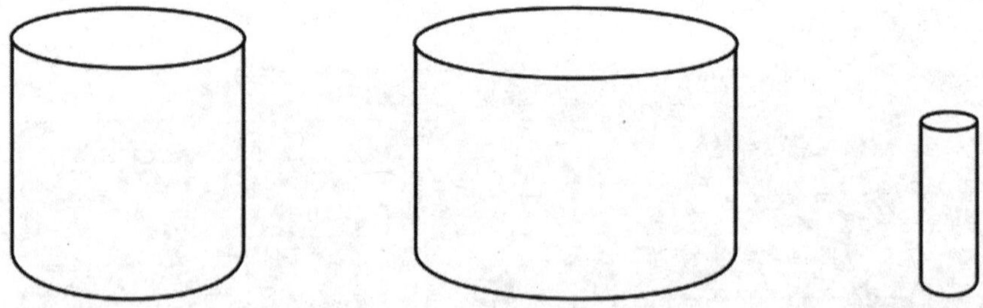

$V = 25\pi \text{ in}^3$ $\quad$ $V = 99.4 \text{ in}^3$ $\quad$ $V = \sqrt{200} \text{ in}^3$

$$25\pi = 78.5 \text{ in}^3$$
$$99.4 = 99.4 \text{ in}^3$$
$$\sqrt{200} = 14.1 \text{ in}^3$$

Now that all three values are expressed in the same form, they can be arranged from least to greatest: $\sqrt{200}$ in$^3$, $25\pi$ in$^3$, $99.4$ in$^3$.

**Review Video: Ordering Rational Numbers**
Visit mometrix.com/academy and enter code: 419578

## EXAMPLE

Order the real numbers from least to greatest.

$80\frac{3}{4}$, 80.72, 65, $\sqrt{81}$

The correct order is $\sqrt{81}$, 65, 80.72, $80\frac{3}{4}$

Start by converting all the numbers into the same form. Decimal form is a great way to efficiently compare values that are rounded to the same place value. Convert $80\frac{3}{4}$, 80.72, 65, and $\sqrt{81}$ into decimal form to the hundredths place.

$$80\frac{3}{4} = 80.75$$
$$80.72 = 80.72$$
$$65 = 65.00$$
$$\sqrt{81} = 9.00$$

Listed from least to greatest: 9.00, 65.00, 80.72, 80.75

Listed from least to greatest: $\sqrt{81}$, 65, 80.72, $80\frac{3}{4}$

### EXAMPLE

Order the real numbers from greatest to least.

$\pi, \sqrt{20}, 0.01, -5$

The correct order is $\sqrt{20}, \pi, 0.01, -5$

Start by converting all the numbers into the same form. Decimal form is a great way to efficiently compare values that are rounded to the same place value. Convert $\pi$, $\sqrt{20}$, 0.01, and -5 into decimal form to the hundredths place.

$$\pi \approx 3.14$$
$$\sqrt{20} \approx 4.47$$
$$0.01 = 0.01$$
$$-5 = -5.00$$

Ordered from greatest to least: 4.47, 3.14, 0.01, -5.00

Ordered from greatest to least: $\sqrt{20}$, $\pi$, 0.01, -5

# Expressions and Equations

## Exponents

An **exponent** is a superscript number placed next to another number at the top right. It indicates how many times the base number is to be multiplied by itself. Exponents provide a shorthand way to write what would be a longer mathematical expression, Example: $2^4 = 2 \times 2 \times 2 \times 2$. A number with an exponent of 2 is said to be "squared," while a number with an exponent of 3 is said to be "cubed." The value of a number raised to an exponent is called its power. So $8^4$ is read as "8 to the 4th power," or "8 raised to the power of 4."

**Review Video: Exponents**
Visit mometrix.com/academy and enter code: 600998

### Properties of Exponents

The properties of exponents are as follows:

| Property | Description |
|---|---|
| $a^1 = a$ | Any number to the power of 1 is equal to itself |
| $1^n = 1$ | The number 1 raised to any power is equal to 1 |
| $a^0 = 1$ | Any number raised to the power of 0 is equal to 1 |
| $a^n \times a^m = a^{n+m}$ | Add exponents to multiply powers of the same base number |
| $a^n \div a^m = a^{n-m}$ | Subtract exponents to divide powers of the same base number |
| $(a^n)^m = a^{n \times m}$ | When a power is raised to a power, the exponents are multiplied |
| $(a \times b)^n = a^n \times b^n$<br>$(a \div b)^n = a^n \div b^n$ | Multiplication and division operations inside parentheses can be raised to a power. This is the same as each term being raised to that power. |
| $a^{-n} = \frac{1}{a^n}$ | A negative exponent is the same as the reciprocal of a positive exponent |

Note that exponents do not have to be integers. Fractional or decimal exponents follow all the rules above as well. Example: $5^{\frac{1}{4}} \times 5^{\frac{3}{4}} = 5^{\frac{1}{4}+\frac{3}{4}} = 5^1 = 5$.

**Review Video: Properties of Exponents**
Visit mometrix.com/academy and enter code: 532558

## Roots

Linear equations use inverse operations to solve by isolating the variable. Solving an equation of the form $x^2 = p$ or $x^3 = p$, where $p$ is a positive rational number, requires the same use of inverse operations to isolate the variable. A root (or radical) is used to undo the power on the variable. A square root undoes a power of 2 because $\sqrt{x^2}$ simplifies to $x$. A cube root undoes a power of 3 because $\sqrt[3]{x^3}$ simplifies to $x$.

To solve these types of equations, get rid of the exponent by taking the square root, if the variable has an exponent of 2, or the cube root, if the variable has an exponent of 3, of both sides. For the equation to stay balanced, the same root must be taken on both sides. If a square root is used, a plus or minus sign ($\pm$) must be placed in front of the square root of the rational number to indicate there are two possible values for the variable. The square of a negative number results in the same value as the square of the corresponding positive number, so both possibilities must be accounted for when finding the solution. For example, both $(2)^2$ and $(-2)^2$ equal 4. With cube roots, only one solution is possible because cubing a negative number does not result in the same answer as cubing the corresponding positive number. So, a plus or minus sign is not needed. For example, $(2)^3 = 8$ while $(-2)^3 = -8$. After taking the square or cube root of both sides of the equation, simplify each side to find the final solution(s).

The solution(s) to an equation of the form $x^2 = p$ or $x^3 = p$, where $p$ is a positive rational number, may simplify to a rational or an irrational number. The solution(s) will be a rational number if $p$ is a perfect square, if the variable has an exponent of 2, or a perfect cube, if the variable has an exponent of 3. A **perfect square** is a number whose square root is an integer. The number 100 is a perfect square because its square root is 10: $\sqrt{100} = \pm 10$ and $10^2 = (-10)^2 = 100$. A **perfect cube** is a number whose cube root is an integer. The number 8 is a perfect cube because its cube root is 2: $\sqrt[3]{8} = 2$ and $2^3 = 8$. Note that -8 is also a perfect cube: $\sqrt[3]{-8} = -2$ and $(-2)^3 = -8$.

To solve $x^2 = 36$, take the square root of both sides to undo the power of 2 on the variable. Because a square root was taken, place a plus or minus sign in front of $\sqrt{36}$. $\sqrt{x^2}$ simplifies to $x$ and $\pm\sqrt{36}$ simplifies to $\pm 6$.

$$x^2 = 36$$
$$\sqrt{x^2} = \pm\sqrt{36}$$
$$x = \pm 6$$

The solution to these types of equations is an irrational number if $p$ is not a perfect square or perfect cube as is the case in the equation $x^3 = 15$. Taking the cube root of both sides results in a solution of $x = \sqrt[3]{15}$. Since 15 is not a perfect cube, the solution is irrational. The solution is typically expressed in terms of the cube root.

Just like other types of equations, the solution(s) can be checked by substituting the value(s) found for the variable back into the original equation. For the equation $x^2 = 36$, both 6 and $-6$ should be verified:

$$(6)^2 = 36$$
$$(-6)^2 = 36$$

When $\sqrt[3]{15}$ is plugged in for $x$ in the equation $x^3 = 15$, the left side is $\left(\sqrt[3]{15}\right)^3$. The power of 3 cancels out the cube root, so it simplifies to 15, which is the same as the right side and confirms the solution.

**Review Video: Roots**
Visit mometrix.com/academy and enter code: 795655

**Review Video: Perfect Squares and Square Roots**
Visit mometrix.com/academy and enter code: 648063

## Scientific Notation

A number is in scientific notation when it is expressed as the product of a number, $a$, and a power of 10 in the form of $a \times 10^p$ where $1 \leq |a| < 10$ and $p$ is an integer. A power of 10 is used because place values in the number system are based on 10's. To convert a standard number to scientific notation, move the decimal point until there is a single non-zero digit in front of the decimal. The value of $a$ is the single non-zero digit in front of the decimal and any digits after the decimal until the last non-zero digit. The number $a$ may include a zero digit within it, but not at the beginning or end. The power, $p$, keeps track of zeros, or decimal places, and its absolute value is equal to the number of places the decimal moved. If the standard number is greater than or equal to 10, the decimal moved to the left and $p$ is positive. If the standard number is less than 1, the decimal moved to the right and $p$ is negative.

The diameter of the Earth is around 8,000 miles. To find the scientific notation form of the diameter, the understood decimal after the last 0 moves to the left 3 times before having the single digit of 8 in front of it. The zero digits after 8 are dropped and accounted for in the power of 10. 10 is raised to the power of 3 to show the decimal moved 3 places to the left. The earth's diameter can be written as 8,000 miles or $8 \times 10^3$ miles.

$$8{,}000 = 8\underbrace{0}\underbrace{0}\underbrace{0.} = 8 \times 10^3$$

The diameter of a red blood cell in the human body is around 0.0003 inches. To find the scientific notation form of the diameter, the decimal moves to the right 4 times before having the single digit of 3 in front of it. The zero digits before 3 are dropped and accounted for in the power of 10. 10 is raised to the power of $-4$ to show the decimal moved 4 places to the right. A red blood cell's diameter can be written as 0.0003 inches or $3 \times 10^{-4}$ inches.

$$0.0003 = 0.\underbrace{0}\underbrace{0}\underbrace{0}\underbrace{3} = 3 \times 10^{-4}$$

The purpose of scientific notation is to represent a number that is extremely large or extremely small in a way that is easier to understand. Scientific notation does not change the value of the number. It is the same number, expressed in a more practical way. Scientific notation allows a convenient estimation to be found of how many times as much one number is than another by comparing each part of the number (the non-exponential value and the power of 10). For example, suppose we are comparing the sizes of Earth and Jupiter. Jupiter has a diameter around $8.9 \times 10^4$ miles. Jupiter's diameter is larger than Earth's, but how much larger? The non-exponential value for Earth's diameter, 8, is similar to Jupiter's value of 8.9 with Jupiter's being about 1.1 times as large, $8 \times 1.1 = 8.8$. Looking at the powers of 10, Jupiter's is one larger than Earth's. With Jupiter's non-exponential value being a about 1.1 times as large and its power being one power of 10 larger, Jupiter's diameter is about 11, or $1.1 \times 10^1$, times as large as Earth's diameter.

### Converting from Decimal Form to Scientific Notation

Converting decimals to scientific notation follows a two-step process.

Place the decimal.

Express as a power of 10.

Consider the decimal 73,500. Start by moving the decimal point. In scientific notation the decimal needs to go to the right of the first non-zero number. In this case, the decimal needs to be moved 4 places to the left. 73,500 becomes 7.3500.

Now, address the power of 10. To determine the power of 10, start at the original decimal point and count how many spaces it takes to arrive at the new decimal location. In this case, the decimal point in 73,500.0 moved 4 spaces to the left in order to create the number 7.3500.

This means the power of 10 will be 4. 73,500 in scientific notation is $7.35 \times 10^4$. Notice how the zeros that are not significant are dropped. $7.35 \times 10^4$ as opposed to $7.3500 \times 10^4$.

It is important to note that powers of 10 can be negative. For example, if the given number is smaller than 1, and the decimal point moves to the right, then the power of 10 will be negative.

0.00000082 is smaller than 1, and the decimal point needs to be moved to the right. The decimal needs to move 7 places to the right, therefore the power of 10 will be −7. 0.00000082 becomes $8.2 \times 10^{-7}$.

### Converting from Scientific Notation to Decimal Form

When a number is in scientific notation, the power of 10 will be used to determine how many places to move the decimal point, and in which direction. For example, consider the value $7.2 \times 10^5$. The value of 7.2 is multiplied by 10 raised to the power of positive 5. This means the decimal in 7.2 needs to move 5 places to the right. $7.2 \times 10^5$ becomes 720,000. In contrast, the value $7.2 \times 10^{-5}$ would result in a decimal movement of 5 places to the left. $7.2 \times 10^{-5}$ would become 0.000072.

**Review Video: Scientific Notation**
Visit mometrix.com/academy and enter code: 976454

### Operations with Numbers in Scientific Notation

Numbers expressed in scientific notation can be multiplied or divided. When finding a product or quotient with one or more numbers in scientific notation, it is best if all numbers are either in scientific notation or in standard form before carrying out the operation. If that is not the case, re-write any numbers as necessary so that the forms of all numbers are the same. To find the product of two numbers in scientific notation, re-arrange and re-group the non-exponential terms together as well as the exponential terms together. To carry out the multiplication, multiply the non-exponential numbers and the exponential numbers separately. When multiplying the exponential numbers, apply the product of powers rule which states to add the exponents if multiplying terms with the same base. For example, to find the product of 0.02 and $4.1 \times 10^7$in scientific notation, 0.02 can be re-written as $2 \times 10^{-2}$. To multiply, group 2 and 4.1 together and multiply them as usual. Group $10^{-2}$ and $10^7$ together and apply the product of powers rule.

$$(2 \times 10^{-2}) \times (4.1 \times 10^7) = (2 \times 4.1) \times (10^{-2} \times 10^7) = 8.2 \times 10^5$$

In a similar way, to divide two numbers in scientific notation, group the non-exponential terms together as well as the exponential terms. To carry out the division, divide the non-exponential numbers and the exponential numbers separately. When dividing the exponential terms, apply the quotient of powers rule which states to subtract the exponents if dividing terms with the same base. For example, to divide $1.6 \times 10^9$ by $6.4 \times 10^2$, group 1.6 and 6.4 together and divide them as usual. Group $10^9$ and $10^2$ together and apply the quotient of powers rule.

$$\frac{1.6 \times 10^9}{6.4 \times 10^2} = \left(\frac{1.6}{6.4}\right) \times \left(\frac{10^9}{10^2}\right) = 0.25 \times 10^7$$

The product or quotient of numbers in scientific notation may not result in a number in scientific notation as is the case in the quotient above. To re-write the result so that it is in scientific notation, find the scientific notation form of the non-exponential term and then apply the product of powers rule to combine the two powers of 10. 0.25 written in scientific notation is $2.5 \times 10^{-1}$. $10^{-1}$and $10^7$ are combined by adding exponents.

$$0.25 \times 10^{-7} = (2.5 \times 10^{-1}) \times 10^7 = 2.5 \times (10^{-1} \times 10^7) = 2.5 \times 10^6$$

While having a large or small number written in scientific notation is more convenient, there may be a unit that is more reasonable for that quantity. When possible, it is better to express a quantity in terms of a unit that is logical for its size rather than a quantity in terms of a unit that requires scientific notation. For example, the duration of a car ride described as $1.44 \times 10^4$ seconds may be accurate, but it is not practical. It is more appropriate to express the length of this car ride in terms of hours not seconds. $1.44 \times 10^4$ can be converted from seconds to hours using the fact that 60 seconds equals 1 minute and 60 minutes equals 1 hour. With the conversion factors in standard form, it may be easier to re-write $1.44 \times 10^4$ as 14,400 before carrying out the conversion.

$$14{,}400\ \cancel{\text{sec}} \times \frac{1\ \cancel{\text{min}}}{60\ \cancel{\text{sec}}} \times \frac{1\ \text{hr}}{60\ \cancel{\text{min}}} = \frac{14{,}400}{3600}\ \text{hr} = 4\ \text{hr}$$

Unlike the imperial system, the metric system is based on powers of 10. With numbers in scientific notation also containing powers of 10, a conversion within the metric system to a more appropriate unit is less cumbersome. For example, to convert $3 \times 10^6$ mm to km, the fact that 1 mm equals $1 \times 10^{-6}$ km is used.

$$\begin{aligned} \frac{3 \times 10^6\ \cancel{\text{mm}}}{1} \times \frac{1 \times 10^{-6}\ \text{km}}{1\ \cancel{\text{mm}}} &= \frac{(3 \times 10^6)(1 \times 10^{-6})}{1}\ \text{km} \\ &= (3 \times 1) \times (10^6 \times 10^{-6})\ \text{km} \\ &= 3 \times 10^0\ \text{km} \\ &= 3\ \text{km} \end{aligned}$$

Scientific notation will sometimes be reported using a different convention. Many graphing calculators and computer-based applications report scientific notion using a capital E to indicate what power of 10 to multiply the base number by: $a \times 10^p = a\text{E}p$. More examples:

$$\begin{aligned} 5.4 \times 10^6 &= 5.4\text{E}6 \\ -2.9 \times 10^{11} &= -2.9\text{E}11 \\ 7.1 \times 10^{-3} &= 7.1\text{E-}3 \end{aligned}$$

# One-Variable Equations and Inequalities

## Writing One-Variable Equations and Inequalities

Some scenarios require **variables** to be on both sides of the equality or the inequality symbol. This is common when setting up equations or inequalities to compare two rates.

For example, consider the two scenarios: Phone company A charges a fee of $20 each month and 5 cents per text message. Phone company B charges a fee of $22 each month and 4 cents per text message. How many text messages need to be sent for the monthly cost for both companies to be the same?

An equation with variables on both sides can be set up in order to determine when the prices will be the same.

Company A: The total monthly cost of $20 plus 5 cents per text message can be written as an expression where $t$ represents text messages: $20 + 0.05t$

Company B: The total monthly cost of $22 plus 3 cents per text message can be written as an expression where $t$ represents text messages: $22 + 0.03t$

Set the expressions equal to each other, then solve to find the value of $t$.

$$\begin{aligned} 20 + 0.05t &= 22 + 0.03t \\ 0.05t &= 2 + 0.03t \\ 0.02t &= 2 \\ t &= 100 \end{aligned}$$

This means that the monthly cost for each company will be the same when 100 text messages are sent.

A similar process applies for inequalities. For example, consider the two scenarios: Electric bike company A charges an initial fee of $3 to rent a bike and then 5 cents for every minute of riding. Electric bike company B charges an initial fee of $2 to rent a bike and then 10 cents for every minute of riding. For how many minutes of riding will company B be more expensive than company A?

An inequality with variables on both sides can be set up to solve for the unknown number of minutes.

Company A: The total cost of a fee of $3 and then 5 cents per minute can be written as an expression with $m$ representing the number of minutes: $3 + 0.05m$
Company B: The total cost of a fee of $2 and then 10 cents per minute can be written as an expression with $m$ representing the number of minutes: $2 + 0.1m$

Set up an inequality to determine the number of minutes that need to expire for company B to be "greater than" company A. Set company B greater than company A.

$$2 + 0.1m > 3 + 0.05m$$

Solve for the number of minutes, $m$.

$$0.1m > 1 + 0.05m$$
$$0.05m > 1$$
$$m > 20$$

So, when the number of minutes is greater than 20, company B is more expensive.

## WRITING WORD PROBLEMS BASED ON ONE-VARIABLE EQUATIONS AND INEQUALITIES

It is important to see the **connection** and **correlation** between equations and inequalities and real-world scenarios. Sometimes a scenario is provided and an equation or inequality needs to be determined. Other times, an equation or inequality is provided and a real-world scenario needs to be applied.

### *EQUATIONS*

Consider the following equation with variables on both sides.

$$100 + 40h = 75 + 45h$$

When writing a real-world problem to match an equation, consider the format of the equation as well as the variable. In this case, there is an $h$ on both sides of the equal sign, and a constant of 100 on the left side and a constant of 75 on the right side. If the constants represent dollar amounts, 100 represents a flat fee of \$100 and 75 represents a flat fee of \$75. If the variable $h$ represents hours, then $40h$ could represent \$40 per hour, and $45h$ could represent \$45 per hour. This equation could represent a scenario where one plumbing company is represented on the left side of the equation and one company is represented on the right side of the equation. For example, plumbing company A charges a flat fee of \$100 and then \$40 per hour, and plumbing company B charges a flat fee of \$75 and then \$45 per hour.

The equation is set up in a way that sets both companies equal to each other. This means that when the equation is solved for the variable $h$, it will describe the number of hours that need to expire for both company A and B to have an equal price.

In this case, $100 + 40h = 75 + 45h$ simplifies to $25 = 5h$ and then $5 = h$. This means that after 5 hours of work, the total price for both companies will be the same.

### *INEQUALITIES*

A similar process applies for writing real-world problems that corelate to inequalities with variables on both sides. Start by identifying the significance of the variables and study the format of the inequality. For example, consider the following inequality.

$$3 + 0.4m < 2 + 0.8m$$

The variable $m$ is on both sides. Perhaps this variable represents miles.

There is also a constant on both sides of the inequality. Perhaps 3 and 2 represent a flat fee.

Start to build a problem around the features of the inequality. For example, consider the left and right side of the inequality as comparisons. The left side of the inequality could represent taxi company A. This company charges a flat fee of \$3 and then 40 cents per mile. The right side of the inequality could represent taxi company B. This company charges a flat fee of \$2 and then 80 cents per mile. The inequality is set up in a way that shows company A "less than" company B. This means that when the variable $m$, miles, is solved for, it will indicate the number of miles that need to be driven for company A to be less expensive than company B.

$3 + 0.4m < 2 + 0.8m$ becomes $1 < 0.4m$ which simplifies to $2.5 < m$. This means that taxi company B will be more expensive than company A when the number of miles exceeds 2.5.

## MODELING AND SOLVING ONE-VARIABLE EQUATIONS

It is important to become familiar with the process of modeling and solving one-variable equations with variables on both sides. Many real-world scenarios can be represented and solved using one-variable equations which makes this skill relevant and important. Many one-variable equations will contain coefficients, constants, fractions, and decimals. Coefficients are numbers multiplied by a variable, such as the coefficient 3 in the term $3x$. Constants are numbers on their own, such as the number 25 in the expression $2y + 25$. It is common to encounter equations with coefficients and constants on both sides of the equation. For example, consider the following equation:

$$1.5x - 5 = -0.5x$$

When solving equations with variables on both sides, start by collecting all the variables on one side. Variables can be moved using inverse operations. Add $0.5x$ to both sides.

$$2x - 5 = 0$$

Now, move the constant to right side of the equation. Add 5 to both sides.

$$2x = 5$$

Divide both sides by 2 and the variable $x$ will be isolated.

$$x = \frac{5}{2} \text{ or } x = 2.5$$

This means that when the value of $x$ is 2.5, the original equation is balanced. Check the accuracy of the answer by substituting 2.5 into the original equation for all $x$-variables.

Check:

$$\begin{aligned} 1.5x - 5 &= -0.5x \\ 1.5(2.5) - 5 &= -0.5(2.5) \\ -1.25 &= -1.25 \end{aligned}$$

The equation is balanced, so the solution of $x = 2.5$ is correct.

Consider another equation:

$$\frac{4(x-2)+1}{12} = \frac{5x}{12}$$

The same process applies for equations with variables on both sides involving fractions. Sometimes it is necessary to distribute before combining elements. In this equation, start by multiplying 4 by $(x - 2)$. Follow the order of operations to simplify the equation.

$$\frac{4x - 8 + 1}{12} = \frac{5x}{12}$$
$$\frac{4x - 7}{12} = \frac{5x}{12}$$

Simplify the left side of the equation by multiplying by 12. What you do to one side, you must do to the other side, so multiply both sides by 12.

$$4x - 7 = \frac{60x}{12}$$
$$4x - 7 = 5x$$

Now, subtract $4x$ from both sides.

$$-7 = x$$

The solution to the equation is $x = -7$.

### EXAMPLE

Two homeowners spent the same amount of money on an electrical project. Homeowner A paid their electrician an inspection fee of $200 and then $60 per hour. Homeowner B paid their electrician an inspection fee of $175 and then $65 per hour. Both homeowners pay the same total amount after how many hours of work?

Let $x$ represent the number of hours of work.

Homeowner A: The electrician charges $200 plus $60 per hour: $200 + 60x$

Homeowner B: The electrician charges $175 plus $65 per hour: $175 + 65x$

Set the expressions equal to each other to solve for the unknown number of hours that makes the equation balanced.

$$200 + 60x = 175 + 65x$$

Solve for $x$ using the order of operations and inverse operations. Collect all $x$-terms on one side and all constants on the other side.

$$25 + 60x = 65x$$
$$25 = 5x$$
$$5 = x$$

This means that after 5 hours of work, the payment to each electrician will be the same for both homeowners.

### EXAMPLE

Alice and Brent select two different taxi companies. The company Alice used charged an initial fee of $30 and then 25 cents per mile. The company Brent used charged an initial fee of $40 and then 20 cents per mile. How many miles need to be driven for the prices of both companies to be the same?

Let $x$ represent the number of miles.

Write an equation, then solve for the variable $x$ to determine the number of miles.

Price of Alice's taxi: $30 + 0.25x$

Price of Brent's taxi: $40 + 0.2x$

Set the expressions equal to each other, then isolate the variable $x$.

$$\begin{aligned} 30 + 0.25x &= 40 + 0.2x \\ 0.25x &= 10 + 0.2x \\ 0.05x &= 10 \\ x &= 200 \end{aligned}$$

The prices for both taxi companies will be the same when 200 miles are driven.

## Identifying Proportional Situations

A proportional relationship involves two quantities that vary directly. In an equation, this follows the form $y = kx$, where $x$ and $y$ vary directly based on the value of $k$. For example, the equation $y = 0.5x$ represents a proportional relationship. Every value of $y$ is directly related to the corresponding value of $x$. Values for $y$ are calculated by multiplying the corresponding values of $x$ by 0.5.

In contrast, non-proportional relationships follow the form $y = mx + b$, where $m$ represents the slope, and $b$ is not equal to zero. The value of $y$ is determined by multiplying or dividing the corresponding $x$-value by a consistent amount, but then a constant will be added or subtracted (the value of $b$). The difference between proportional, $y = kx$, and non-proportional relationships, $y = mx + b$, in equation form is that the variable $b$ is not 0 in non-proportional relationships.

Consider the following scenario:

Martha's parents will pay her 50 cents for every weed she pulls in the garden

This relationship can be displayed in a table, and its proportionality will be evident.

| $x$-variable<br>Number of Weeds Pulled | $y$-variable<br>Amount of Money Earned (Dollars) |
|---|---|
| 0 | 0 |
| 1 | 0.5 |
| 2 | 1 |
| 3 | 1.5 |

Notice how each $y$-value is the result of multiplying the corresponding $x$-value by the same amount each time. This will always be true in proportional situations. In this case, each $x$-value is multiplied by 0.5 to determine the $y$-value. When using a table to check for proportionality, simply check that each $x$-value is consistently multiplied (or divided) by the same amount in order to calculate the corresponding $y$-value. If this is true, then the situation follows the form $y = kx$, and is therefore proportional.

**Review Video: Proportions**
Visit mometrix.com/academy and enter code: 505355

### TABLES

To illustrate a non-proportional relationship within a table, consider this slight alteration to the original scenario:

"Martha's parents pay her $3 upfront for pulling weeds and then 25 cents for each weed she pulls in the garden."

Two things will be noticeably different within the new table.

There will no longer be the ordered pair (0, 0).

The $y$-values are calculated by multiplying $x$ by a consistent amount and then adding the constant 3.

| $x$-variable<br>Number of Weeds Pulled | $y$-variable<br>Amount of Money Earned (Dollars) |
|---|---|
| 0 | 3 |
| 1 | 3.25 |
| 2 | 3.5 |
| 3 | 3.75 |

Notice how each $y$-value is now the result of multiplying $x$ by 0.25 and then adding 3. The fact that each $y$-value is not simply the result of multiplying the $x$-value by a consistent amount indicates that it is not proportional.

## GRAPHS

When proportional relationships are graphed, they have key characteristics. The graphed line will pass through the origin (0,0), and the line will be linear, rising or falling at a steady rate. In the original weed pulling scenario, the line will pass though the origin (0,0) because when Martha pulls 0 weeds, she earns 0 dollars. The graphed line will be linear, or rise at a steady rate, because the amount of money she earns is proportional to the number of weeds she pulls.

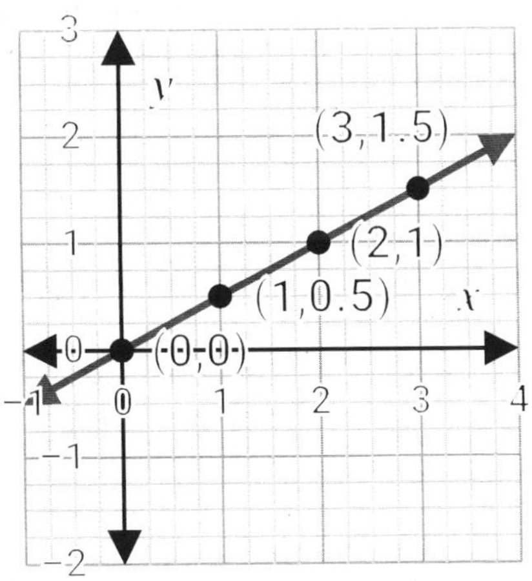


A quick check for determining if a graph is displaying a proportional relationship is to check that it passes through the origin, and check that it is linear.

In contrast, if a graphed line is linear but does not pass through the origin, it is non-proportional. For example, compare the two graphs. The graph below models the scenario where Martha is paid \$3 and then 25 cents for each weed she pulls. Notice how the $y$-intercept is 3, not 0. This is because

Martha earns $3 upfront, even though she has pulled 0 weeds. The line is still linear, but it does not pass through the point (0,0), so it is not proportional.

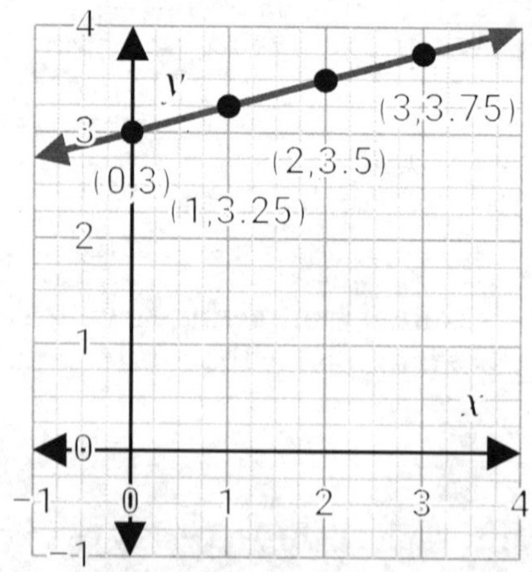


## Proportionality in Similar Shapes

Figures are considered **similar** when they have the **same shape**, but their sizes are different. In order to determine if two figures are similar, their corresponding side lengths need to be proportional. For example, consider the triangles $FLO$ and $HIT$ below.

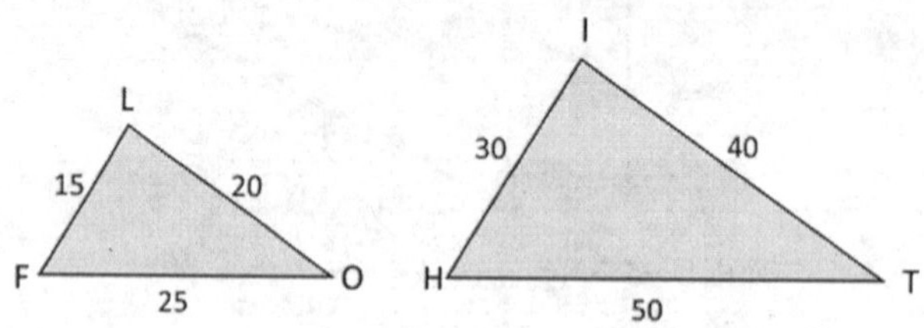


If the **corresponding** side lengths are **proportional**, then the figures are similar. In other words, if corresponding sides are all multiplied or divided by the same value, then the shapes are similar.

$FL$ is 15, and $HI$ is 30. The ratio of $\frac{FL}{HI}$ is $\frac{15}{30} = \frac{1}{2}$.

$LO$ is 20, and $IT$ is 40. The ratio of $\frac{LO}{IT}$ is $\frac{20}{40} = \frac{1}{2}$.

$OF$ is 25, and $TH$ is 50. The ratio of $\frac{OF}{TH}$ is $\frac{25}{50} = \frac{1}{2}$.

The ratio for all three corresponding side lengths is the same, therefore, the figures are similar.

The process of increasing or decreasing the size of a shape using a specific scale factor is known as a dilation. When a scale factor is less than 1, the new shape will be smaller. When a scale factor is greater than 1, the new shape will be larger. In this case, the scale factor used to form triangle $HIT$ from triangle $FLO$ is 2. Every side length of triangle $FLO$ is multiplied by 2 in order to form the corresponding side of triangle $HIT$.

Another way to use scale factors to prove two figures are similar is to set up a proportion. Consider the two rectangles below. A proportion can be set up that relates the corresponding side lengths.

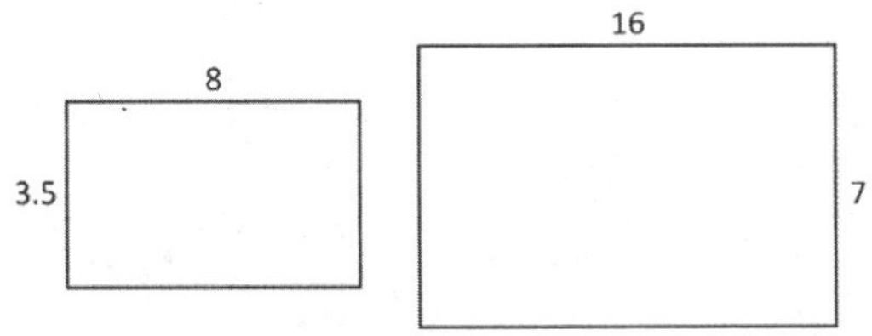


If the ratio of 3.5 to 8 is proportional to the ratio of 7 to 16, then the figures are similar. In this case, $\frac{3.5}{8} = 0.4375$ and $\frac{7}{16} = 0.4375$. This means that $\frac{3.5}{8}$ is proportional to $\frac{7}{16}$. Figures are similar if they are the same shape and corresponding side lengths are proportional, so the two rectangles are similar.

## Comparing a Shape and Its Dilation

Two figures are similar if their **corresponding angle measures** are the **same** and their **corresponding side lengths** are **proportional**. The coordinate plane below shows two triangles, $ABC$ and $A'B'C'$. The marks ' in $A'B'C'$ indicated "prime" which means this is the "new" shape. In this case, triangle $ABC$ is the original shape and $A'B'C'$ is the new shape.

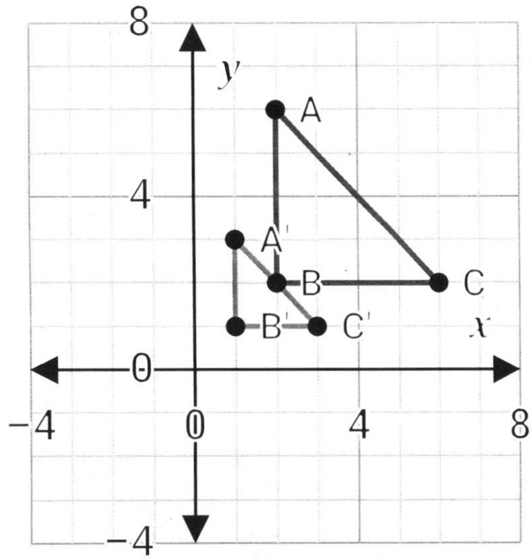


In order to determine if the figures are similar, it needs to be determined that a dilation has occurred using a specific scale factor.

For example, list the corresponding side lengths.

Side $A'B'$ is 2 units long, and side $AB$ is 4 units long. The ratio of the new side length to the old side length is $\frac{2}{4} = \frac{1}{2}$.

Side $B'C'$ is 2 units long, and side $BC$ is 4 units long. The ratio of the new side length to the old side length is $\frac{2}{4} = \frac{1}{2}$.

Side $A'C'$ is $2\sqrt{2}$ units long, and side $AC$ is $4\sqrt{2}$ units long. The ratio of the new side length to the old side length is $\frac{2\sqrt{2}}{4\sqrt{2}} = \frac{1}{2}$.

Since the ratio between all three sides is $\frac{1}{2}$, the original figure has been dilated by a scale factor of $\frac{1}{2}$.

Since all the corresponding side lengths are proportional, all the corresponding angle measures will be the same.

Angle $ABC$ is equal to angle $A'B'C'$.

Angle $BCA$ is equal to angle $B'C'A'$.

Angle $CAB$ is equal to angle $C'A'B'$.

## Scale Factor

Scale factor is the **ratio** of corresponding sides of two **similar** figures. In other words, **scale factor** indicates how many times bigger or smaller a new figure becomes after a dilation. **Dilation** is the process of changing the size of a shape using a scale factor. A shape will decrease in size when the scale factor is less than 1 and increase in size when the scale factor is greater than 1.

A scale factor can be expressed algebraically to describe the dilation that has occurred between two figures. This can be done by comparing "old" points to "new" points, or "old" side lengths to "new" side lengths. For example, consider the figure graphed below.

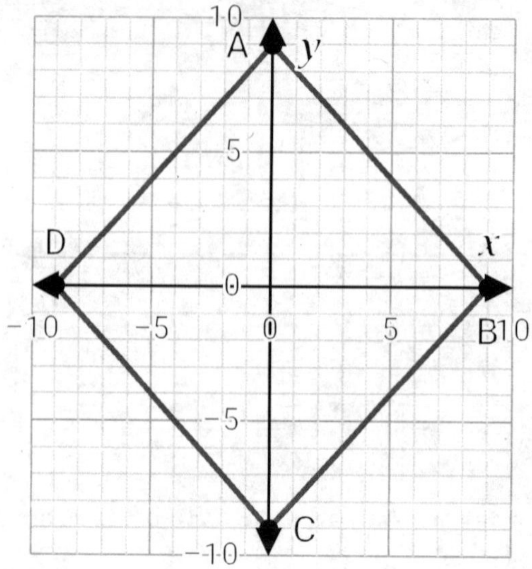


The four points on the graph include (0,9), (9,0), (0, −9), and (−9,0). This figure can be reduced or enlarged based on the scale factor that is applied. For example, if the scale factor is $\frac{1}{2}$, each $x$ and $y$ point will be $\frac{1}{2}$ of its original value. If the scale factor is 2, each $x$ and $y$ point will be 2 times its original value.

If a scale factor of $\frac{1}{2}$ is applied:

Point $A$: (0,9) becomes (0,4.5)

Point $B$: (9,0) becomes (4.5,0)
Point $C$: (0, −9) becomes (0, −4.5)
Point $D$: (−9,0) becomes (−4.5,0)

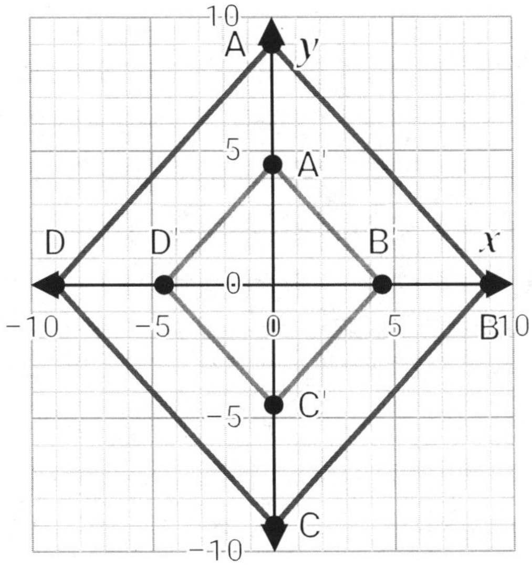


An algebraic rule can be written to represent the dilation that has occurred. Each original $x$ and $y$ point is now half the original value. This means that the algebraic rule will be stated as $(x, y) \rightarrow \left(\frac{1}{2}x, \frac{1}{2}y\right)$.

If a scale factor of 2 is applied:

Point $A$: (0,9) becomes (0,18)

Point $B$: (9,0) becomes (18,0)

Point $C$: (0, −9) becomes (0, −18)

Point $D$: $(-9,0)$ becomes $(-18,0)$

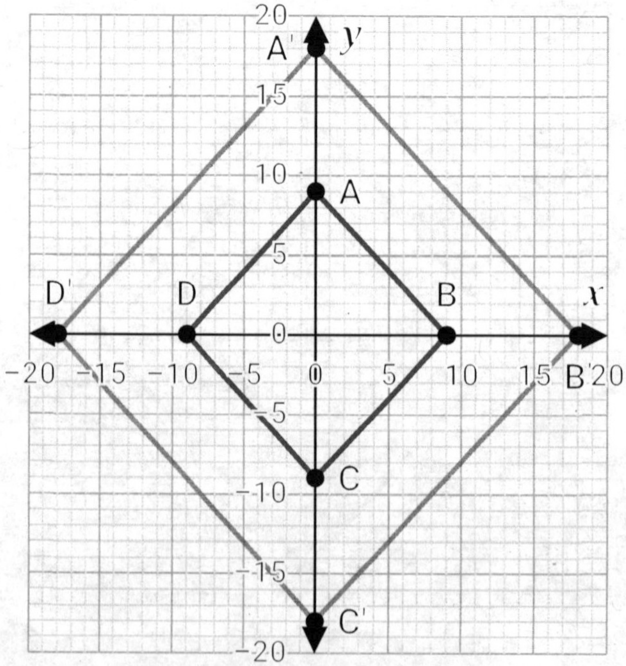


An algebraic rule can be written to represent the dilation that has occurred. Each original $x$ and $y$ point is now twice the original value. This means that the algebraic rule will be stated as $(x, y) \rightarrow (2x, 2y)$.

### *EXAMPLE*

Write a rule that represents the dilation that is applied to the triangle.

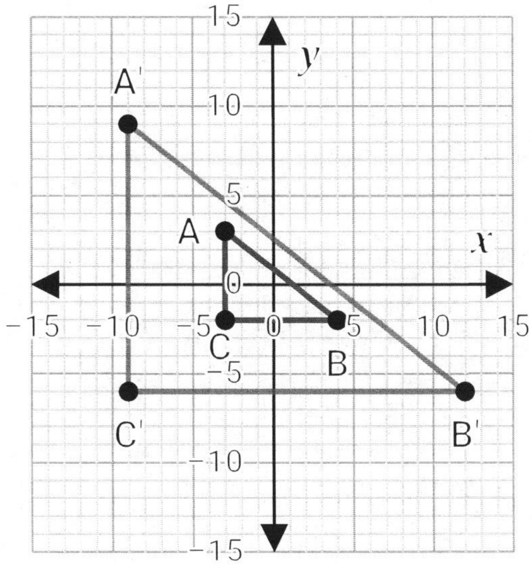


$A$ became $A'$: $(-3,3)$ became $(-9,9)$

$B$ became $B'$: $(4,-2)$ became $(12,-6)$

$C$ became $C'$: $(-3,-2)$ became $(-9,-6)$

Triangle $A'B'C'$ is larger than triangle $ABC$. This means that the scale factor will be greater than 1. In this case, the coordinates of triangle $A'B'C'$ are 3 times larger than the coordinates of triangle $ABC$. This means the scale factor is 3. The rule can be expressed as $(x, y) \rightarrow (3x, 3y)$ in algebraic form.

$(x, y) \rightarrow (3x, 3y)$

### *EXAMPLE*

Plot 4 new points so that the rule $(x, y) \rightarrow (0.5x, 0.5y)$ is applied to quadrilateral $ABCD$.

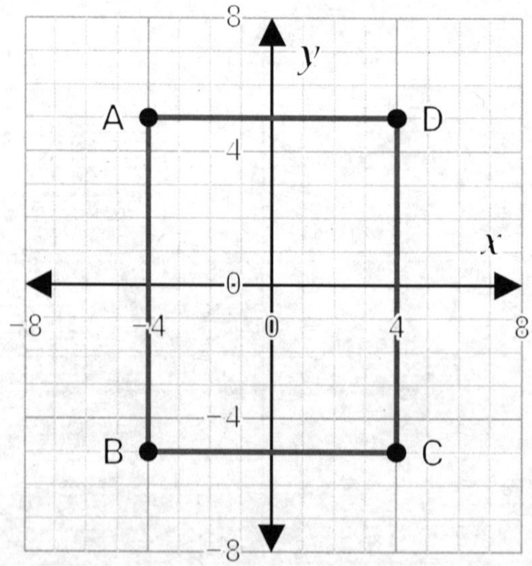


The rule $(x, y) \rightarrow (0.5x, 0.5y)$ indicates that the four coordinates of quadrilateral $ABCD$ will be $\frac{1}{2}$ their original value. The scale factor is less than one (0.5), so the new figure will be smaller than the original. Calculate each new coordinate by multiplying all $x$- and $y$-values by 0.5.

$A$ becomes $A'$: $(-4,5)$ becomes $(-2,2.5)$

$B$ becomes $B'$: $(-4,-5)$ becomes $(-2,-2.5)$

$C$ becomes $C'$: $(4,-5)$ becomes $(2,-2.5)$

$D$ becomes $D'$: $(4,5)$ becomes $(2,2.5)$

$A'$: $(-2,2.5)$ $B'$: $(-2,-2.5)$ $C'$: $(2,-2.5)$ $D'$: $(2,2.5)$

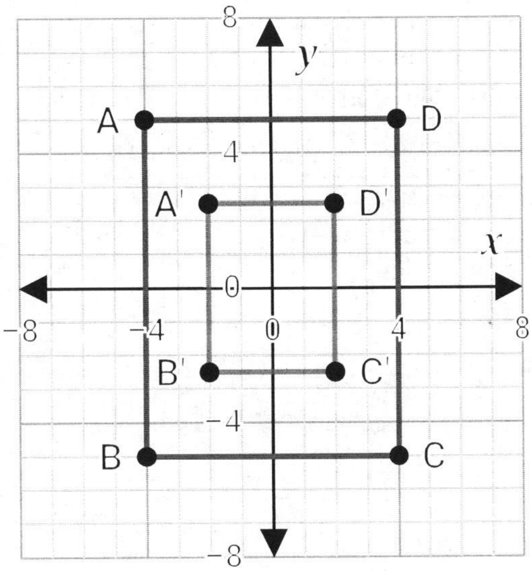


## SLOPE AND SIMILAR RIGHT TRIANGLES

The slope of a line refers to its steepness. In other words, **slope** is the vertical change compared to the horizontal change. This relationship can be described using the formula $m = \frac{y_2 - y_1}{x_2 - x_1}$, where $m$ represents the slope, and $x$ and $y$ represent ordered pairs on the line. For example, consider the line below.

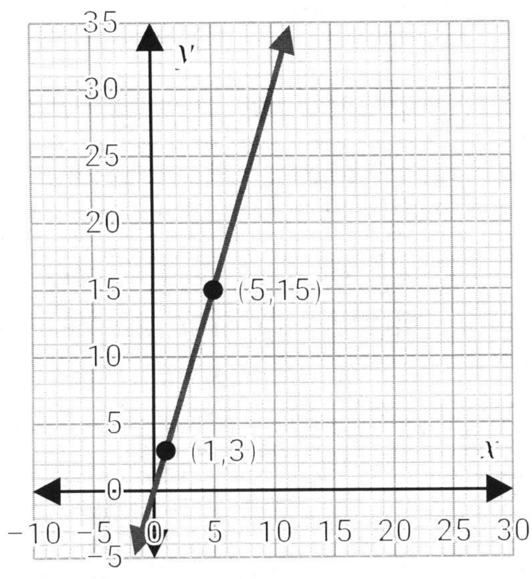


Two points are labeled on the line, (1,3) and (5,15). These ordered pairs represent $(x_1, y_1)$ and $(x_2, y_2)$ in the slope formula $m = \frac{y_2 - y_1}{x_2 - x_1}$. Substitute these points and simplify to find the slope of the line.

$$m = \frac{y_2 - y_1}{x_2 - x_1} = \frac{15 - 3}{5 - 1} = \frac{12}{4} = 3$$

The slope of the line is 3, or $\frac{3}{1}$.

It is important to note that if a graphed line is linear, the slope will remain the same regardless of which two points are selected. For example, the point (10,30) is also on the line. If the points (5,15) and (10,30) are substituted into the slope formula, the slope is still 3.

$$m = \frac{y_2 - y_1}{x_2 - x_1} = \frac{30 - 15}{10 - 5} = \frac{15}{5} = 3$$

This is can be explained with similar triangles.

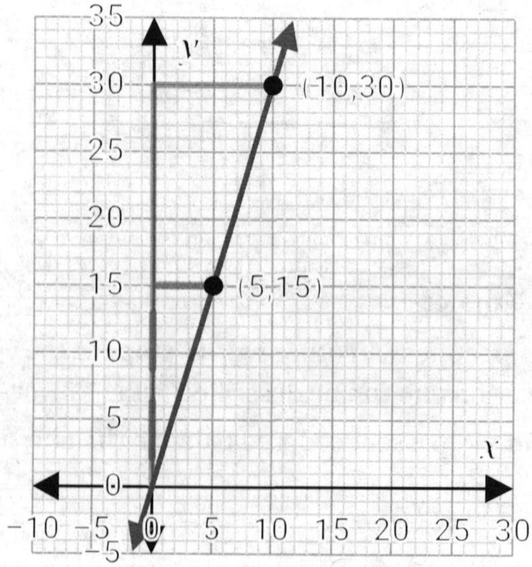


When multiple triangles are built from the same line, as in this scenario, the triangles are similar. This means that the slope of the hypotenuse will always be the same, regardless of the size of the right triangle. When any two points are plotted on a line, the ratio of the vertical change compared to the horizontal change for each right triangle that is formed will always be the same.

**Review Video: Finding the Slope of a Line**
Visit mometrix.com/academy and enter code: 766664

## Graphing Proportional Relationships

When a relationship contains two variables with ratios that are equivalent, the relationship is considered **proportional**. For example, if a chef takes 2 hours to cook 18 meals, the ratio $\frac{18}{2}$ can be used to describe the scenario. The ratio $\frac{18}{2}$ is proportional to $\frac{9}{1}$ because both fractions are the same when reduced to simplest form. "18 meals cooked in 2 hours," can be simplified to "9 meals cooked in 1 hour." 9 meals cooked in 1 hour is considered a unit rate. When a rate is "out of one" or "per one" it is a unit rate. The following scenarios are examples of unit rates.

Driving 55 miles per hour

Selling 26 t-shirts each day

Earning $400 each day

Heating up 1 degree each minute

Situations involving unit rates can be graphed by determining the slope. In a scenario involving a proportional relationship, the unit rate is the slope. For example, if a chef can cook 18 meals in 2 hours, or 9 meals in 1 hour, the unit rate is $\frac{9}{1}$, so the slope is also $\frac{9}{1}$, or 9. Slope can be thought of as the "steepness" of a line. The steepness of the line will be consistent because the relationship is proportional.

Slope is often referred to as $\frac{\textbf{rise}}{\textbf{run}}$, where the vertical change is divided by the horizontal change. In reference to the chef scenario, the unit rate is $\frac{9}{1}$, so the slope of the line representing the situation is $\frac{9}{1}$. This means that the "rise" is 9, and the "run" is 1. In other words, from the origin (0,0), the slope of the line will rise up 9 vertical units and run to the right 1 horizontal unit. From the point (1,9), another point can be plotted by "rising 9" and "running 1". When two or more points are plotted, a line is formed.

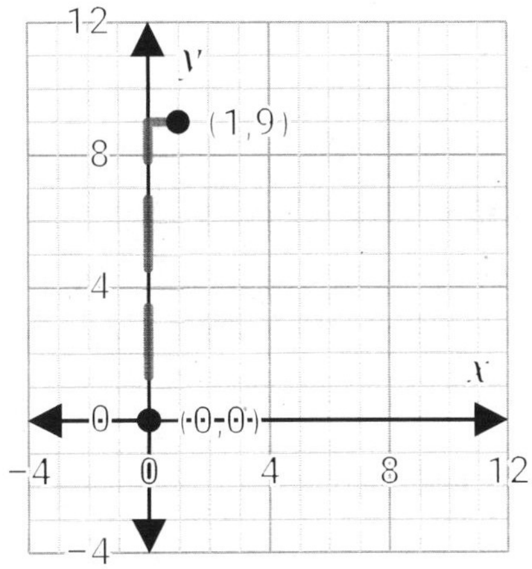

In this scenario, the graph will only be represented in the first quartile, where $x$- and $y$-values are always positive. This is because, realistically, a chef cannot cook a negative number of meals, or work within a negative amount of time.

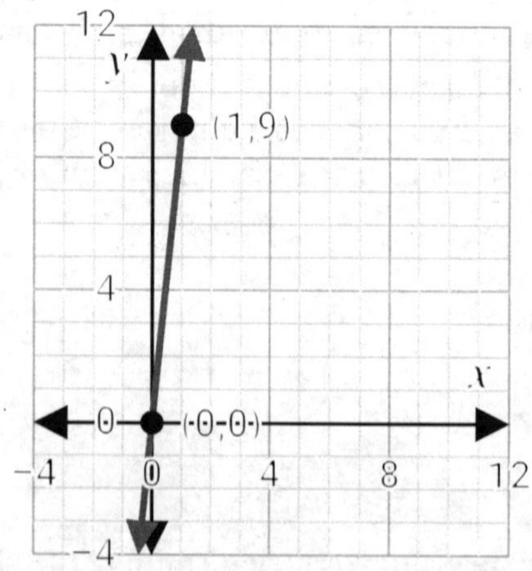


Slope will not always be positive (a line extending from the lower left to the upper right). Some scenarios will exhibit a negative proportional relationship.

For example, if a diving team starts at the surface of the water and dives down towards the ocean floor at a steady rate, the scenario will represent a negative proportional relation. If the diver descends 2 feet each second, the equation $y = -2x$ can be used to represent the scenario. The diver descends 2 feet (rise of −2) each second (run of 1). This means that the slope of the line is −2. Starting at the point (0,0) the plotted points will "rise" 2 units in the negative direction, and "run" 1 unit in the positive direction. The points (0,0) and $(1, -2)$ can be connected to form a line representing the negative proportional relationship.

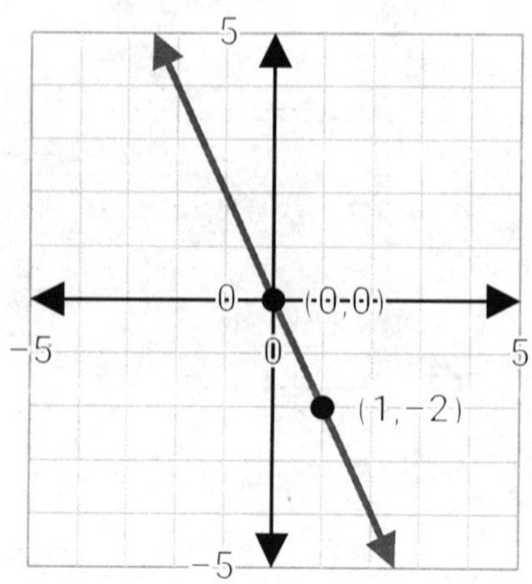

### EXAMPLE

Sam's Corner Store is having a produce sale. During the sale, a customer purchased 3 pounds of apples for $3.60. Use a unit rate to determine the slope, and then graph the scenario.

It costs $3.60 to purchase 3 pounds of apples. Divide to find the unit rate.

$$3.6 \div 3 = 1.2$$

This means it costs $1.20 to purchase 1 pound of apples. So, $1.20 per pound is a unit rate. The slope will be the same as the unit rate. The slope is $\frac{1.2}{1}$. The "rise" is 1.2, and the "run" is 1. Start at the point (0,0) and "rise" 1.2 units and "run" 1 unit.

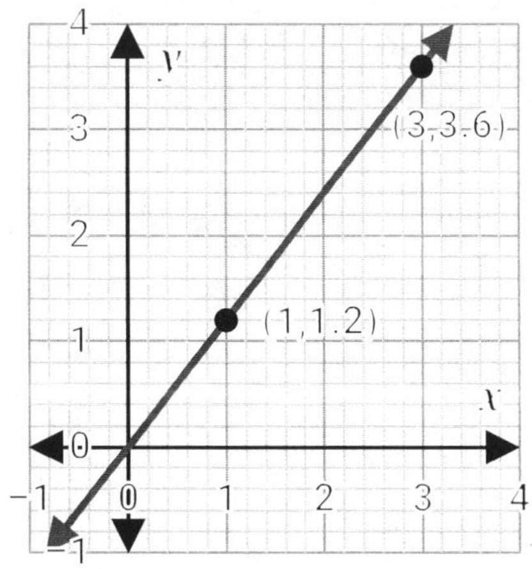

### EXAMPLE

It costs $1.25 to play five games of pinball. Use a unit rate to determine the slope, and then graph the scenario.

It costs $1.25 to play 5 games of pinball. Divide to find the unit rate.

$$1.25 \div 5 = 0.25$$

This means it costs $0.25 to play one game. So, $0.25 cents per game is a unit rate. The slope will be the same as the unit rate. This means the slope is $\frac{0.25}{1}$. The "rise" is 0.25 and the "run" is 1. Start at the point (0,0) and "rise" 0.25 and "run" 1.

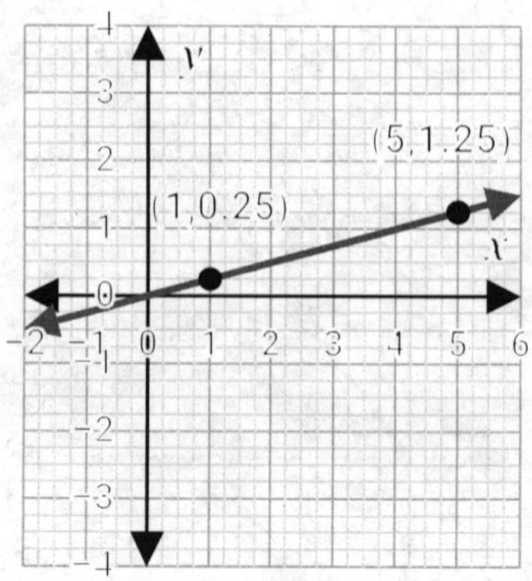

# Determining Rates and Slopes

Rate of change problems are often accompanied by a graph or a table. Rates can be determined from graphs and tables by identifying aspects such as slope and $y$-intercept.

## Determining a Rate from a Graph

The **rate** is the **slope** of the line. For example, a rate of 4 miles per hour would be graphed with a slope of 4. To determine the slope of a line, identify the vertical change and the horizontal change. This can be done by drawing a right triangle over the line. Plot points on two coordinates of the line, and identify the vertical change, or "rise" and the horizontal change, or "run."

For example, for the line below, points can be plotted at (0,1) and (4,4).

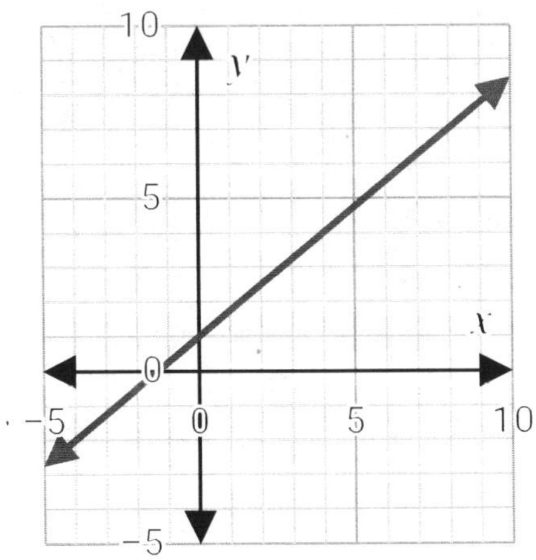


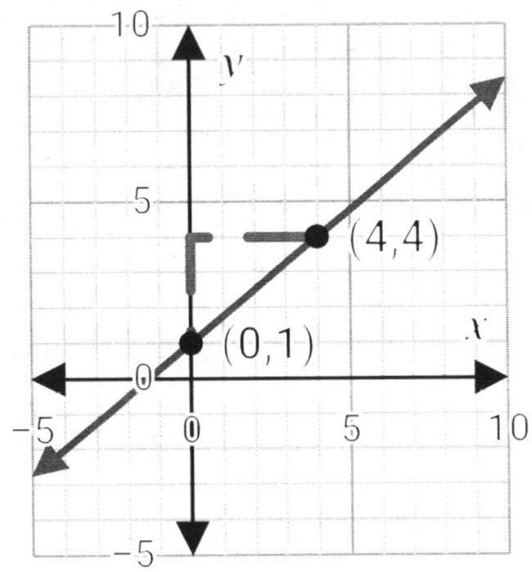


Connect the points to form a right triangle. Notice how the triangle has a "rise" of 3 and a "run" of 4. Slope is defined as the vertical change divided by the horizontal change, so the slope of the line is $\frac{3}{4}$. This can also be done using the slope formula, $m = \frac{y_2 - y_1}{x_2 - x_1}$, where $x$ and $y$ represent ordered pairs, and $m$ represents the slope.

$$m = \frac{y_2 - y_1}{x_2 - x_1} = \frac{4 - 1}{4 - 0} = \frac{3}{4}$$

A rate of $\frac{3}{4}$ could represent a scenario such as a plant growing at a steady rate of $\frac{3}{4}$ centimeters each month. In this case, the height of the plant depends on the number of months it has been growing. This means the dependent variable ($y$-variable) is the height of the plant. The independent variable ($x$-variable) is the number of months the plant has been growing. The $y$-intercept is where the line intersects the $y$-axis. The line has a $y$-intercept of 1 at the point (0,1). For this scenario, a $y$-intercept of 1 represents an initial plant height of 1 centimeter prior to tracking growth.

### EXAMPLE

Use the graph to determine the slope and $y$-intercept of the line.

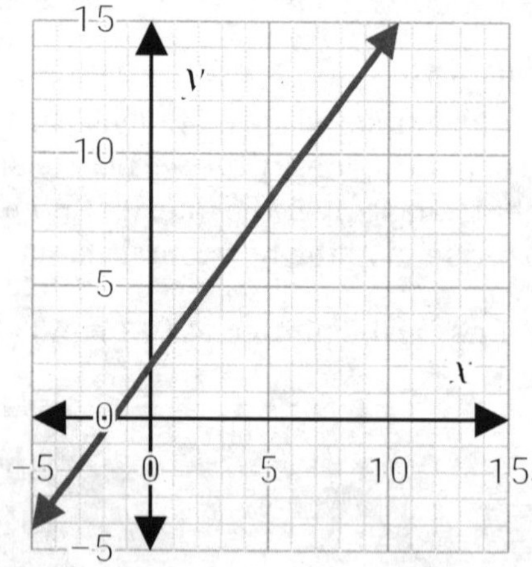


The slope is $\frac{5}{4}$ and the $y$-intercept is 2.

Pick two points on the line. For example, (0, 2) and (4, 7). Use the points to form a right triangle. The triangle has a vertical distance of 5 units and a horizontal distance of 4 units. The "rise" over the "run" is $\frac{5}{4}$. This means the slope of the line is $\frac{5}{4}$.

Using the slope formula: $m = \frac{y_2-y_1}{x_2-x_1} = \frac{7-2}{4-0} = \frac{5}{4}$

On a graph, the $y$-intercept is located at the point where the line intersects the $y$-axis. In this case, the line intersects the $y$-axis at the point (0,2). This means the $y$-intercept is 2.

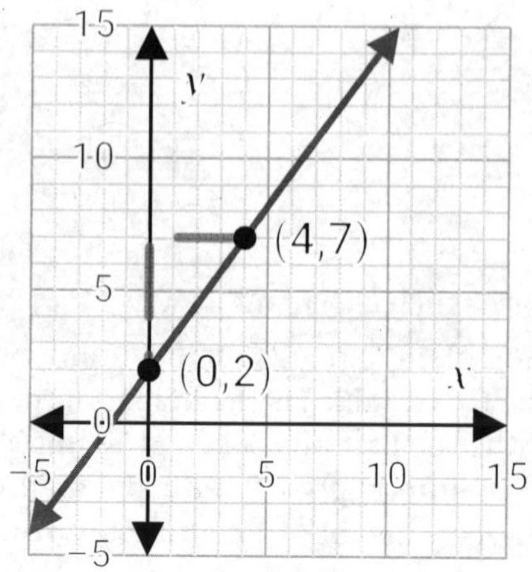

### DETERMINING A RATE FROM A TABLE

To determine slope from a table of values that represents a linear relationship, chose two points and apply the slope formula. Slope is calculated as the vertical change over the horizontal change using the formula, $m = \frac{y_2 - y_1}{x_2 - x_1}$. Select two ordered pairs from the table, and substitute these $x$- and $y$-values into the formula. It does not matter which pair is $y_1$ and $y_2$, or $x_1$ and $x_2$, as long as the arrangement is consistent. Consider the ordered pairs $(-5, 6)$ and $(-2,0)$. If 0 is designated as $y_2$, then -2 needs to be designated $x_2$.

| $x$ | $y$ |
|---|---|
| -5 | 6 |
| -4 | 4 |
| -3 | 2 |
| -2 | 0 |

$$m = \frac{y_2 - y_1}{x_2 - x_1} = \frac{0 - 6}{-2 - (-5)} = -\frac{6}{3} = -2$$

The slope, or rate of change, of the table of values is -2. The means that the rate of change in the table is -2. Every time the $x$-value increases by 1, the $y$-value decreases by 2. The $y$-intercept can be determined by locating the point where $x$ is equal to 0. Work backwards to find the value of $y$ when $x = 0$. The table shows that $y = 0$ when $x = -2$. First, find the value of $y$ when $x = -1$ by using the slope and subtracting 2 from 0 to get -2. Repeat this method one more time to find the value of $y$ when $x = 0$. Subtract 2 from -2 to get -4. This means the $y$-intercept is -4.

#### *EXAMPLE*

Use the table to determine the slope and $y$-intercept of the linear relationship.

| $x$ | $y$ |
|---|---|
| 1 | 7 |
| 2 | 14 |
| 3 | 21 |
| 4 | 28 |

Slope is 7 and $y$-intercept is 0

The table contains $(x, y)$ ordered pairs that form a line when graphed. Substitute two ordered pairs into the slope formula. For example, use the points (1,7) and (3,21).

$$m = \frac{y_2 - y_1}{x_2 - x_1} = \frac{21 - 7}{3 - 1} = \frac{14}{2} = 7$$

The slope of the line is 7.

The $y$-intercept of a graph is the location where the graphed line intersects the $y$-axis. In other words, when $x$ is 0, the corresponding $y$-value represents the $y$-intercept. The $y$-intercept can be identified even if $x = 0$ is not listed in a table. One way to do this is to identify the consistent rate of change for both the $x$- and they $y$-variables. For example, in this table the $x$-values are increasing by 1 and the $y$-values are increasing by 7. This means that if $x$ is reduced by 1, then $y$ should be reduced by 7. In this case, when $x$ is reduced by 1 and $y$ is reduced by 7, the result is (0,0). This means the line passes through the origin (0,0), and the $y$-intercept is 0.

| $x$ | $y$ |
|---|---|
| 0 | 0 |
| 1 | 7 |
| 2 | 14 |
| 3 | 21 |
| 4 | 28 |

## Representing Linear Proportions

Equations that represent **proportional** relationships follow the form $y = kx$, where $k$ represents the **constant of proportionality**, and $x$ and $y$ represent an **ordered pair** in the corresponding graph or table. For example, consider the unit rate "55 miles per hour." This value is considered $k$, the constant of proportionality. When 55 is substituted in for $k$, the equation $y = kx$ becomes $y = 55x$.

### Determining the Constant of Proportionality from a Graph

Proportional relationships in the form of a graph can be expressed in the form $y = kx$ by identifying the constant of proportionality, $k$. The constant of proportionality determines the relationship between $x$ and $y$. On a graph, this is observed as the slope. For example, consider the graph below. When two points are plotted, the slope can be determined.

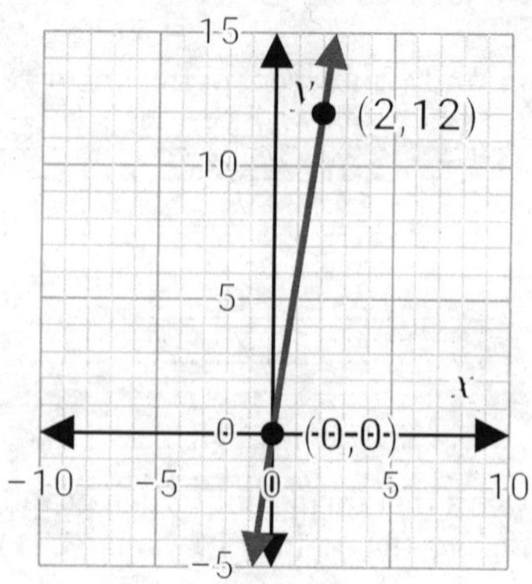


The line passing through the two points (0,0) and (2,12) forms the hypotenuse of a right triangle. The vertical side length of this triangle is 12 units, and the horizontal side length of this triangle is 2 units. Slope is defined as the vertical change over the horizontal change, so the slope of this line is $\frac{12}{2}$

or 6. Each $y$-value is determined by multiplying the corresponding $x$-value by 6. This means that the constant of proportionality is 6. The equation $y = kx$ becomes $y = 6x$.

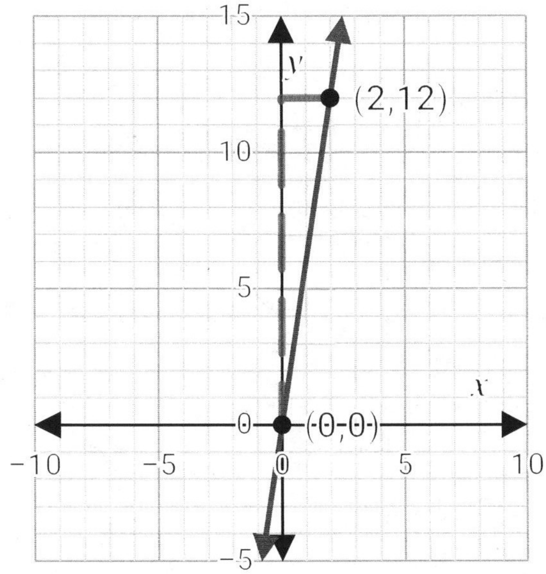


### Determining the Constant of Proportionality from a Table

A table can be used to determine $k$, the constant of proportionality, by identifying what amount $x$ is being multiplied by in order to produce $y$. This value will be the same for any row in the table if the relationship is directly proportional. Another key feature of directly proportional relationships is that they must include the point (0,0).

For example, consider the table below. What are the $x$-values multiplied by in order to produce the $y$-values? In this case each $x$-value is multiplied by 12. This means that the value of $k$ is equal to 12. The equation $y = kx$ becomes $y = 12x$.

| $x$ | $y$ |
|---|---|
| 0 | 0 |
| 1 | 12 |
| 2 | 24 |

## Representing Linear Non-Proportions

**Linear** situations form a **straight line** when graphed. For example, an employee that earns \$40 per hour represents a linear scenario. The money that the employee earns is calculated by multiplying their hours worked by 40. If they work 5 hours, they earn $5 \times \$40 = \$200$. This can be expressed as the equation $y = 40x$. When this kind of proportional relationship is graphed the $y$-intercept passes through the origin (0,0). However, not all linear scenarios will pass through the origin. **Non-proportional linear situations** form a line when graphed but do not pass through the origin.

### Non-Proportional Linear Situations in Graphs

For example, consider the following scenario. An employee receives a \$50 signing bonus when they are initially, and then they earn \$40 per hour. This relationship will form a straight line when graphed, but the $y$-intercept will not be (0,0). This is because the employee earned \$50 after 0 hours of work. In this case, the $y$-intercept will be (0,50). The line still has a consistent slope, but the line does not pass through the origin. This kind of linear non-proportional situation is expressed in equation form as $y = mx + b$, where $x$ and $y$ represent an ordered pair on the graphed line, $m$ represents the slope, and $b$ represents the $y$-intercept. In this case, the equation would be $y = 40x + 50$.

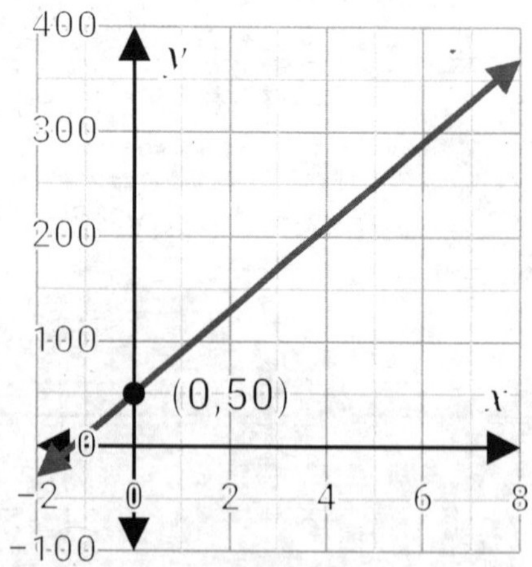


### Non-Proportional Linear Situations in Tables

Consider a similar scenario where an employee earns \$60 per hour and received a \$100 signing bonus. The employee earned \$100 for 0 hours of work, which means the $y$-intercept is (0,100). The employee also earns \$60 each hour, which means the total earnings can be calculated by adding 100, to 60 times the number of hours. For example, if the employee worked for 4 hours, he or she would earn $(4 \times 60) + 100 = \$340$. The equation $y = 60x + 100$ applies to the scenario. A table of values can be filled in for any number of hours.

| Hours Worked | Total Earnings |
|---|---|
| 0 | 100 |
| 1 | 160 |
| 2 | 220 |

The biggest difference between proportional linear situations and non-proportional linear situations is that the $y$-intercept for non-proportional situations is not (0,0). Linear proportional scenarios follow $y = kx$ and linear non-proportional scenarios follow $y = mx + b$.

## Writing Equations to Represent Linear Relationships

Linear relationships can be presented in the form of a table, graph, or verbal description. It is important to be able to interpret relationships presented in these three forms, and then write an equation in the form $y = mx + b$ that represents the scenario. In the equation $y = mx + b$, $m$ represents the slope, $b$ represents the $y$-intercept, and $x$ and $y$ represent an ordered pair that falls on the graphed line of the equation.

## Writing an Equation Based on a Table

| $x$ | $y$ |
|---|---|
| -1 | 9 |
| 0 | 11 |
| 1 | 13 |
| 2 | 15 |

The table shows $x$- and $y$-values. These values represent ordered pairs that can be graphed. When writing an equation from a table of values, two key pieces of information need to be identified: $y$-intercept and slope.

When $x = 0$, the corresponding $y$-value represents the $y$-intercept. In this scenario, when $x = 0$, $y = 11$. This means that the $y$-intercept, $b$, is 11.

Now determine the slope using the slope formula $m = \frac{y_2 - y_1}{x_2 - x_1}$. Select any two ordered pairs, for example, $(-1, 9)$ and $(0,11)$.

$$m = \frac{11 - 9}{0 - (-1)} = \frac{2}{1} = 2$$

The slope, $m$, is 2.

The $y$-intercept and slope are identified, so the equation can be expressed in the form $y = mx + b$. Substitute in values for $m$ and $b$. The table can be represented using the equation $y = 2x + 11$.

### *Example*

Write an equation that can be used to describe the relationship displayed in the table.

| $x$ | $y$ |
|---|---|
| 3 | 40 |
| 4 | 45 |
| 5 | 50 |
| 6 | 55 |

$y = 5x + 25$

Identify the $y$-intercept, $b$, and the slope, $m$.

The $y$-intercept is the value of $y$, when $x$ equals 0. The value for $x = 0$ is not listed in the table, so use the pattern to identify the value of $y$ when $x$ is 0. The $y$-values increase by 5 and the $x$-values increase by 1. Apply this pattern in reverse. When $x = 2$ then $y = 35$. When $x = 1$ then $y = 30$. When $x = 0$ then $y = 25$. The $y$-intercept is 25.

$$b = 25$$

The slope can be calculated using the slope formula $m = \frac{y_2 - y_1}{x_2 - x_1}$. Select any two ordered pairs and substitute the values into the formula. When (3,40) and (4,45) are selected, $m = \frac{y_2 - y_1}{x_2 - x_1}$ becomes $m = \frac{45-40}{4-3}$, which simplifies to $\frac{5}{1}$ or 5. The slope is 5, so $m = 5$.

$$y = 5x + 25$$

## WRITING AN EQUATION BASED ON A GRAPH

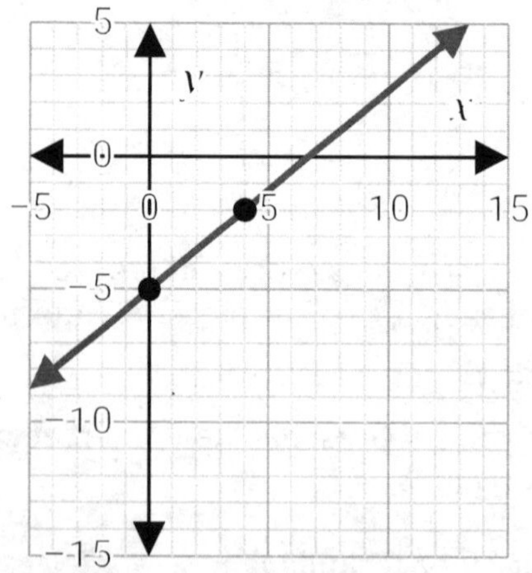


To write the equation in $y = mx + b$ form start by identifying the $y$-intercept. This is the location where the graphed line intersects the $y$-axis. The $y$-intercept of this line is $(0, -5)$, so $b$ is -5.

Now identify the slope. Slope is defined as the vertical change divided by the horizontal change. In other words, $\frac{\text{rise}}{\text{run}}$. Pick two points on the line. For example, $(0, -5)$ and $(4, -2)$. Use the slope formula $m = \frac{y_2 - y_1}{x_2 - x_1}$. The formula becomes $m = \frac{-2-(-5)}{4-0}$, which simplifies to $m = \frac{3}{4}$. The slope of the line is $\frac{3}{4}$. This means that $m$, in the equation $y = mx + b$, is $\frac{3}{4}$.

The $y$-intercept and slope are identified, so the equation can be expressed in $y = mx + b$ form.

$$y = \frac{3}{4}x - 5$$

Writing an equation to model a relationship within a verbal description:

When writing equations from verbal descriptions, it is important to determine which variable is independent and which is dependent. The independent variable is represented by $x$, and the dependent variable is represented by $y$. For example, consider the following verbal scenario.

A medium pizza costs $24, plus 50 cents for each topping. Express the cost of a medium pizza using an equation.

Start by identifying the independent ($x$) and dependent ($y$) variables. Ask yourself, does price depend on the number of toppings, or does the number of toppings depend on the price? The price depends on the number of toppings so the independent variable is the number of toppings. This means that in the equation, $x$ will represent toppings and $y$ will represent price.

Now identify the $y$-intercept. In other words, when $x$ is 0, what is the value of $y$? In this case, when there are 0 toppings on the pizza, the price is $24. This means that when $x$ is 0, $y$ is 24. 24 is the $y$-intercept, $b$, in the equation $y = mx + b$.

The number of toppings, $x$, is multiplied by the price per topping, which is 50 cents. The value that is multiplied by $x$ is considered the slope. This means that the slope, or $m$, in this scenario is 0.5.

The $y$-intercept and slope are identified, so the equation can be expressed in the form $y = mx + b$.

$$y = 0.5x + 24$$

### *EXAMPLE*

Write an equation that can be used to describe the relationship displayed in the graph.

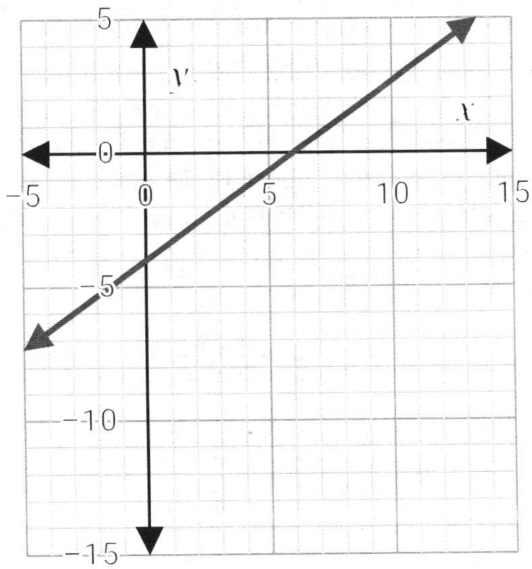


$y = \frac{2}{3}x - 4$

Identify the $y$-intercept and slope.

The $y$-intercept is the location where the graphed line intersects the $y$-axis. The line passes through the $y$-axis at the point $(0, -4)$. The $y$-intercept is −4.

The slope can be determined using the slope formula $m = \frac{y_2 - y_1}{x_2 - x_1}$. Select two points on the line such as $(0, -4)$ and $(3, -2)$.

$$m = \frac{-2 - (-4)}{3 - 0} = \frac{2}{3}$$

The slope, $m$, is $\frac{2}{3}$.

$$y = \frac{2}{3}x - 4$$

# Intersections of Graphed Linear Equations

**Linear equations** form a straight line when graphed. When two linear equations are graphed, and the lines **intersect**, the point of intersection is the **solution**. To solve a system of two linear equations in two variables means to find all ordered pairs that satisfy both equations. The solution to a system may be one ordered pair, infinitely many ordered pairs, or no ordered pairs. Solving can be done graphically, numerically using a table, or algebraically using substitution or elimination. To solve graphically, graph both linear equations on the same coordinate plane to find if the lines intersect at one point, never intersect, or are the same line. It is helpful if both equations are in slope-intercept form so that the lines can be graphed using the slope and $y$-intercept. Before graphing the system $2x - y = -3$ and $y = 3x + 8$, put the first equation in slope-intercept form. Move $2x$ using subtraction then move the coefficient of $-1$ on $y$ using division. The equation becomes $y = 2x + 3$, so the line has a slope of 2 and a $y$-intercept at (0,3). The second equation, $y = 3x + 8$, has a slope of 3 and a $y$-intercept at (0,8). The graph shows the system has one solution because the lines intersect at $(-5, -7)$.

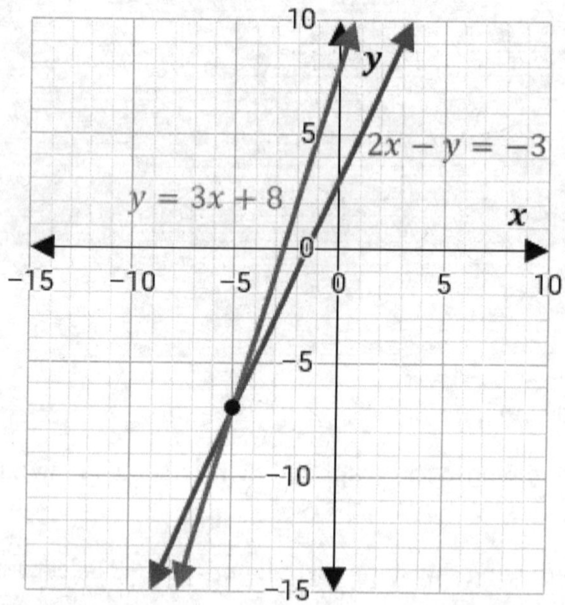


To solve numerically using a table, substitute $x$ values into both equations to find if the equations have the same $y$ value for one value of $x$, all values of $x$, or no values of $x$. Just like when graphing, it is helpful if the equations are in slope-intercept form to make substituting $x$ values easier. Before creating a table for the system $y = -\frac{1}{2}x + 3$ and $-x + y = 6$, move $-x$ in the second equation to the opposite side using addition to make it $y = x + 6$. When creating a table of values, choose both positive and negative numbers to substitute into the equations.

| $x$ | $-3$ | $-2$ | $-1$ | $0$ | $1$ | $2$ | $3$ |
|---|---|---|---|---|---|---|---|
| $y = -\frac{1}{2}x + 3$ | $\frac{9}{2}$ | 4 | $\frac{7}{2}$ | 3 | $\frac{5}{2}$ | 2 | $\frac{3}{2}$ |
| $y = x + 6$ | 3 | 4 | 5 | 6 | 7 | 8 | 9 |

The equations have the same $y$ value of 4 when $x = -2$, therefore the system has one solution, $(-2,4)$.

To solve algebraically using substitution, choose one equation and solve for one of the variables. This step may be skipped if one of the equations already has a variable isolated such as $y = 3x + 2$. Substitute the expression for the solved variable in the other equation so that there is now an equation in one variable. Solve the resulting equation to find the value of the one variable. Substitute this answer into the equation found in the first step to find the value of the other variable.

Example: Solve $\begin{cases} x - 3y = 15 \\ 3x + 2y = 1 \end{cases}$ using substitution.

When possible, solve for a variable with a coefficient of 1. In this case, the variable $x$ in the first equation is the easiest to solve for by moving $-3y$ using addition. The result of $x = 15 + 3y$ gives an expression for $x$ in terms of $y$ that can be substituted into the second equation for $x$. The resulting equation has one variable, $y$.

$$\begin{gathered} 3(15 + 3y) + 2y = 1 \\ 45 + 9y + 2y = 1 \\ 45 + 11y = 1 \\ -45 \quad\quad -45 \\ \frac{11y}{11} = \frac{-44}{11} \\ y = -4 \end{gathered}$$

To find the value of $x$, substitute $-4$ for $y$ into $x = 15 + 3y$. $x = 15 + 3(-4) = 15 - 12 = 3$. $(3,-4)$ is the one solution to the system.

To solve algebraically using elimination, choose a variable to eliminate. Create an equivalent system of equations so that when the two equations are added together, the chosen variable is eliminated. To create an equivalent system, multiply one or both of the equations by a nonzero number so that the coefficients on the chosen variable are opposites in each equation. This step may be skipped if the two original equations already have opposite coefficients on one of the variables. Once the equations have opposite coefficients on the chosen variable, add the two equations together and eliminate that variable. The resulting equation will be an equation in one variable. Solve the resulting equation to find the value of one variable. Substitute this answer into one of the original equations and solve for the value of the other variable.

Example: Solve $\begin{cases} 3x + 7y = -1 \\ x + 4y = 3 \end{cases}$ using elimination. To eliminate $x$, multiply the second equation by $-3$ to create the equivalent equation $-3x - 12y = -9$. Add the first equation and the equivalent equation together. The result is an equation with one variable, $y$.

$$\begin{gathered} \begin{cases} 3x + 7y = -1 \\ -3x - 12y = -9 \end{cases} \\ \frac{-5y}{-5} = \frac{-10}{-5} \\ y = 2 \end{gathered}$$

To find the value of $x$, substitute 2 for $y$ into either original equation. The easiest choice is $x + 4y = 3$.

$$\begin{aligned} x + 4(2) &= 3 \\ x + 8 &= 3 \\ -8 \quad & \quad -8 \\ x &= -5 \end{aligned}$$

$(-5,2)$ is the solution to the system.

When solving systems of equations algebraically, a result of infinitely many solutions or no solution is recognized similarly to solving a linear equation with those results. There will be infinitely many solutions if solving for one of the variables results in a term or expression equal to itself. There will be no solution if solving for one of the variables results in a false statement. It is also possible to recognize these solutions by inspecting the two equations. For example, the system $x + y = 4$ and $2x + 2y = 8$ has infinitely many solutions because the equations are equivalent and will coincide on the graph. The second equation is the first equation multiplied by 2. The system $x + 3y = 7$ and $x + 3y = -3$ has no solution because $x + 3y$ cannot equal both 7 and $-3$.

## Application of Systems of Linear Equations

A real-world problem involving a system of linear equations has two unknown quantities, and two linear equations are created from the information given in the problem. The following steps provide a plan for creating a system of equations from a real-world scenario.

1. Define the two variables by identifying the unknown quantities. In most cases, the unknown quantities are what the question asks you to find.
2. Identify any quantities representing a total amount. If there are fewer than 2 totals given, see step 4.
3. Use the information given to write an equation that equals each total amount found in step 2. Pay careful attention to what the total amount represents to ensure both sides of the equation describe the same thing. For example, if the total is a dollar amount and the variables represent number of items, the variables need to have coefficients that are dollar amounts so that the units on both sides of the equation are dollars.
4. If less than 2 totals are given, write the remaining equation(s) using a relationship given in the scenario between the two unknown quantities. For example, "the width of a rectangle is 4 more than twice the length" describes a relationship from which the equation $w = 2l + 4$ can be created.

While a system of equations can be solved graphically, using a table, or algebraically using substitution or elimination, real-world problems are best solved using substitution or elimination. If the solutions are not integers, it becomes difficult to find the solution by graphing or with a table of values.

# Functions

## Identifying Functions

A **relation** defines a relationship between two sets of elements. A relation may be represented in a variety of ways, such as a table, a mapping diagram, a collection of ordered pairs, or a graph. The first set of elements is called the **inputs** or **domain**. The second set of elements is called the **outputs** or **range**. If a relation is in the form of ordered pairs or a graph, the $x$ values are the inputs, and the $y$ values are the outputs. Examples of four types of relations are shown below.

**Relation 1**

| Input | Output |
|---|---|
| 4 | -2 |
| -3 | 0 |
| 5 | -2 |
| 1 | 1 |

**Relation 2**

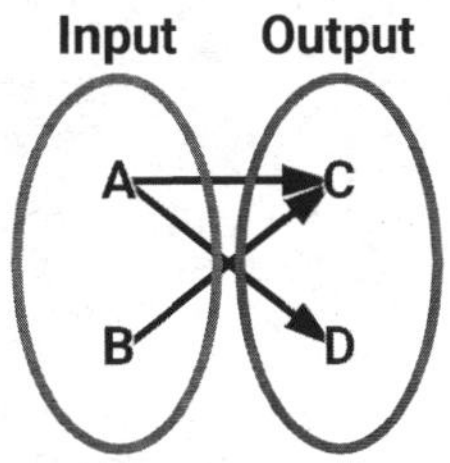


**Relation 3**

$\{(9,3), (-4,2), (0,-1)\}$

**Relation 4**

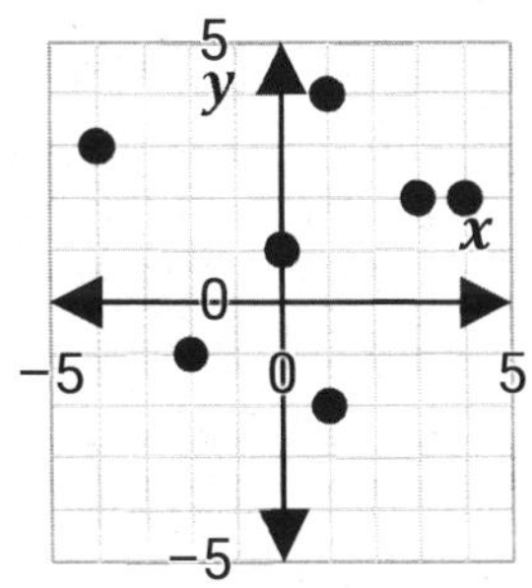


A **function** is a type of relation that assigns each input to exactly one output. In other words, a function cannot have more than one output assigned to any single input. It is possible for a function to have two or more inputs that all have the same output. Relations 1 and 3 are functions because every input has exactly one output. Relation 2 is not a function because the input A has two outputs: C and D. Relation 4 is not a function because the $x$-value 1 has two $y$-values: $-2$ and 4. Notice that if a vertical line was drawn at $x = 1$, the line would touch two points: $(1,-2)$ and $(1,4)$. The **vertical line test** can be used to quickly determine if a graph is a function. A graph represents a function if no vertical line intersects the graph at more than one point. If a vertical line intersects the graph at more than one point anywhere on the graph, it does not represent a function.

A function may also be given as a rule in the form of a verbal description or equation. For example, suppose a rule for a function is to divide the input by 2 then add 6. If 8 is an input for this function, then the output can be calculated by dividing 8 by 2 and adding 6, which results in an output of 10. This same function could also be written as $y = \frac{x}{2} + 6$.

**Review Video: Definition of a Function**
Visit mometrix.com/academy and enter code: 784611

## Representation of Functions

Functions do not have to be represented in the same way to compare properties between them, provided that the property being compared can be found from each representation of the function. For example, the rate of change and $y$-intercepts of linear functions can be compared even if the functions are in different forms. Consider the three functions below:

**Function A**

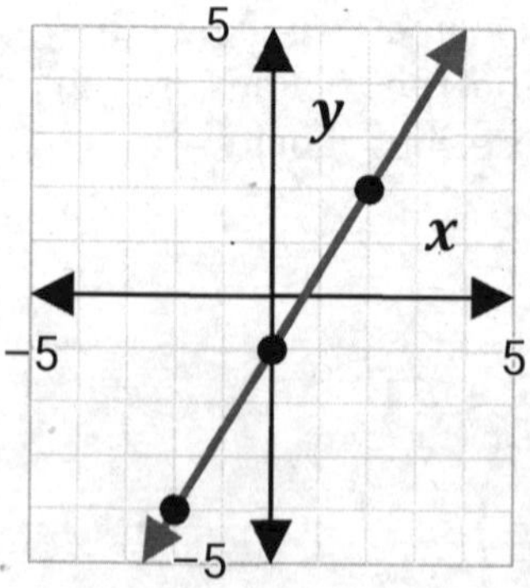


**Function B**

$y = 5x - 1$

**Function C**

| $x$ | $y$ |
|---|---|
| −4 | 1 |
| 0 | 3 |
| 4 | 5 |

The rate of change, also known as slope, of a linear function is the ratio of the vertical change to the horizontal change. It is the same between any two distinct points on a linear function. Beginning at $(0, -1)$, Function A rises 3 and runs right 2 to the point $(2,2)$; therefore, the rate of change is $\frac{3}{2}$. When given a linear equation in the form of $y = mx + b$, also known as slope-intercept form, $m$ is the rate of change. For Function B, the rate of change is 5. In the table, Function C's $y$-values increase by 2, and the $x$-values increase by 4 resulting in a rate of change of $\frac{2}{4}$ which simplifies to $\frac{1}{2}$. Function C has the smallest rate of change while Function B has the largest rate of change.

The $y$-intercept of a function is the point at which the function intersects the $y$-axis. The $x$-value is 0 at the $y$-intercept. Function A has a $y$-intercept at $(0, -1)$. When given a linear equation in the form of $y = mx + b$, $(0, b)$ is the $y$-intercept. Function B has a $y$-intercept at $(0, -1)$. Function C has a $y$-intercept at $(0,3)$. Functions A and B have the same $y$-intercept while Function C has a larger $y$-intercept.

### *Ordered Pairs*

Ordered pairs consist of $x$- and $y$-values. The $x$-values represent the **independent variable**, or the input. The $y$-values represent the **dependent variable**, or the output. For example, the ordered pair $(8,10)$ has an $x$-value of 8 and a $y$-value of 10. When $x$ is 8 the value of $y$ is 10.

A set of ordered pairs can be used to determine if a relationship is a function. No input can have more than one output. If no two ordered pairs have the same $x$-value with differing $y$-values, the relation is a function. A common example to illustrate this rule is to compare a function to a restaurant menu. A menu can contain multiple items for the same price, but a menu cannot contain the same item for differing prices. This makes a restaurant menu a function.

These points represent a function: $(2,6)$, $(5,30)$, $(10,30)$

Each input is associated with one output. There are two ordered pairs with a $y$-value of 30, and this is fine because there is not the same input aligned with more than one output.

These points do not represent a function: $(10, -20)$, $(-20, 10)$, $(-10, 8)$, $(10, 18)$

This is not a function because one of the input values has more than one output value. The input value of 10 is listed twice, with two different output values, –20 and 18. The points $(10, -20)$ and $(10,18)$ prove that the relationship is not a function.

### TABLES

Tables can be used to identify whether a relationship is a function. If each input has only one output value, then the relationship is a function. If an input has more than one different output value, then the relationship is not a function. For example, consider the tables below.

This table represents a function:

| Input | Output |
|---|---|
| 1 | 15 |
| 2 | 45 |
| 3 | 23 |
| 4 | 33 |

The relationship modeled in the table is function because each input is paired with only one output.

This table is not a function:

| Input | Output |
|---|---|
| 2 | 20 |
| 4 | 40 |
| 3 | 30 |
| 2 | 40 |

The relationship modeled in the table is not a function because the input 2 has more than one output. The table shows that the input 2 can have an output of 20 or 40. This means the relationship is not a function.

#### EXAMPLE

Does the table represent a function? Explain.

| $x$ | -3 | 3 | 0 | -5 | -3 |
|---|---|---|---|---|---|
| $y$ | 9 | 3 | 5 | -2 | -9 |

No. The table does not represent a function. The $x$-value of –3 has more than one corresponding $y$-value. When $x$ is –3, and the corresponding $y$-values are 9 and –9. A function cannot have more than one output for the same input.

## MAPS

Mapping diagrams are useful when studying the relationship between input and output values. Maps usually appear as two circles containing elements or values. Arrows point from one set of values to the other set of values, noting the relationship between input and output. For example, consider the map below.

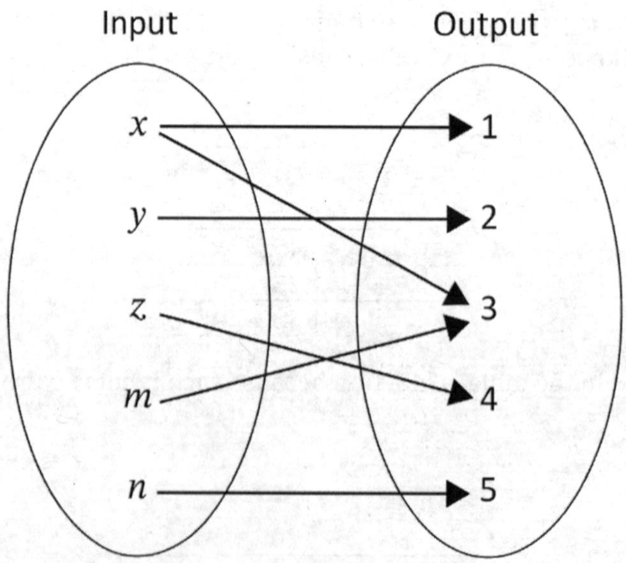


Notice how $x$ in the input has more than one output value, 1 and 3. This indicates that the relationship is not a function.

However, consider the map below. Notice how each input has a unique output value. This indicates that the relationship IS a function.

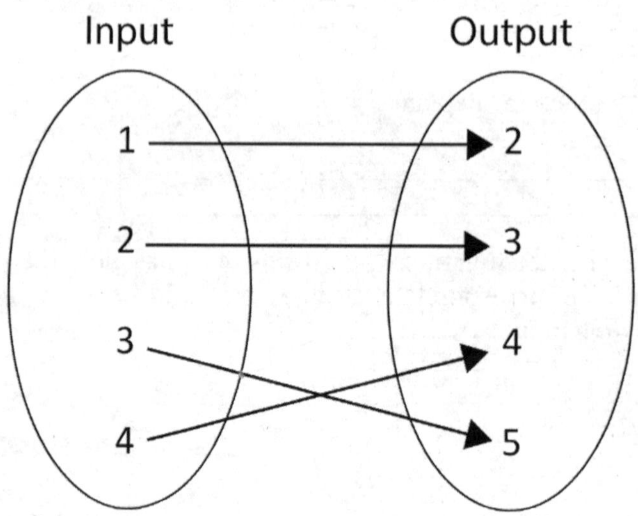

### *Graphs*

Functions have only one output value for each input value. This can be tested on a graph using what is referred to as the vertical line test. To determine if a graph represents a function, draw multiple vertical lines through the graph. If any of the lines pass through the graphed line more than once, the relationship does not represent a function. If each drawn line only passes through the graphed line at one point each, then the relationship represents a function.

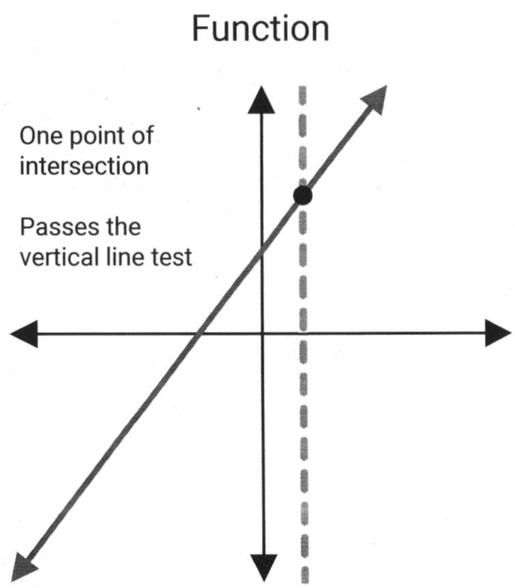


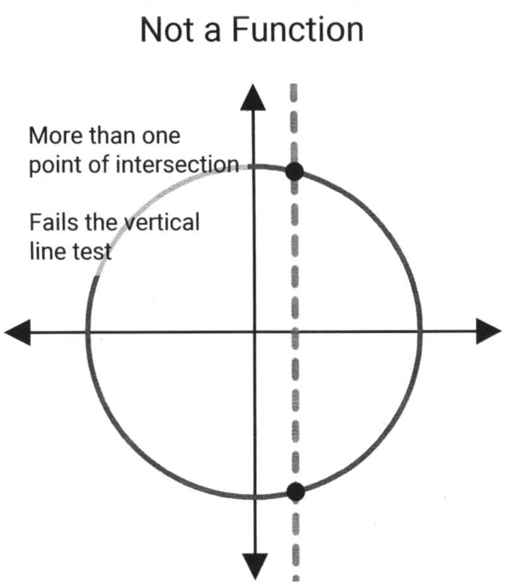

EXAMPLE

**Which graph represents a function? Explain.**

a. 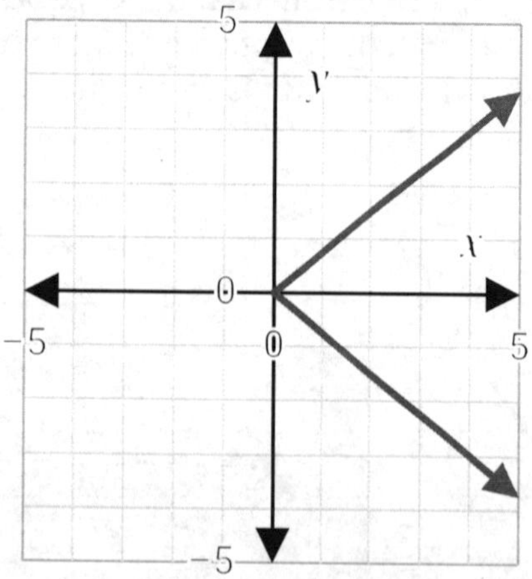 b. 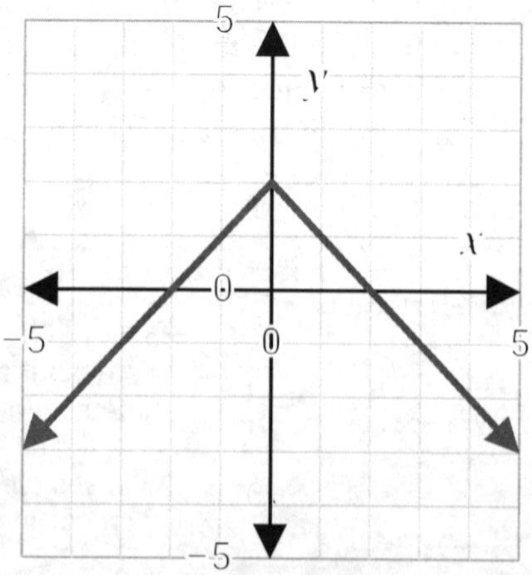

Graph B is a function. Graph B satisfies the vertical line test. Graph A fails the vertical line test because a vertical line can be drawn that intersects the graph at more than one location.

## LINEAR AND NON-LINEAR FUNCTIONS

Functions can be classified as linear or non-linear. A continuous function whose inputs are the set of all real numbers is **linear** if it can be represented as an equation in the form $y = mx + b$, also known as slope-intercept form, where $m$ and $b$ are real numbers. The graph of a linear function is a straight line. A function that cannot be written as an equation in slope-intercept form and whose graph does not form a straight line is called **nonlinear**. Consider the 4 continuous functions below:

| **Function A** | **Function B** | **Function C** |
|---|---|---|
| $4x + 3y = 7$ | $y = 3x^2 - 2$ | $y = \|x + 1\|$ |

**Function D**

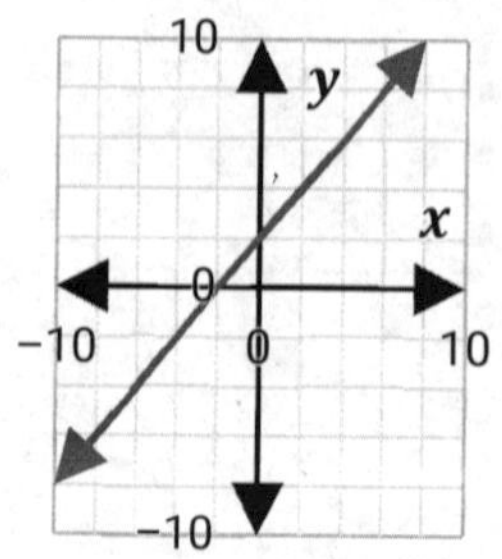

**Function E**

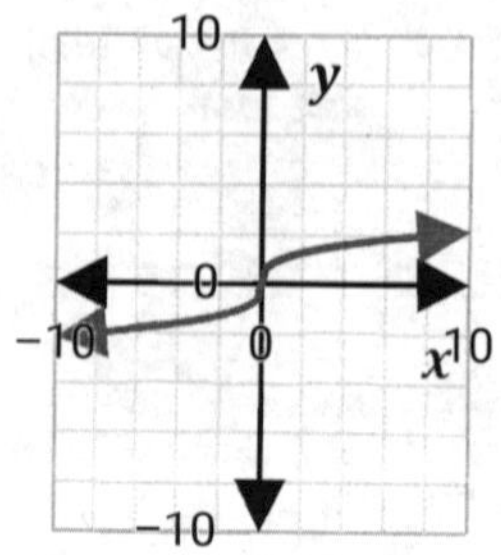

Function A is linear despite not being in slope-intercept form. It can be re-written by moving $4x$ using subtraction then dividing by 3 which results in $y = -\frac{4}{3}x + \frac{7}{3}$. To identify an equation of a linear function not written in slope-intercept form, the exponents on both variables cannot be larger than 1. Neither variable can be inside an operation such as a root or absolute value or be in the denominator of a fraction, and the variables cannot be multiplied by one another. Functions B and C are nonlinear. A function that includes any of the conditions prohibited for linear function is nonlinear. Function D is linear because its graph is a straight line. Function E is nonlinear because its graph is not a straight line.

Discrete functions whose inputs are limited to a set of listed values can also be classified as linear or nonlinear. These types of functions are only linear if the rate of change between any two points is the same. Consider the 3 discrete functions below:

**Function F**

$\{(-3,1), (0,-2), (3,-5)\}$

**Function G**

| $x$ | $y$ |
|---|---|
| 2 | 5 |
| 6 | 7 |
| 10 | 9 |
| 14 | 11 |

**Function H**

| $x$ | $y$ |
|---|---|
| −2 | 5 |
| 0 | 3 |
| 2 | 1 |
| 4 | 4 |

Functions F and G are both linear. For Function F, the $y$-values decrease by 3, and the $x$-values increase by 3 resulting in a constant rate of change of $-1$. For Function G, the $y$-values increase by 2, and the $x$-values increase by 4 resulting in a constant rate of change of $\frac{1}{2}$. Function H is nonlinear because the ordered pairs do not have a constant rate of change. It appears that the $y$-values decrease by 2 as the $x$-values increase by 2, but the last point listed (4,4) deviates from that pattern.

## Increasing and Decreasing Functions

The functional relationship between two quantities may be described as increasing, decreasing, or constant. A function is increasing if its output values increase as input values increase. The graph of an increasing function rises from left to right. For example, a continuous linear function with a positive slope is increasing. A function is decreasing if its output values decrease as input values increase. The graph of a decreasing function falls from left to right. For example, a continuous linear function with a negative slope is decreasing. A function is constant if its outputs are the same for all inputs. A horizontal line is a constant function. While some functions such as linear functions are increasing, decreasing or constant over their entire domain, some functions are not the same over their entire domain.

A function may contain different intervals within its domain that are increasing, decreasing, and/or constant. For these functions, the interval is described using $x$-values. For example, the function $y = |x + 1|$ represented on the graph below is decreasing until $x = -1$, at which point, it changes to increasing.

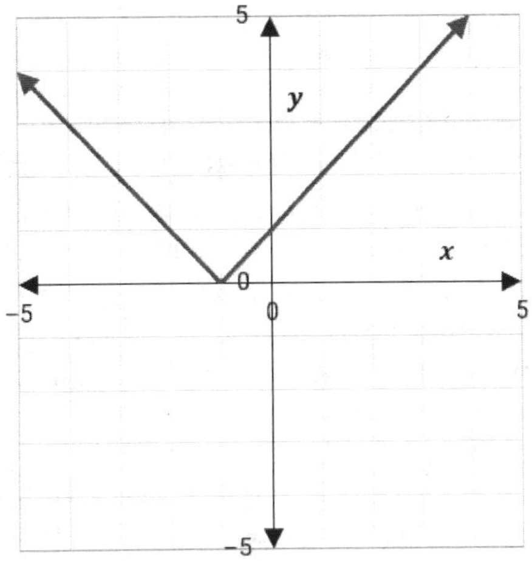

Not all functions are defined by a single equation. A piecewise function is a function that has a different equation for each specified interval or "piece" of the domain. Consider the piecewise function graphed below:

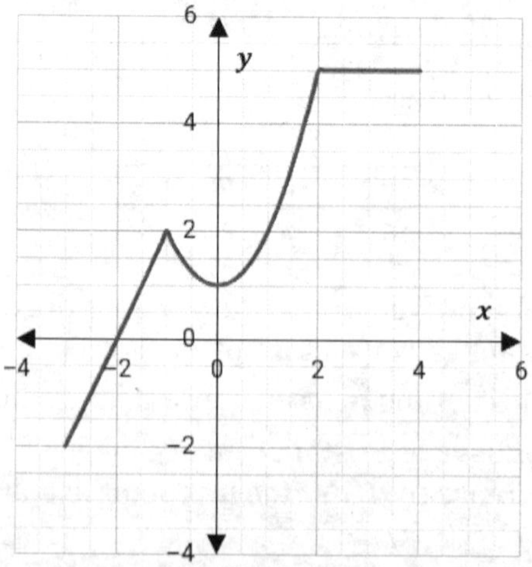


This piecewise function is increasing from $x = -3$ to $x = -1$ and from $x = 0$ to $x = 2$. It is decreasing from $x = -1$ to $x = 0$. It is constant from $x = 2$ to $x = 4$. In addition to describing the increasing, decreasing, or constant intervals, linear or nonlinear intervals of a function can also be described using $x$-values. A linear interval is where the function's graph is a straight line. A nonlinear interval is where the function's graph is not a straight line. The piecewise function above is linear from $x = -3$ to $x = -1$ and from $x = 2$ to $x = 4$. It is nonlinear from $x = -1$ to $x = 2$.

## Constructing Linear Functions

Linear functions (represented by an equation of the form $y = mx + b$) can be used to model the relationship between many real-world quantities. The quantity that is **independent** of the other quantity is the input, $x$, of the function. Its value does not depend on the other quantity. The quantity that is **dependent** on the other quantity is the output, $y$, of the function. The value of $m$ in the function is the rate of change between the two quantities. The rate of change describes how much the output increases or decreases as the input increases. For a scenario depicted by a graph, the slope of the line is the rate of change. The value of the constant $b$ in the equation is the output when the input is 0, which is the same as the $y$-value of the $y$-intercept of its graph.

Many functions that model real-world situations do not have negative inputs (i.e., the domain is real numbers greater than or equal to zero). In those cases, the constant $b$ is also called the **initial value**. The graph of these functions begins at the $y$-axis and go to the right. When setting up a function to model a real-life situation it is important to determine whether the domain is restricted. Does the input represent a quantity of physical objects? If the function is relating the number of hamburgers purchased to the amount of money spent, the domain of the function cannot start less than 0 since it is not possible to purchase a negative number of hamburgers. When making a graph of this function, the graph cannot extend left of the $y$-axis.

Suppose a tank has water being added to it at a constant rate. After 3 minutes, the tank has 31 gallons of water. After 5 minutes, the tank has 49 gallons of water. A linear function can be used to model the number of gallons of water based on the number of minutes. What equation describes this relationship? The number of gallons of water in the tank depends on the number of minutes, so the output is the number of gallons and the input is the number of minutes. The scenario gives two input-output pairs: (3,31) and (5,49). The difference in the outputs is $49 - 31 = 18$ and the difference in the inputs is $5 - 3 = 2$. Dividing these differences results in a rate of change of $\frac{18}{2} = 9$, which is the value of $m$ in the linear equation. The water in the tank increases by 9 gallons per minute. The value of $b$ in the equation is the number of gallons of water in the tank at 0 minutes. To find this initial value, use the linear equation formular $y = mx + b$. After substituting values in, the result would be $31 = 9(3) + b$. The next step would be to solve for $b$, the number of gallons in the tank at 0 minutes, in the equation. The result is that $b = 4$. Therefore, the linear function modeling this situation is $y = 9x + 4$.

## Identifying Proportional Functions

A function is a rule or law that defines a relationship between an independent variable, $x$, and a dependent variable, $y$. Functions can be proportional or non-proportional.

In equation form, functions that are proportional have the form $y = mx$, and functions that are non-proportional have the form $y = mx + b$. This is because proportional relationships always have the same ratio between the two variables.

**Proportional functions:** The ratio of $x$ to $y$ is consistent.

$$y = 2x$$
$$y = \frac{3}{4}x$$
$$y = -6x$$

**Non-proportional functions:** The ratio of $x$ to $y$ is not consistent.

$$y = 5x - 1$$
$$y = -\frac{3}{2}x + 9$$
$$y = 5x + \frac{1}{2}$$

## GRAPHS

It can be helpful to use a graph to determine whether a function is proportional or not. If the function passes through the origin (0,0) and has a consistent slope, it is a proportional function. If not, it is not a proportional function.

Consider the graph below. This graph relates time, $x$, to cost, $y$. As time increases, cost increases proportionally. When 0 hours have elapsed, the cost is \$0. The graphed line passes through the origin and the slope is consistent, so the function is proportional.

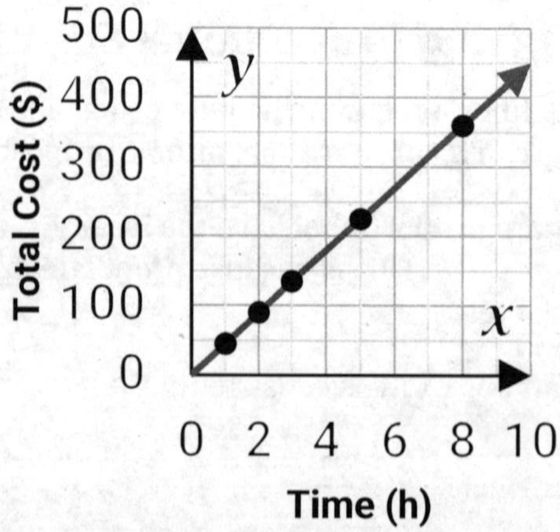


The graph below relates games, $x$, to total cost, $y$. The total cost increases as the number of games increases. However, when the number of games is 0, the cost is not 0. The initial price before playing any games is \$5. The graphed line does not pass through the origin, so the function is not proportional.

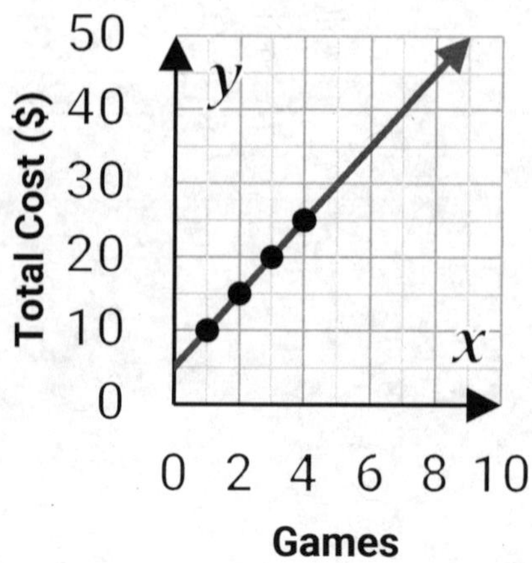

## TABLES

Tables can also be used to determine if a function is proportional. If the ratio of $x$ to $y$ is consistent, then the relationship is proportional. One way to check this is to divide each $x$-value by its corresponding $y$-value. If the ratio is consistent for each pair, and the line passes through the point (0,0), then the relationship is proportional.

For example, consider the table below. When each $x$-value is divided by the corresponding $y$-value, the result is 0.5. The line also passes through the point (0,0), so the relationship between $x$ and $y$ is proportional.

| $x$ | $y$ |
|---|---|
| −2 | −4 |
| −1 | −2 |
| 0 | 0 |
| 1 | 2 |
| 2 | 4 |

$$\frac{-2}{-4} = 0.5$$
$$\frac{-1}{-2} = 0.5$$
$$\frac{1}{2} = 0.5$$
$$\frac{2}{4} = 0.5$$

The ratio of $x$ to $y$ is consistent, and the line passes through (0,0). Therefore, the table represents a proportional function.

If the ratio of $\frac{x}{y}$ is not consistent, or the line does not pass through the origin (0,0), then the function is not proportional.

| $x$ | $y$ |
|---|---|
| 0 | 1 |
| 1 | 3 |
| 2 | 5 |
| 3 | 7 |

$$\frac{1}{3} = 0.3333$$
$$\frac{2}{5} = 0.4$$
$$\frac{3}{7} = 0.4285$$

This table does not represent a proportional function because the line does not pass through the origin (0,0) and the ratio between $x$ and $y$ is not consistent.

# Geometry

## Transformations

Transformations move, flip, or change a figure in order to create a new figure. Four common **transformations** are rotations, reflections, translations, and dilations.

### ROTATIONS

A **rotation** can be visualized as a "turn."

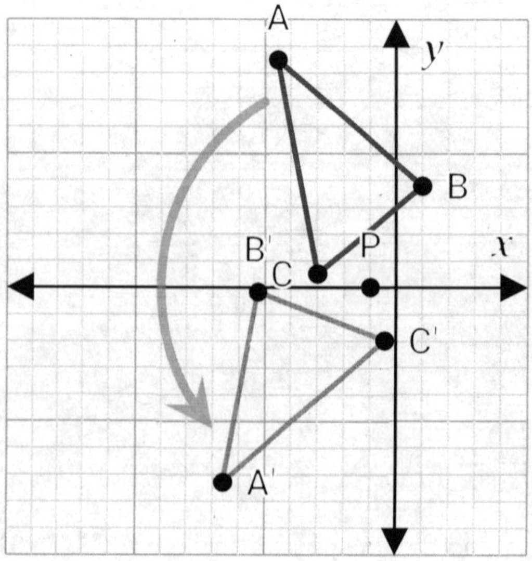


When a geometric figure is turned around a fixed point, the figure is rotated. The distance from the central fixed point and any point on the shape will always stay the same during a rotation. When a figure is rotated, the original figure will be congruent to the new figure. The triangle to the left has been rotated around the point marked with a P.

**Review Video: Rotation**
Visit mometrix.com/academy and enter code: 602600

## Reflections

A **reflection** can be visualized as a "flip."

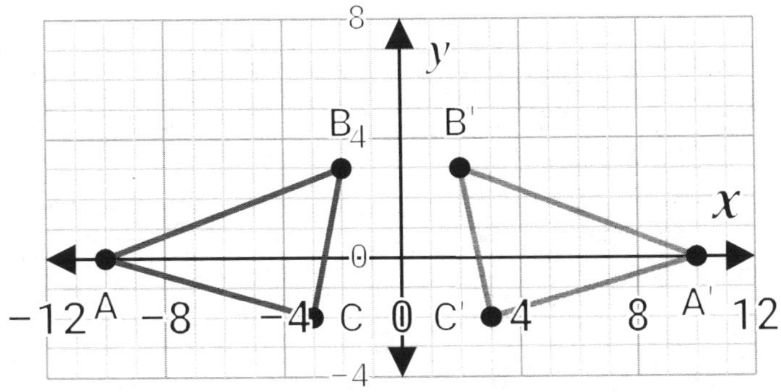


When a figure is mirrored across a line or a plane, the figure has been reflected. The line that an image is reflected across is referred to as the mirror line. Mirror lines can be in any direction. Each point on the reflected figure will be the same distance from the mirror line as the point on the original figure. A reflected image will remain the same size as the original image.

**Review Video: Reflection**
Visit mometrix.com/academy and enter code: 955068

## Translations

A **translation** can be visualized as a "slide."

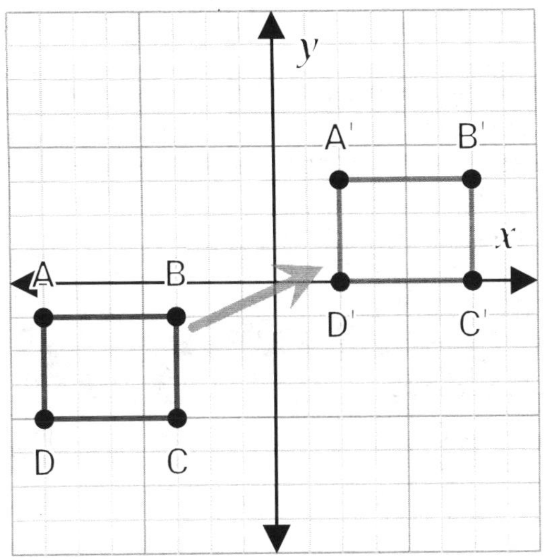

In a translation, every point of the figure must be moved the same distance, in the same direction. For example, all points on the original rectangle $ABCD$ have moved 9 units to the right and 4 units up in order to form the new rectangle. The new and original figures remain congruent when translated.

**Review Video: Translation**
Visit mometrix.com/academy and enter code: 718628

## DILATIONS

A **dilation** can be visualized as resizing.

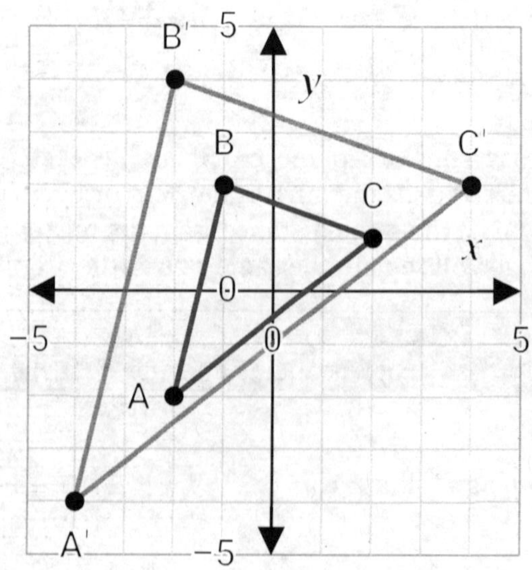


Dilations change the size of figure based on a scale factor. A scale factor is the amount by which the size of the figure is changed from its original size. A figure is enlarged if the scale factor is greater than 1. An image is contracted if the scale factor is less than 1 and greater than 0. Dilation occurs around a center point of dilation which is a fixed point on the coordinate plane where all points are expanded or contracted from. Dilation changes the position and size of a figure but not the overall shape.

**Review Video: Dilation**
Visit mometrix.com/academy and enter code: 471630

## Preserving Congruence in Transformations

When a transformation is applied to a figure, a new figure is created. Common transformations include rotations, reflections, translations, and dilations.

When rotations, reflections, and translations occur the new figure is the same shape and size as the original figure, which means it is **congruent** to the original figure. The new shape has a new orientation on the coordinate plane.

Consider the rotation, reflection, and translation in the graphics. Notice how the original and new shapes are congruent despite having a new orientation on the coordinate plane.

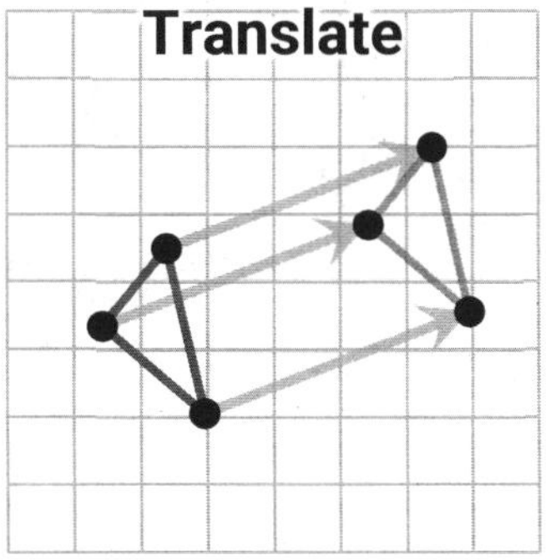


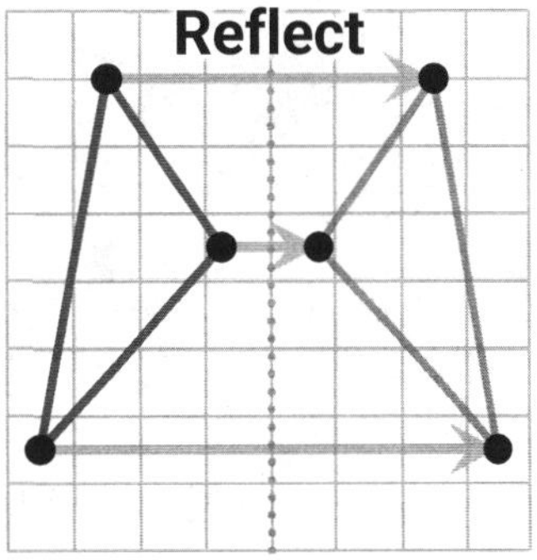


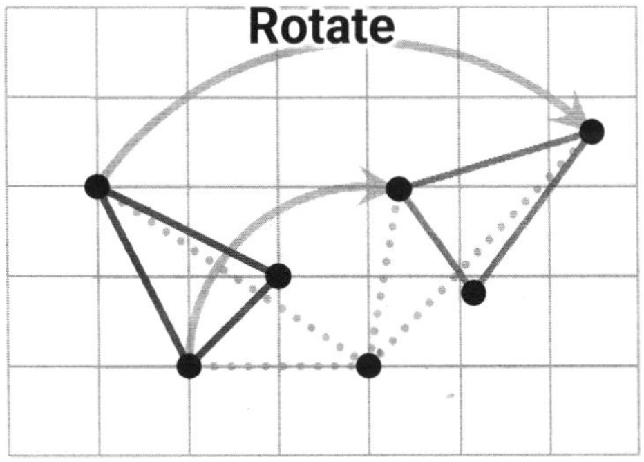


A translation "slides", a reflection "flips", and a rotation "spins." Regardless of the new orientation of the shape on the coordinate plane, the new shapes are all the same shape and size as the originals. This means that when a shape is translated, reflected, or rotated it will maintain congruency.

When a dilation occurs, the new figure will not be congruent to the original figure. There is one exception to this rule, and that is if the scale factor of the dilation is equal to 1. A dilation maintains its orientation on the coordinate plane, but the original figure is enlarged or reduced.

If the scale factor is greater than 1 then the figure will be enlarged. If the scale factor is less than 1 but greater than 0 then the figure will be reduced.

Consider the dilations below.

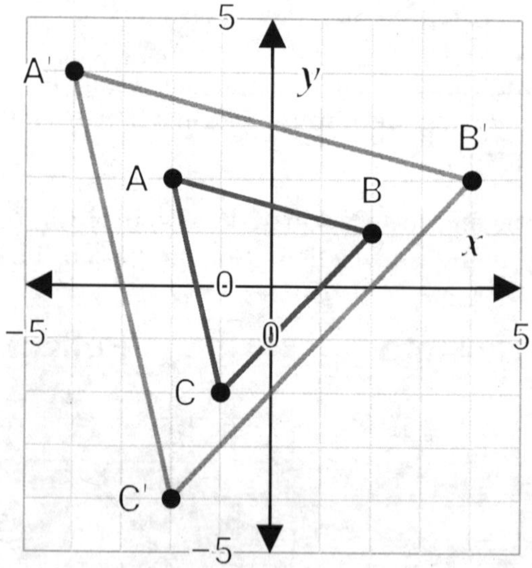


The original image contains the following points:

$$A\ (-2, 2)$$
$$B\ (2,1)$$
$$C\ (-1, -2)$$

All $x$- and $y$-coordinates are multiplied by a scale factor of 2 in order to create the new coordinates.

$$A'(-4,4)$$
$$B'\ (4,2)$$
$$C'(-2, -4)$$

The new figure is an enlargement based on a scale factor of 2. The new figure is not congruent to the original figure.

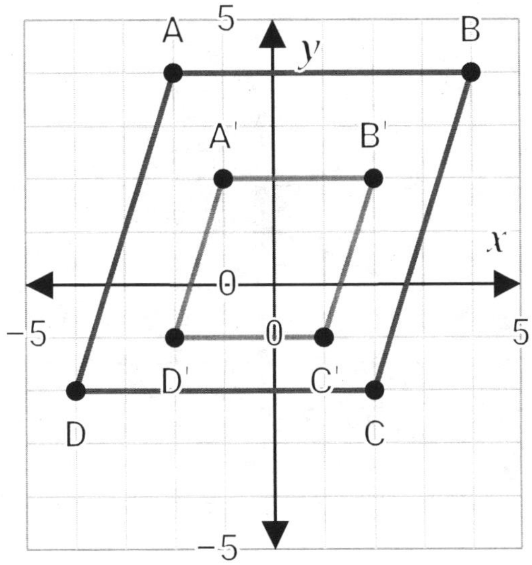


The original image contains the following points:

$$A\ (-2,4)$$
$$B\ (4,4)$$
$$C\ (2,-2)$$
$$D\ (-4,-2)$$

All $x$- and $y$-coordinates are multiplied by a scale factor of $\frac{1}{2}$ in order to create the new coordinates.

$$A'\ (-1,2)$$
$$B'\ (2,2)$$
$$C'\ (1,-1)$$
$$D'\ (-2,-1)$$

The new figure is a reduction. The new figure is not congruent to the original figure.

## Representing Transformations

Translations, reflections, and rotations are all examples of **transformations**. In general, reflections occur over the $x$-axis or $y$-axis, and rotations are limited to 90°, 180°, 270°, and 360° with the origin as the center of rotation. Transformations can be expressed verbally or algebraically.

### *TRANSLATIONS*

A translation is a type of transformation. **Translations** move or **slide** a figure from one location to another. When a translation occurs, the new figure is congruent to the original figure. The size and shape do not change, just the location on the coordinate grid.

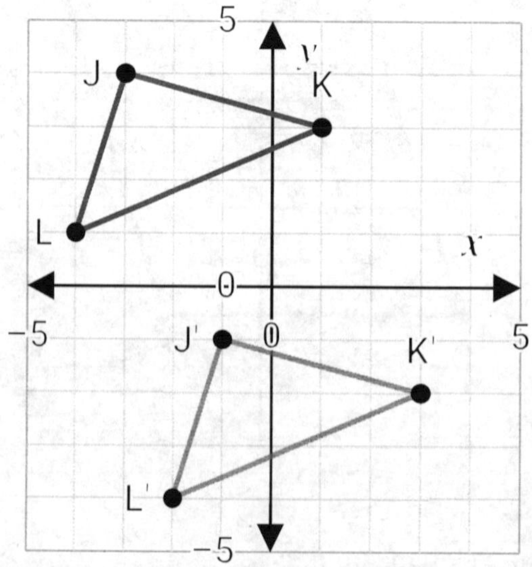


Triangle $JKL$ has been translated. The original triangle contained the points $J(-3,4)$, $K(1,3)$, and $L(-4,1)$. The new triangle contains the points $J'(-1,-1)$, $K'(3,-2)$ and $L'(-2,-4)$. This can be described as a translation of 2 units to the right and 5 units down. This can be tested by counting the movements of each point. Notice how each point, $J$, $K$, and $L$, move 2 units to the right and 5 units down.

A translation can be described using an algebraic representation. In the translation above, each point, $J$, $K$, and $L$ have moved 2 units to the right and 5 units down. Algebraically, "2 units to the right" is equivalent to the $x$-coordinate moving 2 units in the positive direction, or +2. "5 units down" is equivalent to the $y$-coordinate moving 5 units in the negative direction, or –5. The original points $(x, y)$ now become $(x + 2, y - 5)$. An arrow is used to indicate how the original points are translated into the new points. The transformation is expressed as $(x, y) \rightarrow (x + 2, y - 5)$ algebraically.

### REFLECTIONS

A **reflection** is a transformation that can be visualized as a **flip**. Shapes are reflected over a line of reflection, which is usually the $x$- or $y$-axis. When a shape is reflected over the $x$- or $y$-axis, each point maintains the same distance from the line of reflection.

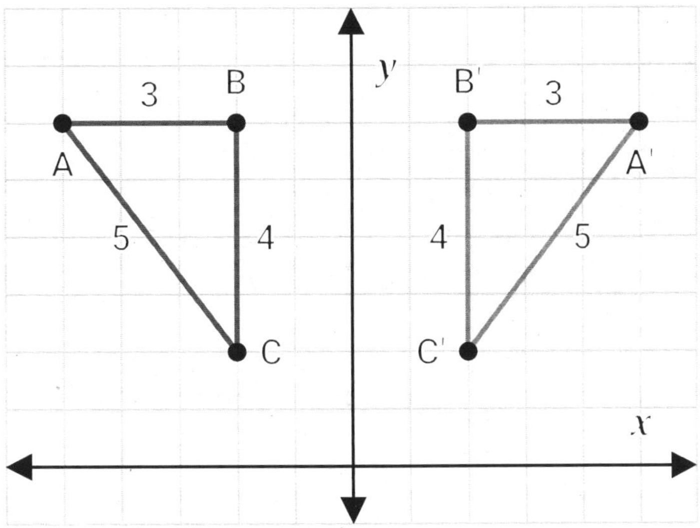


For example, triangle $ABC$ is reflected over the $y$-axis to form the triangle $A'B'C'$. Point $A$ is 5 units from the $y$-axis, and point $A'$ is also 5 units from the $y$-axis. Point $B$ is 2 units from the $y$-axis, and point $B'$ is also 2 units from the $y$-axis. Point $C$ is 2 units from the $y$-axis, and point $C'$ is also 2 units from the $y$-axis. When a reflection occurs over the $y$-axis, the $y$-coordinates stay the same. When a reflection occurs over the $x$-axis, the $x$-coordinates stay the same.

When an $(x, y)$ point is reflected over the $x$-axis, the $x$-value will remain the same, but the sign associated with the $y$-value will change. Similarly, when an $(x, y)$ point is reflected over the $y$-axis, the $y$-value will remain the same, but the sign associated with the $x$-value will change.

For example, in triangle $ABC$ shown above, point $A$ was located at $(-5,6)$. This is reflected over the $y$-axis, so the $y$-value will remain the same, but the sign associated with the $x$-value will change so that the point $(-5,6)$ becomes $(5,6)$.

Point $A$: $(-5,6)$ becomes $(5,6)$

Point $B$: $(-2,6)$ becomes $(2,6)$

Point $C$: $(-2,2)$ becomes $(2,2)$

The table below summarizes the changes that occur to the $x$- and $y$-values when a reflection takes place over the $x$- or $y$-axis.

| Type of Reflection | Point of the pre-image (before reflection) | Point of the image (after reflection) |
|---|---|---|
| Reflection about the $\boldsymbol{x}$-axis | $(x, y)$ | $(x, -y)$ |
| Reflection about the $\boldsymbol{y}$-axis | $(x, y)$ | $(-x, y)$ |

### ROTATIONS

A **rotation** is a type of transformation where a shape is **spun** around a stationary point. Rotations can be visualized as a shape turning around a fixed point. The shape and size of the original figure will not change. This means that the new shape and the original shape will be congruent. Rotations will generally occur at intervals of 90°, 180°, 270°, and 360° clockwise or counterclockwise around the center of rotation (origin). This process can be expressed algebraically.

Consider the rotation of figure $ABC$.

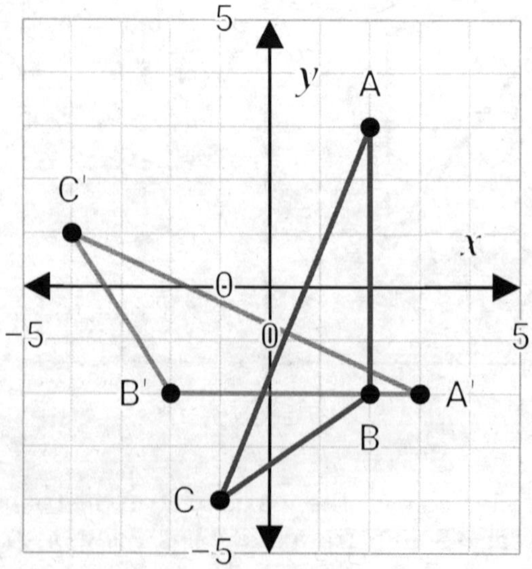


Triangle $ABC$ has been rotated clockwise, 90° around the center of rotation (0,0). Point $A(2,3)$ becomes $A'(3,-2)$. Point $B(2,-2)$ becomes $B'(-2,-2)$. Point $C(-1,-4)$ becomes $C'(-4,1)$. A set of algebraic rules can be utilized to save time. For example, take a close look at point $A$ and point $A'$.

Point $A$: (2,3)

Point $A'$: $(3,-2)$

Notice how the $(x,y)$ becomes $(y,-x)$. In other words, change the sign of the $x$-coordinate then the $x$ and $y$ trade places. This rule, $(x,y) \rightarrow (y,-x)$ applies to all 90° clockwise rotations.

The clockwise rotation of 90° around the origin can be described algebraically as the following:

Point $A$: $(2,3) \rightarrow (3,-2)$

Point $B$: $(2,-2) \rightarrow (-2,-2)$

Point $C$: $(-1,-4) \rightarrow (-4,1)$

Not all rotations are 90° in the clockwise direction. The table below describes the rules for clockwise and counterclockwise rotation of 90°, 180°, and 270°.

| Type of Rotation | Point of the pre-image (before rotation) | Point of the image (after rotation) |
|---|---|---|
| Rotation of 90° (clockwise) | $(x, y)$ | $(y, -x)$ |
| Rotation of 90° (counter clockwise) | $(x, y)$ | $(-y, x)$ |
| Rotation of 180° (clockwise and counter clockwise) | $(x, y)$ | $(-x, -y)$ |
| Rotation of 270° (clockwise) | $(x, y)$ | $(-y, x)$ |
| Rotation of 270° (counter clockwise) | $(x, y)$ | $(y, -x)$ |

### *EXAMPLE*

Triangle $ABC$ was transformed to create triangle $A'B'C'$. Which rule most accurately describes the transformation?

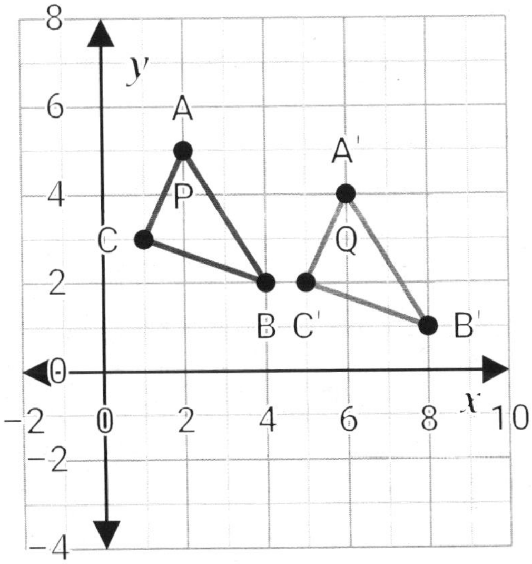


$(x, y) \rightarrow (x + 4, y - 1)$

Each point on the original triangle moves 4 units to the right. This means that each $x$-value moves 4 units in the positive direction, or +4. Algebraically, $x$ becomes $x + 4$.

Each point on the original triangle moves 1 unit down. This means that each $y$-value moves 1 unit in the negative direction, or –1. Algebraically, $y$ becomes $y - 1$.

The translation of triangle $ABC$ can be described using the rule $(x, y) \rightarrow (x + 4, y - 1)$.

### EXAMPLE

A triangle is reflected over the $x$-axis. The original points of the triangle are $P(2,5)$, $Q(6,2)$, and $R(2,2)$. The new points of the triangle are $P'(2,-5)$, $Q'(6,-2)$, and $R'(2,-2)$. Which rule best describes the result of the reflection?

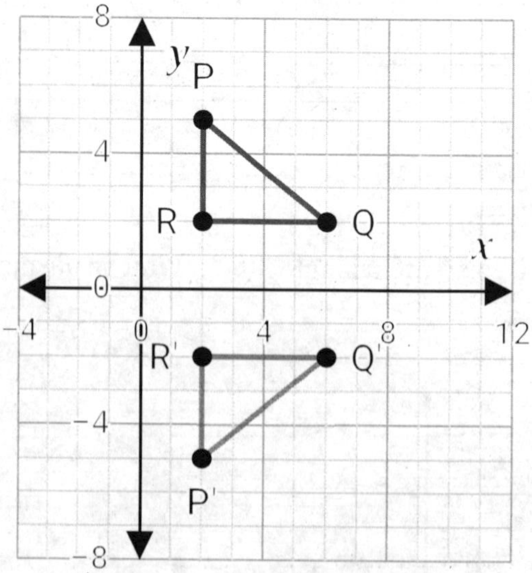


$(x, y) \rightarrow (x, -y)$

The triangle is reflected over the $x$-axis. This means that the new points will maintain the same distance from the $x$-axis as the original points. When a figure is reflected over the $x$-axis, the $x$-values will remain the same. However, the sign associated with the $y$-value will be reversed. Notice how the $y$-value associated with point $P$ was originally 5, and the new $y$-value for $P'$ is –5. This will be true for all $y$-values when reflected over the $x$-axis. This rule can be described algebraically as $(x, y) \rightarrow (x, -y)$.

### MEASUREMENTS OF DILATED SHAPES

A **dilation** is the process of changing the **size** of a figure by applying a **scale factor**. When a scale factor is **greater than 1** the new dilated figure will be an **enlargement**. When a scale factor is **less than 1** and greater than 0 the new dilated figure will be a **reduction**. When a dilation occurs, the area and perimeter of the new and original figures will be different.

When a dilation occurs, the area of the new figure can be determined by multiplying the square of the scale factor by the original area. For example, if the original area of the figure is 36 units squared, and the scale factor is $\frac{1}{4}$, the area of the new figure will be the product of $\left(\frac{1}{4}\right)^2$ and 36 which simplifies to $\frac{1}{16} \times 36 = 2\frac{1}{4}$ The area of the new figure will be $2\frac{1}{4}$ units squared.

When a dilation occurs, the perimeter of the figure can be determined by multiplying the scale factor by the original perimeter. For example, if the original perimeter of the figure is 36 units, and the scale factor is $\frac{1}{4}$, the perimeter of the new figure will be the product of $\frac{1}{4}$ and 36 which is 9. The perimeter of the new figure will be 9 units.

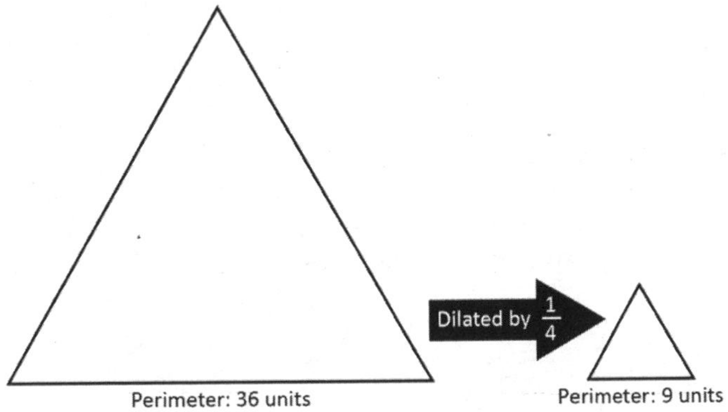


## Mapping Transformations

**Rigid transformations** are transformations in a two-dimensional plane that preserve the size and shape of a figure by preserving the distance and angle between any pair of points in the plane. That is to say, the **preimage**, or the original figure, may change in orientation in the plane but does not get bigger or smaller or change in shape in any way after it has been transformed. There are three types of rigid transformations: **translations, rotations,** and **reflections.**

### Lines Mapped to Lines

A **translation** moves every point in the plane by the same distance in the same direction. Translations move a figure either up, down, left, or right and any combination of those directions. Doing this preserves the shape and size of the figure. Consider the image below. In the preimage, triangle ABC, each of the vertices moved up three units and right two units in the plane. By doing this, the image A'B'C' (pronounced "A prime," "B prime," "C prime") is formed, making ABC and A'B'C' congruent triangles. This also means that line segment AB is equal to line segment A'B', line segment AC is equal to line segment A'C', and line segment CB is equal to line segment C'B'.

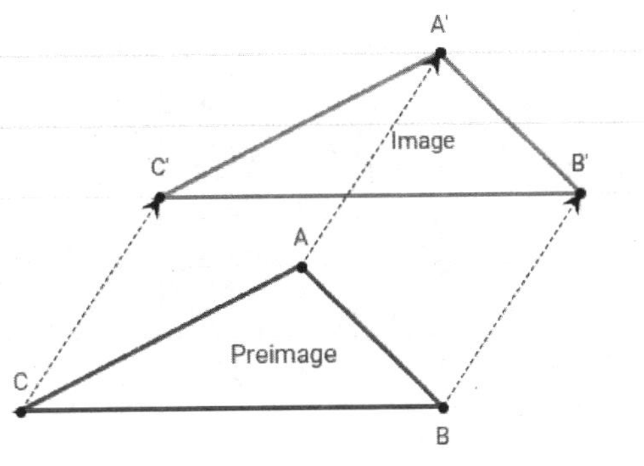

Since a translation operates on each point in the coordinate plane, well-defined rules can be used to transform each point.

| Translation UP $k$ units | Translation DOWN $k$ units | Translation RIGHT $h$ units | Translation LEFT $h$ units |
|---|---|---|---|
| $(x, y) \to (x, y + k)$ | $(x, y) \to (x, y - k)$ | $(x, y) \to (x + h, y)$ | $(x, y) \to (x - h, y)$ |

**Example 1:** If a line segment has endpoints A(0, 1) and B(6, 1), the line segment is 6 units long. If line segment AB is translated three units down and one unit right, $h = 1, k = 3$. Using the rules above, A' is $(0 + 1, 0 - 3) \to (1, -3)$ and B' is $(6 + 1, 0 - 3) \to (7, -3)$. The translated line segment A'B' is also 6 units long. Use the graph below to see this visually.

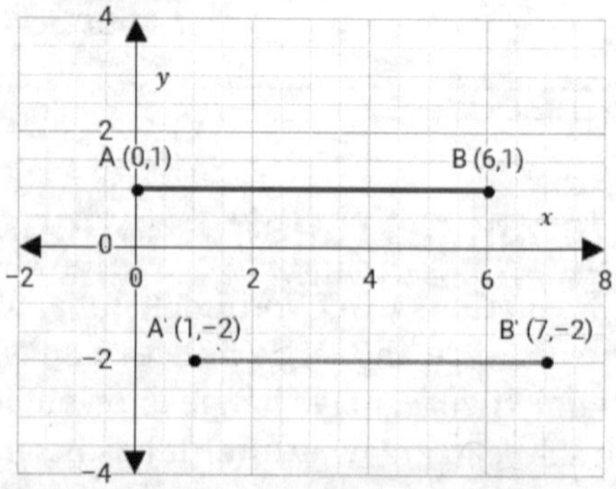


A **rotation** in the plane is a transformation that takes every point in a figure and rotates it a certain number of degrees, called the **angle of rotation,** around a given point or the **center of rotation.** Rotations can be both clockwise and counterclockwise. This is called the **direction of rotation.** Again, the original figure is called the preimage, and the rotated figure is called the image. The image and preimage are congruent as a rotation preserves the size and shape of the figure. The picture below shows triangle ABC and its image triangle A'B'C'. ABC has been rotated counterclockwise by 90° around point P. Therefore, the direction of rotation is counterclockwise, the angle of rotation is 90°, and the center of rotation is point P.

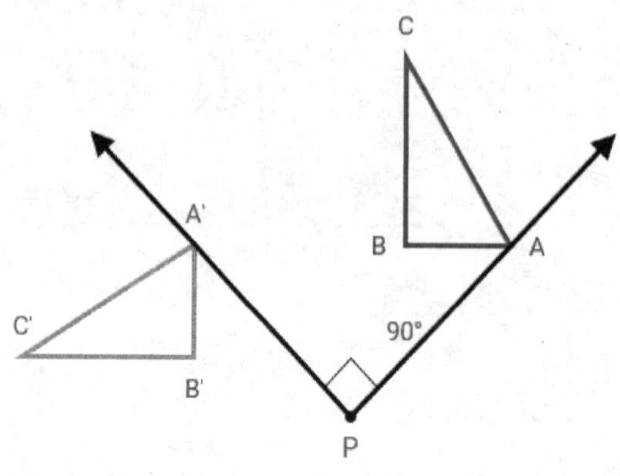


Rules for the most common angles of rotation about the origin can be used to find the coordinates of rotated points.

| | 90° | 180° | 270° |
|---|---|---|---|
| **Clockwise** | $(x, y) \to (y, -x)$ | $(x, y) \to (-x, -y)$ | $(x, y) \to (-y, x)$ |
| **Counterclockwise** | $(x, y) \to (-y, x)$ | $(x, y) \to (-x, -y)$ | $(x, y) \to (y, -x)$ |

**Example 2:** The line segment with endpoints C $(-1,3)$ and D $(-1,5)$ is two units long. To rotate CD about the origin 270° counterclockwise, use the rules above. Find C', $(-1,3) \rightarrow (3,-(-1)) \rightarrow (3,1)$ and D' $(-1,5) \rightarrow (5,-(-1)) \rightarrow (5,1)$. The length of the rotated line segment, C'D', is two units, just like its preimage. Verify graphically using the image below.

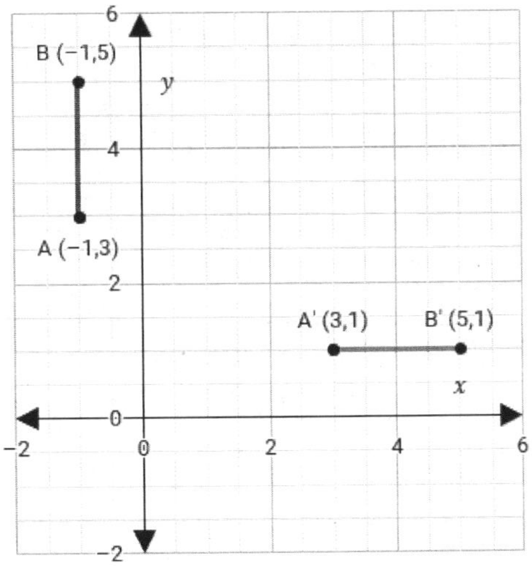


A **reflection** is the mirror image of a figure in the plane. Mathematically, each point in the image is the same distance from the **line of reflection** as its corresponding point in the preimage but on the opposite side of the line of reflection. In the image below, the line of reflection is the vertical line $x = -2$, and point A in the preimage maps to point A' in the image. Notice the distance between point A and the line of reflection is exactly equal to the distance between point A' and the line of reflection. This is true for every point in the plane, including the vertices and sides of the triangles.

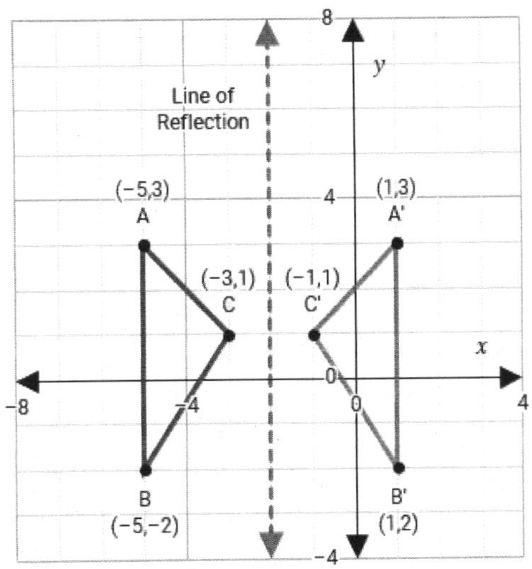


The line of reflection is the **perpendicular bisector** of the line segment connecting each point and its reflected point. For example, the line of reflection meets line segment AA' at a 90° angle and intersects AA' at its midpoint. The same is true for the intersection of the line of reflection and line segments for every pair of points in the plane.

Common lines of reflection include the $x$-axis, the $y$-axis, and the line $y = x$. Rules for reflecting points over these lines can be found in the table below.

| Reflection over $x$-axis | Reflection over $y$-axis | Reflection over $y = x$ |
|---|---|---|
| $(x, y) \rightarrow (x, -y)$ | $(x, y) \rightarrow (-x, y)$ | $(x, y) \rightarrow (y, x)$ |

**Example 3:** Line segment EF is 3 units long with endpoints $E(2, 5)$ and $F(2, 8)$. If EF is reflected over $y = x$ to form the image E'F', the rules in the table above can be used to find the new endpoints E' and F'. Reflecting a point over $y = x$ switches the $x$ and $y$-coordinates of each point: $E'(2, 5) \rightarrow (5, 2)$, $F'(2, 8) \rightarrow (8, 2)$. Verify this reflection using the graph below.

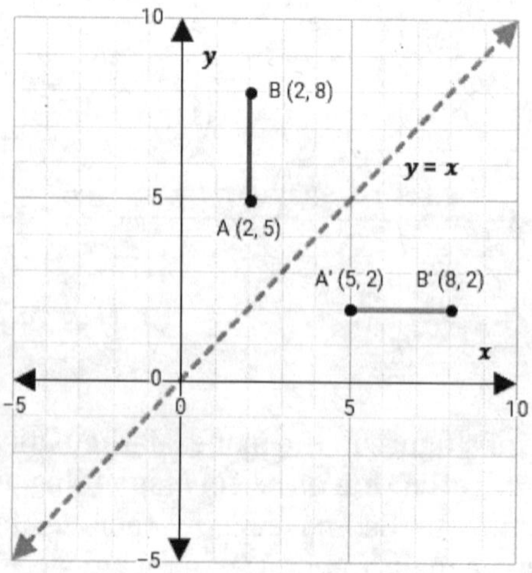

**Linear functions** of the form $y = mx + b$ are a collection of infinite points, and they make a line on a coordinate plane. Because transformations in the plane operate on points, and a linear function is composed of infinitely many points, these functions are translated, rotated, and reflected the same way any figure in the plane would be.

| Translation | Rotation | Reflection |
|---|---|---|
| 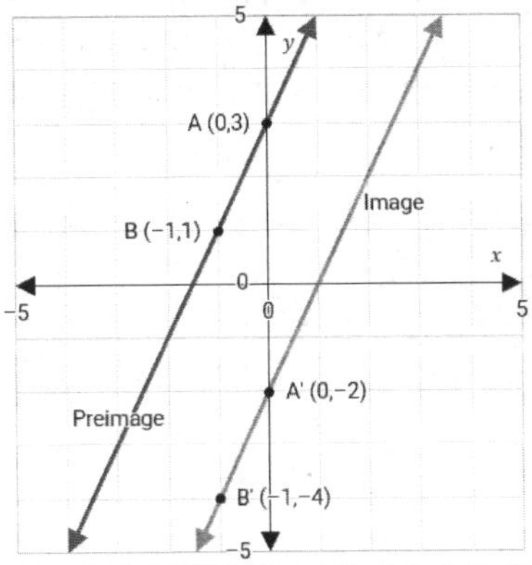 | 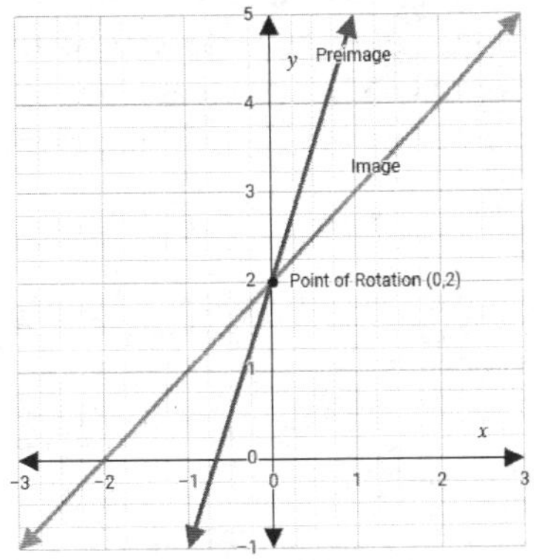 | 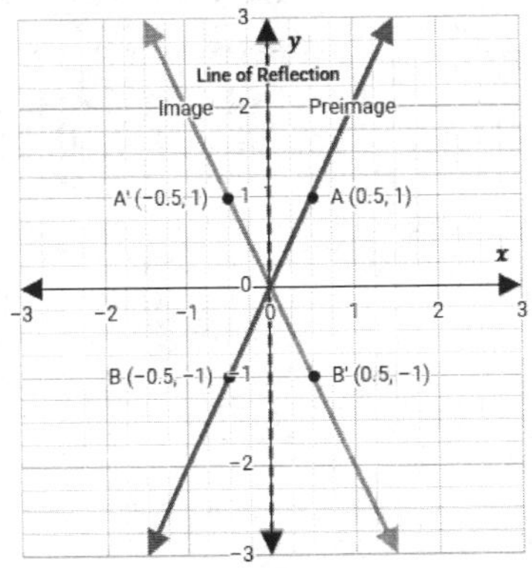 |
| Each point on the preimage line has been translated down five units to each point on the image line, so the preimage maps directly onto the image. Both the preimage and image are linear functions with equal slopes. | Each point on the preimage line has been rotated clockwise about the point of rotation to create the image line. The image and the preimage are both linear functions, so the structure has not changed. | Each point on the preimage line has been reflected over the line of reflection (the $y$-axis) to form the image line, so the preimage maps directly onto the image. The orientation of the line has changed (the slope went from 2 to $-2$), but the structure remains the same. |

## Angles Mapped to Angles

A **translation** moves every point in the plane by the same distance in the same direction. Translations move a figure either up, down, left, or right and any combination of those directions. Doing this should still preserve the shape and size of the figure. Consider the image below. In the preimage, triangle ABC, each of the vertices moved up two units and right five units in the plane. By doing this, the image A'B'C' (pronounced "A prime," "B prime," "C prime") is formed, making ABC and A'B'C' congruent triangles. This also means that the measure of angle A is equal to the measure of angle A', the measure of angle B is equal to the measure of angle B', and the measure of angle C is equal to the measure of angle C'.

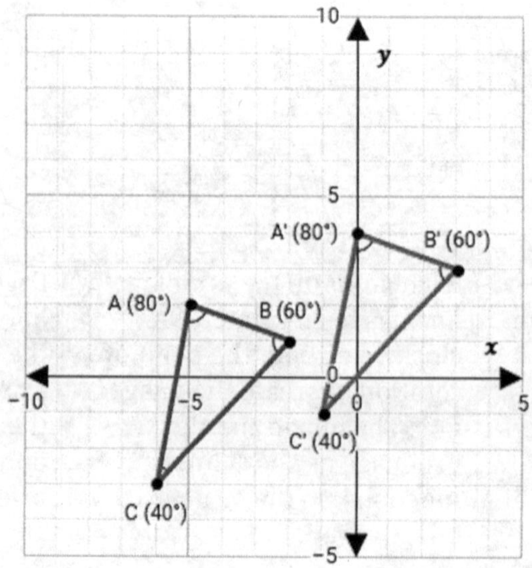


**Example 1:** Triangle DEF is translated two units down and one unit left to create triangle D'E'F'. If $\angle D = 12°$, and $\angle E = 48°$, the measure of $\angle F'$ can be found using properties of triangles and translations. Since the sum of the three interior angles of a triangle must equal 180°, the following is true:

$$\begin{aligned} \angle D + \angle E + \angle F &= 180 \\ 12 + 48 + \angle F &= 180 \\ 60 + \angle F &= 180 \\ -60 \qquad & \quad -60 \\ \angle F &= 120° \end{aligned}$$

Because translations preserve angle measures, $\angle D \cong \angle D'$, $\angle E \cong \angle E'$, and $\angle F \cong \angle F'$. Therefore, $\angle F' = 120°$.

A **rotation** in the plane is a transformation that takes every point in a figure and rotates it a certain number of degrees, called the **angle of rotation,** around a given point or the **center of rotation**. Rotations can be both clockwise and counterclockwise. This is called the **direction of rotation**. Again, the original figure is called the preimage, and the rotated figure is called the image. The preimage and image are congruent to each other since a rotation preserves the size and shape of the figure. The picture below shows triangle ABC and its preimage triangle A'B'C'. ABC has been rotated counterclockwise by 90° around point P. Therefore, the direction of rotation is counterclockwise, the angle of rotation is 90°, and the center of rotation is point P. Notice that each of the angles in the preimage are congruent with each of the corresponding angles in the image: $\angle A \cong \angle A', \angle B \cong \angle B'$, and $\angle C \cong \angle C'$.

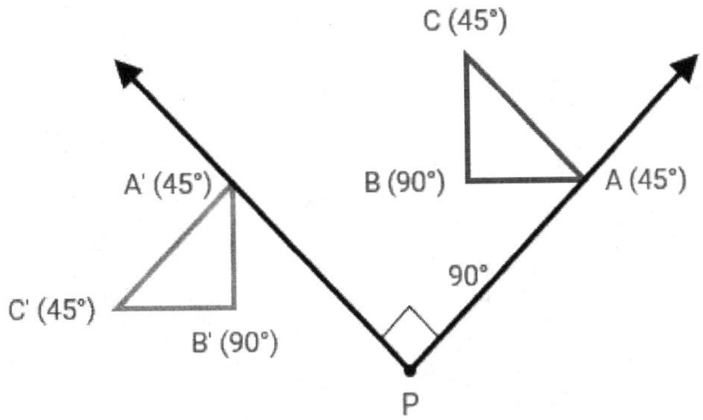


**Example 2:** In the image below, quadrilateral ABCD is rotated around point R to form quadrilateral A'B'C'D'. The angles in the image and preimage are congruent, so $\angle A \cong \angle A', \angle B \cong \angle B', \angle C \cong \angle C'$, and $\angle D \cong \angle D'$. This means that the measure of angle C' is equal to the measure of angle C, and the measure of angle A' is equal to the measure of angle A, so $m\angle C' = 123°$ and $m\angle A = 166°$.

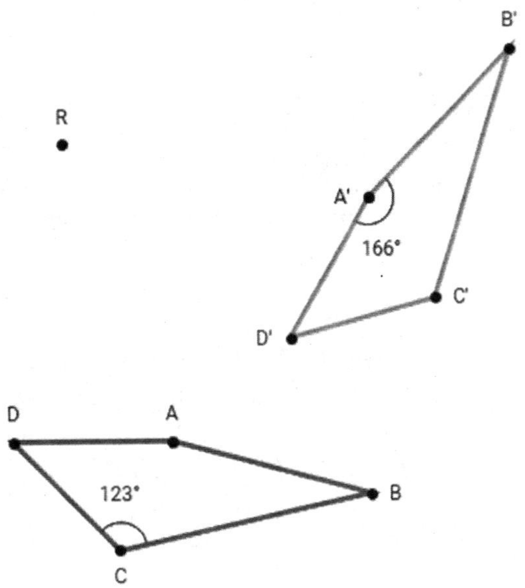


A **reflection** is the mirror image of a figure in the plane. Mathematically, each point in the image is the same distance from the **line of reflection** as its corresponding point in the preimage but on the opposite side of the line of reflection. In the image below, the line of reflection is the vertical line I, and point A in the preimage maps to point A' in the image. Notice the distance between point A and the line of reflection is exactly equal to the distance between point A' and the line of reflection. This is true for every point in the plane, including the vertices and sides of the quadrilaterals. Notice that each angle in the preimage is congruent to each angle in the image, so $\angle A \cong \angle A'$, $\angle B \cong \angle B'$, $\angle C \cong \angle C'$, and $\angle D \cong \angle D'$.

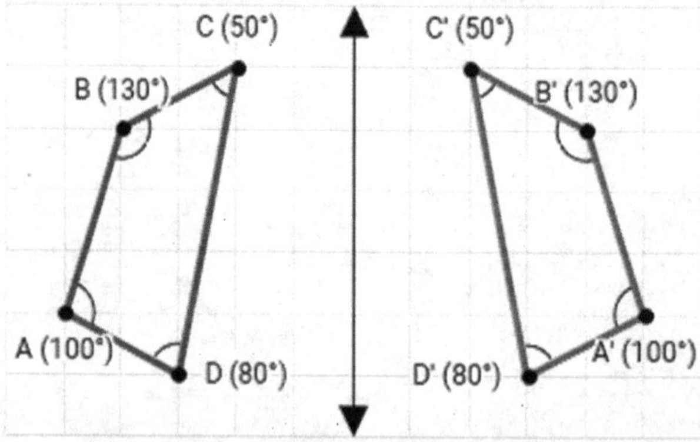


The line of reflection is the **perpendicular bisector** of the line segment connecting each point and its reflected point. For example, the line of reflection meets line segment AA' at a 90° angle and intersects AA' at its midpoint. The same is true for the intersection of the line of reflection and line segments for every pair of points in the plane.

**Example 3:** If the preimage angles are given, how is it possible to find the measures of the angles of the image? Since reflections in the plane preserve angle measures, each angle in the preimage is congruent to each corresponding angle in the image. Therefore, if the preimage has angles A, B, and C, the image will have angles A', B', and C' and the following congruencies are true: $\angle A \cong \angle A'$, $\angle B \cong \angle B'$, $\angle C \cong \angle C'$.

## Parallel Lines Mapped to Parallel Lines

A **translation** moves every point in the plane by the same distance in the same direction. Translations move a figure either up, down, left, or right and any combination of those directions. Doing this should still preserve the shape and size of the figure. **Parallel lines** have the same slope, meaning they never cross or touch. Another way to think about parallel lines is lines that are at a constant distance from one another in the plane. Lines $a$ and $b$ in the picture below are 3 units apart at any given point on the lines, and they both have a slope equal to zero. Thus, they are parallel. Within parallel lines $a$ and $b$, each point was translated up seven units. By doing this, the image, lines $a'$ and $b'$ (pronounced "a prime," "b prime") is formed. Because the distance between any pair of points in the plane is preserved in a translation, the distance between lines $a'$ and $b'$ remains constant, and thus, $a'$ and $b'$ are also parallel lines.

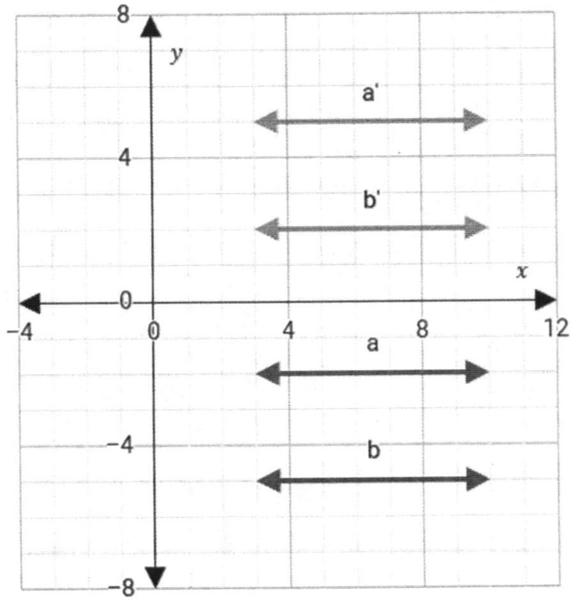


A **rotation** in the plane is a transformation that takes every point in a figure and rotates it a certain number of degrees, called the **angle of rotation,** around a given point called the **center of rotation**. Rotations can be both clockwise and counterclockwise. This is called the **direction of rotation**. Again, the original figure is called the preimage, and the rotated figure is called the image. Rotation preserves the size and shape of a figure as well as the distance between any two points in the plane. The picture below shows parallel lines *c* and *d* and its image parallel lines *c'* and *d'*. The preimage has been rotated 90° clockwise about the origin. Therefore, the direction of rotation is clockwise, the angle of rotation is 90°, and the point of rotation is the origin, point (0,0). Notice that lines $c'$ and $d'$ are also parallel, as the rotation has preserved the distance between the lines.

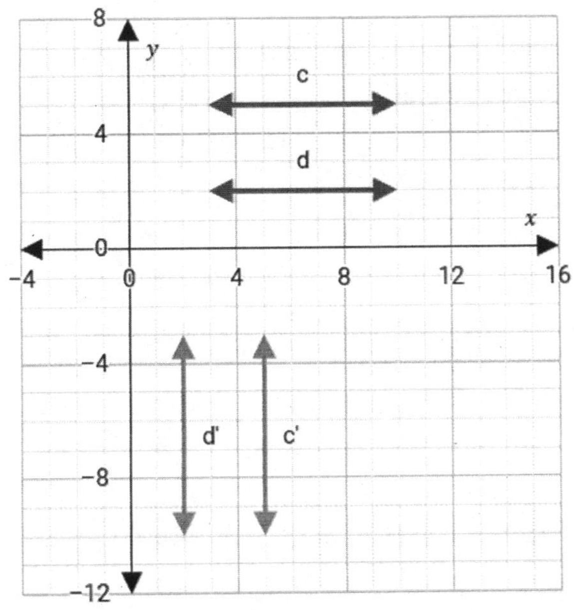

A **reflection** is the mirror image of a figure in the plane. Mathematically, each point in the image is the same distance from the **line of reflection** as its corresponding point in the preimage, but the points are on the opposite side of the line of reflection. In the image below, the line of reflection is the $x$-axis, and point A in the preimage maps to point A' in the image. Notice the distance between point A and the line of reflection, five units, is exactly equal to the distance between point A' and the line of reflection, also five units. This is true for every point in the plane, including the infinitely many points on each of the lines AB and CD. Notice that parallel lines in the preimage, AB and CD, are mapped to parallel lines A'B' and C'D' in the image. This happens because reflections preserve the distance between any two points in the plane, so lines A'B' and C'D' are equidistant at every point and thus parallel.

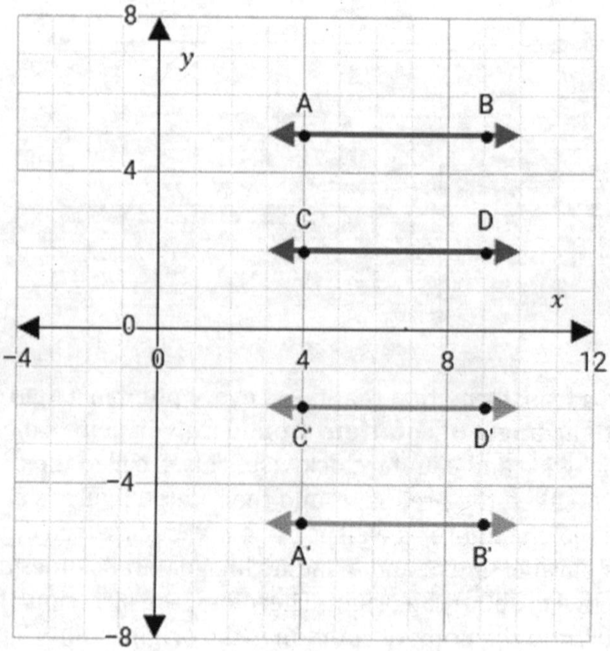


The line of reflection is the **perpendicular bisector** of the line segment connecting each point and its reflected point. For example, the line of reflection meets line segment AA' at a 90° angle and intersects AA' at its midpoint. The same is true for the intersection of the line of reflection and line segments for every pair of points in the plane.

## Similarity in Transformations

In math, two figures are **congruent** if they are exactly equal in shape and size. This means that two congruent figures in the plane will have corresponding angles of equal measure, corresponding line segments of equal length, and the same number of sides and angles. If two figures in the plane have congruent **corresponding** sides and angles, then the figures themselves are congruent. For example, in the figure below, triangle ABC is congruent to triangle EFG. The angle congruency is expressed as $\angle A \cong \angle E$, $\angle B \cong \angle F$, $\angle C \cong \angle G$, the line segment congruency is expressed as $\overline{AB} \cong \overline{EF}$, $\overline{AC} \cong \overline{EG}$, and $\overline{BC} \cong \overline{FG}$, and the triangle congruency is expressed as $\Delta ABC \cong \Delta EFG$.

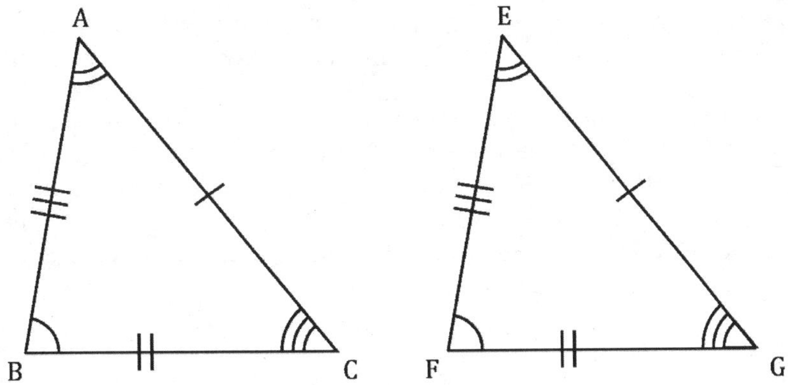


**Example 1:** To determine if triangle ABC is congruent to triangle DEF below, verify that the corresponding angles and corresponding sides are congruent. The largest angle in each triangle, $\angle A$ and $\angle E$, are congruent based on the two arcs marked on the angles. Further, the two smallest angles of each triangle, $\angle C$ and $\angle F$, are congruent based on the three arcs marked on the angles. Similarly, corresponding angles B and E are congruent based on the single arc marked on the angles. Corresponding sides are also congruent, as shown by the hash marks on each triangle. The segment connecting the largest and smallest angles on each triangle, $\overline{AC}$ and $\overline{DF}$, are congruent because each has two hash marks. Line segment AB corresponds to line segment DE, and both are equal in length, as shown by the single hash mark. Line segments FE and CB are the same length, as shown by the three hash marks on each. Thus, they are also congruent sides. Since every corresponding angle and side length are congruent, triangle ABC and triangle DEF are congruent.

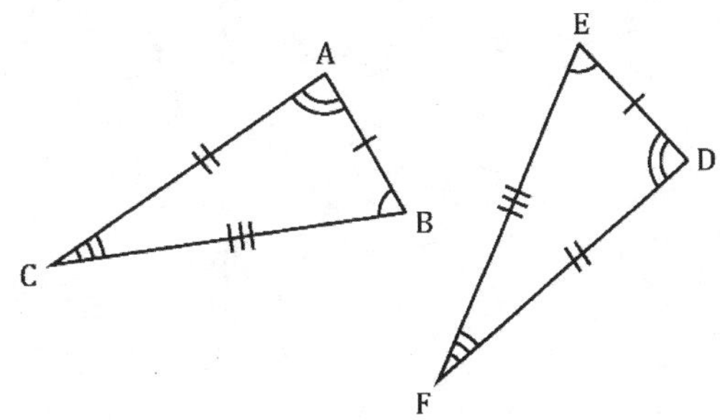


**Rigid transformations** are transformations in a two-dimensional plane that preserve the size and shape of a figure by preserving the distance and angle between any pair of points in the plane. That is to say, the **preimage**, or the original figure, may change in orientation in the plane but does not get bigger or smaller or change in shape in any way after it has been transformed. The result of any rigid transformation in the plane is two congruent figures; the image is congruent to the preimage. There are three types of rigid transformations: **translations, rotations,** and **reflections.**

A **translation** moves every point in the plane by the same distance in the same direction. Translations move a figure either up, down, left, or right and any combination of those directions. Doing this preserves the shape and size of the figure.

A **rotation** in the plane is a transformation that takes every point in a figure and rotates it a certain number of degrees, called the **angle of rotation,** around a given point or the **center of rotation.** Rotations can be both clockwise and counterclockwise. This is called the **direction of rotation**. Again, the original figure is called the preimage, and the rotated figure is called the image. Rotation preserves the size and shape of a figure as well as the distance between any two points in the plane.

A **reflection** is the mirror image of a figure in the plane. Mathematically, each point in the image is the same distance from the **line of reflection** as its corresponding point in the preimage but on the opposite side of the line of reflection. The line of reflection is the **perpendicular bisector** of the line segment connecting each point and its reflected point. This means that the line of reflection intersects the line between any two points in the plane at a 90° angle, and exactly halfway between the two points.

**Example 2:** If the preimage, triangle ABC, is translated five units left and three units up, the image, triangle A'B'C' (pronounced "A prime," "B prime," "C prime") is congruent to triangle ABC. Since translations in the plane preserve size, shape, and distance between points, each corresponding line segment and angle of triangles ABC and A'B'C' are congruent. Thus, triangle ABC is congruent to triangle A'B'C'.

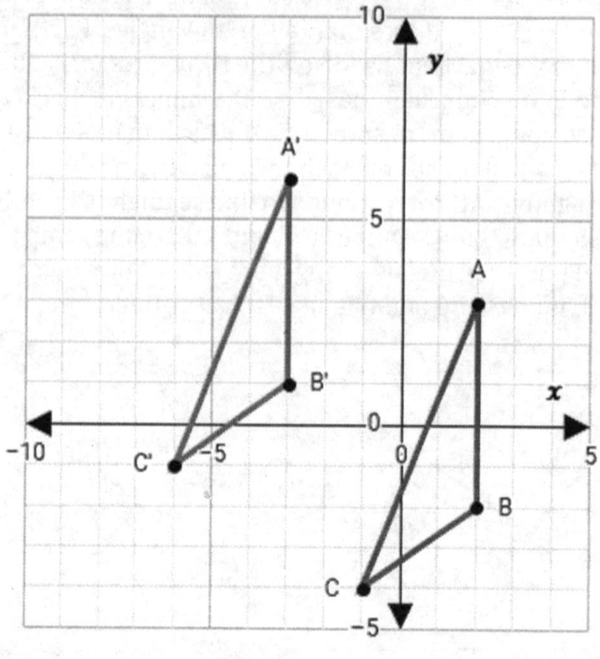


A **transformation sequence** is an ordered series of translations, reflections, and rotations that map a preimage onto an image. A transformation sequence results in two congruent figures in the plane. The sequence's order matters because it affects the final image. For example, translating a figure two units down and then rotating it about the origin will result in a different image than rotating it about the origin and then translating it two units down.

**Example 3:** Given the figures below, it is possible to describe the transformation sequence mapping the preimage, triangle ABC, onto the image, triangle A'B'C'. One transformation sequence involves a reflection over the $y$-axis followed by a translation up two units. This can be verified by looking at each vertex point. Each vertex changed from $(x, y)$ to$(-x, y)$ to $(-x, y + 2)$. For example, point A$(4, -4)$ mapped to point A'$(-4, -2)$: $(4, -4) \to (-4, -4) \to (-4, -4 + 2) \to (-4, -2)$. An alternate sequence begins with a translation two units up and is followed by a reflection over the $y$-axis. Again, this can be verified by looking at each vertex point as they change from $(x, y)$ to $(x, y + 2) \to (-x, y + 2)$. For example, point B$(8, -8)$ mapped to point B'$(-8, -6)$ : $(8, -8) \to (8, -8 + 2) \to (8, -6) \to (-8, -6)$.

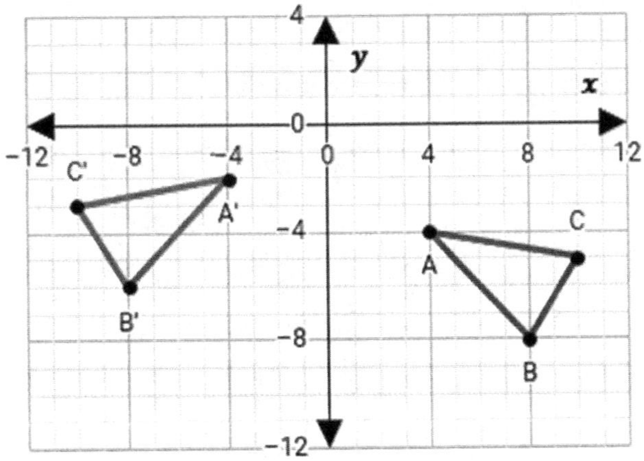


## Angles

An important section of many geometry courses is devoted to the study of **triangles** and their **angle measures**. There are many rules regarding this topic that should be reviewed. For example, consider the rules below.

The sum of the **interior angles** of all triangles is 180°.

**Complementary angles** have a sum of 90°.

**Supplementary angles** have a sum of 180°.

These rules can be helpful when solving for interior and exterior angles of a triangle.

## Parallel Lines Cut by a Transversal

**Parallel lines** are lines in the plane that never touch or intersect. If two parallel lines are cut by a **transversal**, or a single line that intersects both of the parallel lines, important relationships between the resulting angles exist. These relationships are **corresponding angles, alternate interior angles, alternate exterior angles,** and **consecutive interior angles.** The image below illustrates these relationships when parallel lines *a* and *b* are cut by transversal *l*.

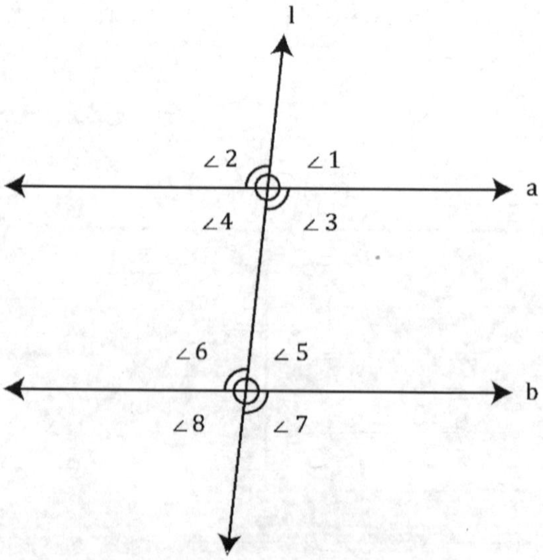


**Corresponding angles** have the same relative position, so in the image above, the corresponding angle pairs are $\angle 1$ and $\angle 5$, $\angle 2$ and $\angle 6$, $\angle 3$ and $\angle 7$, and $\angle 4$ and $\angle 8$. Corresponding angles are **congruent**; they have the same measure, so $\angle 1 \cong \angle 5$, $\angle 2 \cong \angle 6$, $\angle 3 \cong \angle 7$, and $\angle 4 \cong \angle 8$.

**Alternate interior angles** are on the inside of the parallel lines cut by the transversal. In the image above, there are two pairs of alternate interior angles: $\angle 4$ and $\angle 5$, and $\angle 3$ and $\angle 6$. Alternate interior angles are congruent, so $\angle 4 \cong \angle 5$, and $\angle 3 \cong \angle 6$. This is true because, by the definition of corresponding angles, $m\angle 1 = m\angle 5$, and because they are adjacent angles that make a straight line, $m\angle 1 + m\angle 3 = 180$ and $m\angle 5 + m\angle 6 = 180$. Substituting angle 1 for angle 5 gives $m\angle 5 + m\angle 3 = 180$ and $m\angle 5 + m\angle 6 = 180$. Setting the equations equal to each other, $m\angle 5 + m\angle 3 = m\angle 5 + m\angle 6$, and subtracting $m\angle 5$ from both sides gives $m\angle 3 = m\angle 6$ so, $\angle 3 \cong \angle 6$. The same reasoning can be used to show $\angle 4 \cong \angle 5$.

**Alternate exterior angles** are formed on the outside, or the exterior, of the parallel lines cut by a transversal. In the image above, there are two pairs of alternate exterior angles: $\angle 1$ and $\angle 8$, and $\angle 2$ and $\angle 7$. Alternate exterior angles are congruent, so $\angle 1 \cong \angle 8$, and $\angle 2 \cong \angle 7$. This is true because, by definition of **vertical angles,** $\angle 2 \cong \angle 3$ and by definition of corresponding angles, $\angle 7 \cong \angle 3$. If both angle 7 and angle 2 are congruent to angle 3, they must be congruent to each other, so $\angle 2 \cong \angle 7$. The same reasoning can be used to show $\angle 1 \cong \angle 8$.

**Consecutive interior angles** are the angles formed inside the parallel lines and on the same side of the transversal. In the image above, there are two pairs of consecutive interior angles: $\angle 4$ and $\angle 6$, and $\angle 3$ and $\angle 5$. Two consecutive interior angles are **supplementary**; thus, their sum is 180°, so $m\angle 4 + m\angle 6 = 180°$ and $m\angle 3 + m\angle 6 = 180°$. By definition of corresponding angles, $\angle 2 \cong \angle 6$, and because angles 2 and 4 are adjacent and make a straight line, they are supplementary, so $m\angle 2 + m\angle 4 = 180°$. Angle 2 is congruent to angle 6, so substitute the measure of angle 6 for the measure of angle two and arrive at $m\angle 6 + m\angle 4 = 180°$. Thus, angles four and six are supplementary. The same reasoning can show that angles 3 and 5 are supplementary.

**Example 1:** Parallel lines *c* and *d* are cut by transversal *e*. To find the value of *x*, notice that the given angles are alternate interior angles. Alternate interior angles are congruent, so set the angle measures equal and solve for *x*.

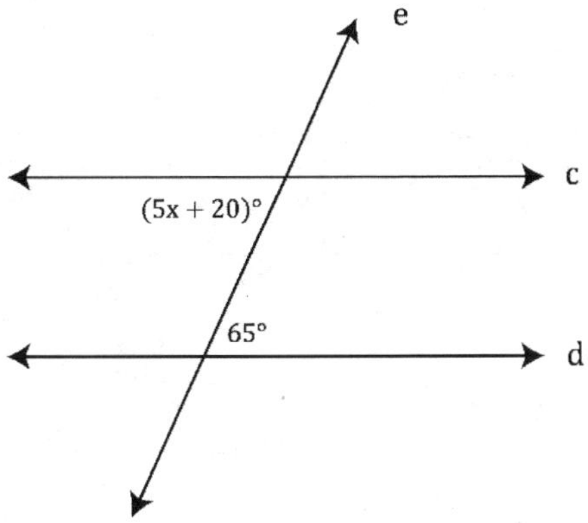


$$\begin{aligned} 5x + 20 &= 65 \\ -20 &\quad -20 \\ \frac{5x}{5} &= \frac{45}{5} \\ x &= 9 \end{aligned}$$

Therefore, $x = 9$.

## Angle Sum Theorem

The **Angle-Sum Theorem,** also called the Triangle Sum Theorem, of triangles states that the sum of the three interior angles of any triangle is equal to 180 degrees. To understand why this is true, consider triangle ABC in Figure 1 below. Notice that the three interior angles of triangle ABC, when placed adjacent to one another, as shown in Figure 2, create a straight line equal to 180 degrees. This is true for any triangle.

To further understand why this is true, consider Figure 3 below. When a line is drawn parallel to the base of triangle ABC, angles p and q are formed. Using the properties of parallel lines when cut by a transversal line, it can be determined that angles p and b are alternate interior angles and are congruent, so $m\angle p = m\angle b$. The same is true for angles q and c, thus $m\angle q = m\angle c$. Angles q, a, and p make a straight line, so $m\angle q + m\angle a + m\angle p = 180°$. Since $m\angle p = m\angle b$ and $m\angle q = m\angle c$, with substitution $m\angle c + m\angle a + m\angle b = 180°$, and the sum of the interior angles of triangle ABC is equal to 180 degrees.

Figure 1

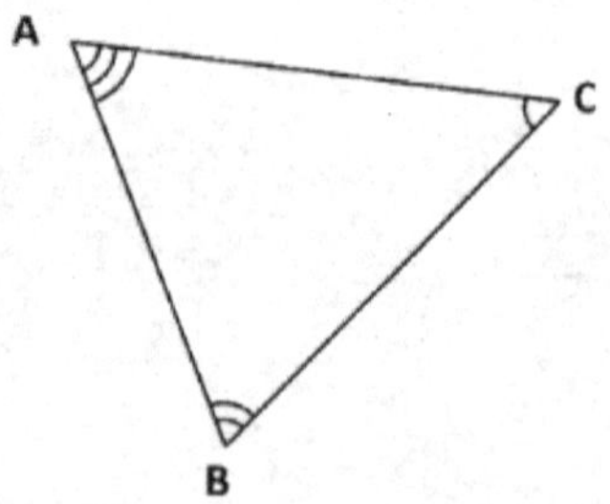


Figure 2

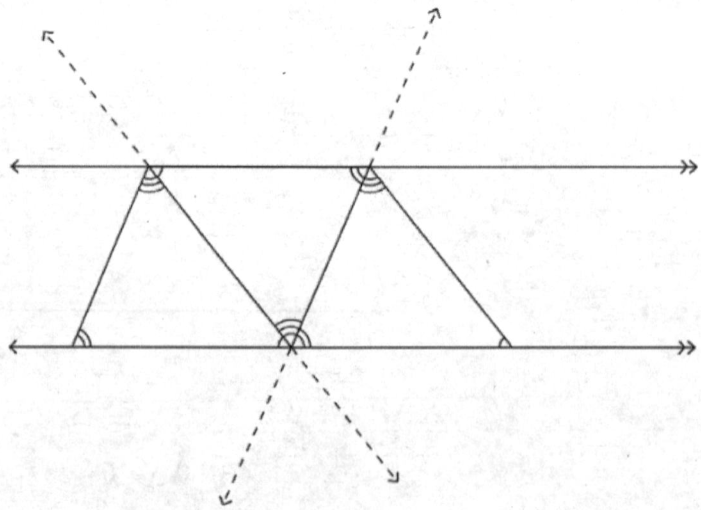

Figure 3

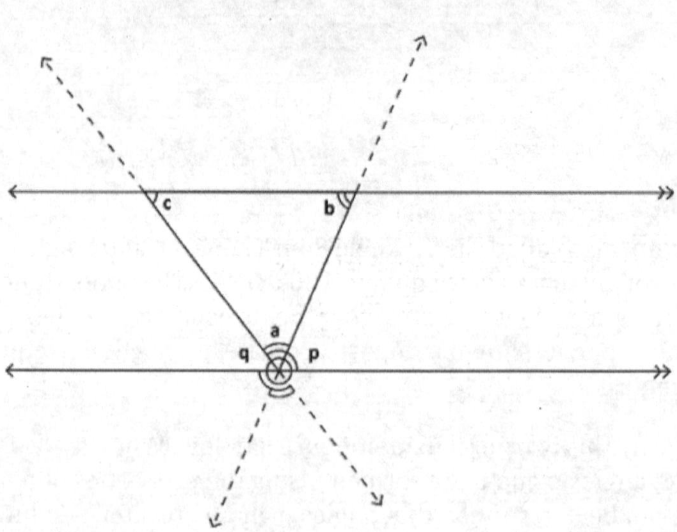


**Example 2:** If triangle ABC has the following angle measures, $m\angle A = 12°, m\angle C = 100°$, it is possible to find the measure of angle B using the Angle-Sum Theorem. This theorem states that the sum of the interior angles of a triangle is equal to 180 degrees, so $m\angle A + m\angle B + m\angle C = 180°$:

$$\begin{aligned} 12 + m\angle B + 100 &= 180 \\ m\angle B + 112 &= 180 \\ -112 &\quad -112 \\ m\angle B &= 68° \end{aligned}$$

Thus, the measure of angle B is 68°.

### Exterior Angle Sum Theorem

A theorem that follows from the Angle-Sum Theorem is the **Exterior Angle Sum Theorem** of triangles. The Exterior Angle Sum Theorem states that a triangle's exterior angle equals the sum of its two **interior opposite angles**. To understand why this is true, consider the image below. Triangle ABC has interior angles a, b, and c and exterior angle e. The interior opposite angles are a and b, as they are not adjacent to exterior angle e. Angles c and e are supplementary because they make a straight line, so $c + e = 180°$. Further, by the Angle-Sum Theorem, $a + b + c = 180°$. These equations are both equal to 180°, so they can be set equal $c + e = a + b + c$. The variable c can be subtracted from both sides of the equation to get $e = a + b$. Therefore, the measure of exterior angle e is equal to the sum of the measures of angles a and b, or the opposite interior angles.

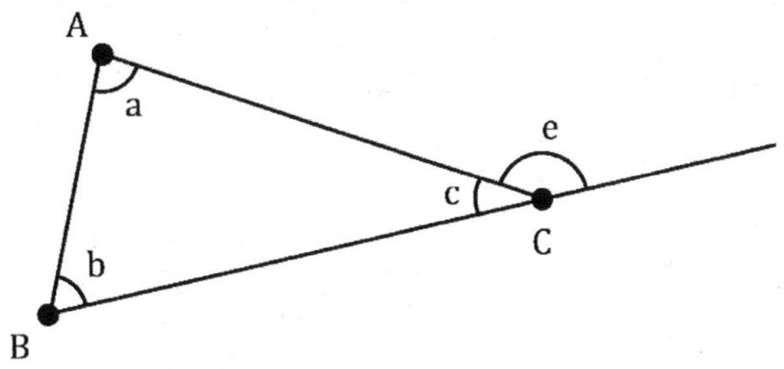


**Example 3:** In triangle ABC below, the Exterior Angle Sum Theorem can be used to solve for the variable *x*.

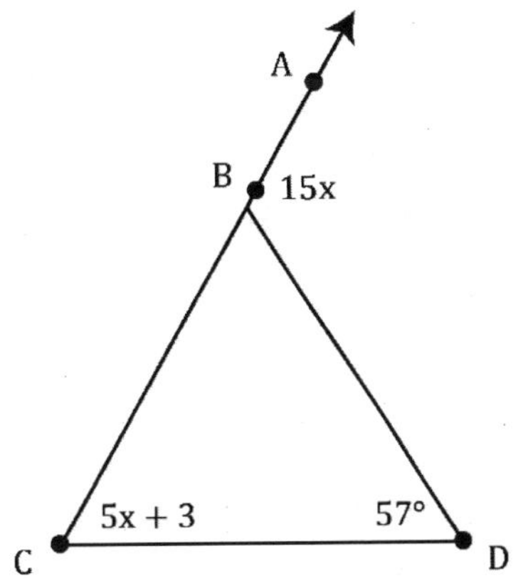


The measure of the exterior angle is the sum of the two opposite interior angles, so the following is true: $m\angle ABD = m\angle C + m\angle D$. Substitute the value of each angle and solve for *x*.

$$m\angle ABD = m\angle C + m\angle D$$
$$15x = (5x + 3) + 57$$
$$\begin{array}{r} 15x \\ -5x \end{array} = \begin{array}{r} 5x + 60 \\ -5x \end{array}$$
$$\frac{10x}{10} = \frac{60}{10}$$
$$x = 6$$

Substitute $x = 6$ to find the measures of angles ABD and C.

$$m\angle ABD = 10x$$
$$m\angle ABD = 10(6)$$
$$m\angle ABD = 60°$$

$$m\angle C = 5x + 3$$
$$m\angle C = 5(6) + 3$$
$$m\angle C = 30 + 3$$
$$m\angle C = 33°$$

The measure of angle C is 33°, and the measure of angle ABD is 60°.

## Angle-Angle Similarity

The **Angle-Angle Similarity** (or AA similarity) of triangles states that if two corresponding angles in two triangles are congruent, the triangles must be **similar**. If any two corresponding angles of a triangle are congruent, the third angle must also be congruent since all three interior angles must add up to be 180°. For example, triangles $ABC$ and $DEF$ are similar.

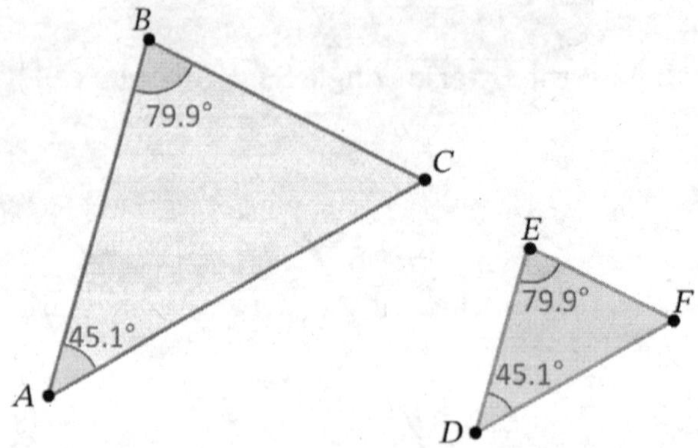

**Example 4:** Triangles RST and UVW are shown below. To determine if these are similar triangles, decide if the corresponding angles are congruent using AA similarity. The corresponding angle pairs are $\angle R$ and $\angle U$, $\angle T$ and $\angle W$, and $\angle S$ and $\angle V$. The image shows $\angle R \cong \angle U$ as they both have a measure of 60°. Find the value of angles S and W using the Angle-Sum Theorem to determine if the remaining pairs are congruent.

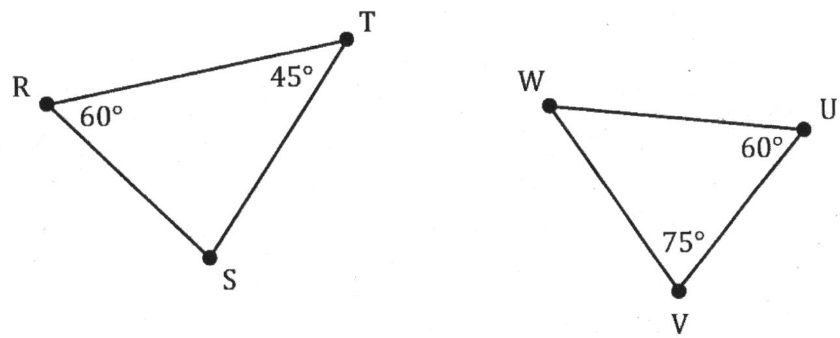


$$m\angle R + m\angle S + m\angle T = 180$$
$$60 + m\angle S + 45 = 180$$
$$\begin{array}{rcr} 105 + m\angle S & = & 180 \\ -105 & & -105 \end{array}$$
$$m\angle S = 75°$$

$$m\angle U + m\angle V + m\angle W = 180$$
$$60 + 75 + m\angle W = 180$$
$$\begin{array}{rcr} 135 + m\angle W & = & 180 \\ -135 & & -135 \end{array}$$
$$m\angle W = 45°$$

Solving for the remaining angle measures in each triangle shows that angles S and V both have a measure of 75°, and angles T and W both have a measure of 45°. This means all corresponding angles are congruent, and triangle RST is similar to triangle UVW.

# Pythagorean Theorem

## Proofs and Its Converse

The **Pythagorean theorem** states that if a **right triangle** has **legs** of length $a$ and $b$, and **hypotenuse** of length $c$, the sum of the squares of the legs is equal to the square of the hypotenuse: $a^2 + b^2 = c^2$.

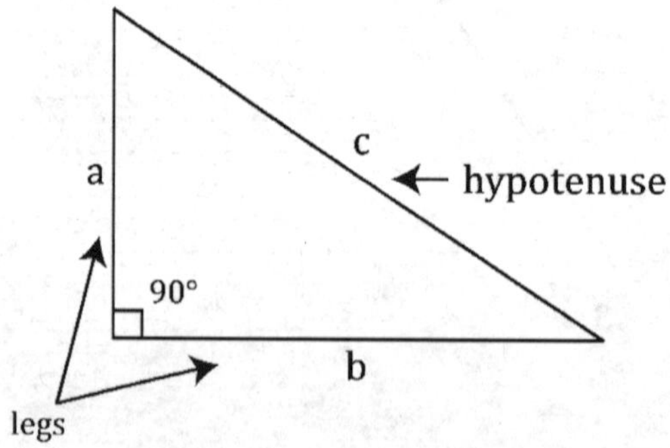


A right triangle is a triangle with one right or 90° angle. The legs of a right triangle are the two sides that meet at a right angle. These are the two shorter sides. The hypotenuse is the side opposite the right angle and is the longest side of the triangle.

To better understand this concept, look at the image below. Three squares are constructed, each with the dimensions of one side of the right triangle with side lengths a, b, and c. The area of the two smaller squares with side lengths a and b add up to equal the area of the third, and largest square, with side length c.

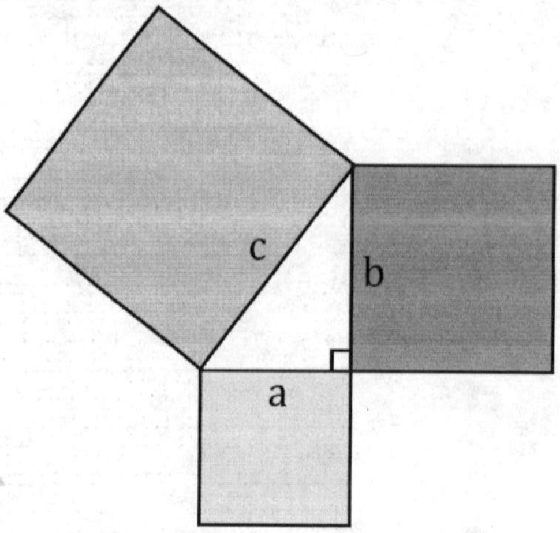


Many proofs of the Pythagorean theorem exist. One proof is shown below. This proof is known as a "proof of rearrangement," and it uses a, b, and c to denote the lengths of the sides of a right triangle with legs a and b, and hypotenuse c. Notice that each of the squares below has dimensions of $(a + b)^2$, and thus equal areas, but each is decomposed into a different number of shapes. Figure 1 consists of four right triangles, each with area $\frac{1}{2}ab$, and two squares, one with an area of $a^2$ and the other with an area of $b^2$. Figure 2 consists of four right triangles, each with an area of $\frac{1}{2}ab$, and it has one large square with an area of $c^2$.

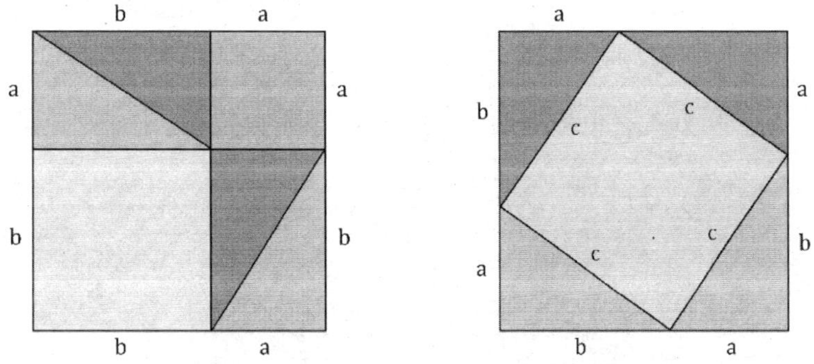


$$Area\ Figure\ 1 = Area\ Figure\ 2$$
$$4\left(\frac{1}{2}ab\right) + a^2 + b^2 = 4\left(\frac{1}{2}ab\right) + c^2$$
$$a^2 + b^2 = c^2$$

Thus, the right triangle with legs of length a and b and hypotenuse of length c has the relationship $a^2 + b^2 = c^2$.

The **converse**, or reverse of the Pythagorean theorem, states that if the sum of the squares of sides $a$ and $b$ of a triangle are equal to the square of the third side $c$, then the triangle is a right triangle.

**Example 1:** If a triangle has side lengths 5, 6, and 10 use the converse of the Pythagorean theorem to determine if it is a right triangle. The converse states if $a^2 + b^2 = c^2$, then the triangle is a right triangle. Substitute the given values for a, b, and c using the shortest two lengths for a and b and the longest side for c. If the resulting equation is true, the triangle must be a right triangle.

$$a^2 + b^2 = c^2$$
$$(5)^2 + (6)^2 = (10)^2$$
$$25 + 36 = 100$$
$$61 \neq 100$$

Since 61 is not equal to 100, the given triangle is not a right triangle.

## APPLICATION OF PYTHAGOREAN THEOREM

The **Pythagorean theorem** states that if a **right triangle** has **legs** of length $a$ and $b$, and **hypotenuse** of length $c$, the sum of the squares of the legs is equal to the square of the hypotenuse: $a^2 + b^2 = c^2$.

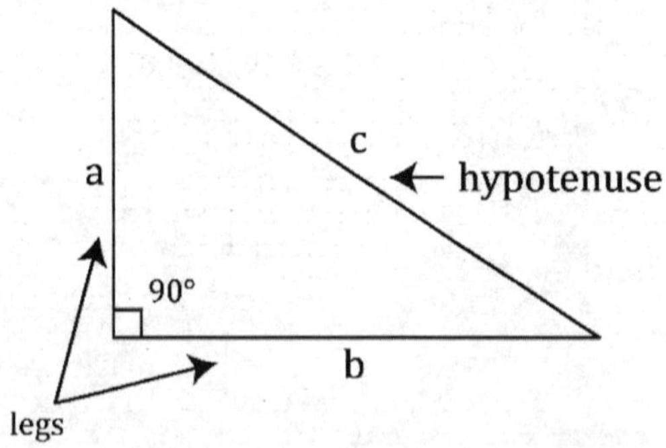


A right triangle is a triangle with one right or 90° angle. The legs of a right triangle are the two sides that meet at a right angle. These are the two shorter sides. The hypotenuse is the side opposite to the right angle, and it is the longest side of the triangle.

**Example 1:** Triangle ABC has a right angle at vertex B. Side AB has a length of 12 inches, and side AC has a length of 18 inches. Because ABC has a right angle at vertex B, it is a right triangle. To find the length of side BC, sketch triangle ABC and use the Pythagorean theorem to find the missing side, BC. Use the drawing of triangle ABC below to see which side lengths are given and which side length is missing.

$$\begin{aligned} AB^2 + BC^2 &= AC^2 \\ (12)^2 + BC^2 &= 18^2 \\ 144 + BC^2 &= 324 \\ -144 \qquad & \quad -144 \\ BC^2 &= 180 \\ BC &= \sqrt{180} \\ BC &\approx 13.4 \end{aligned}$$

Side BC is $\sqrt{180}$ inches, or, when rounded to the nearest tenth, it is approximately 13.4 inches long.

**Example 2:** The image below shows a 20 ft ladder placed on the ground 8 ft from a vertical wall. Assume the wall meets the ground at a right angle. Use the Pythagorean theorem to determine how high the ladder reaches up the wall. The ladder represents the hypotenuse of the right triangle formed, and the distance between the base of the ladder and the wall represents one of the legs. The distance between the ground and the top of the ladder represents the unknown leg of the triangle.

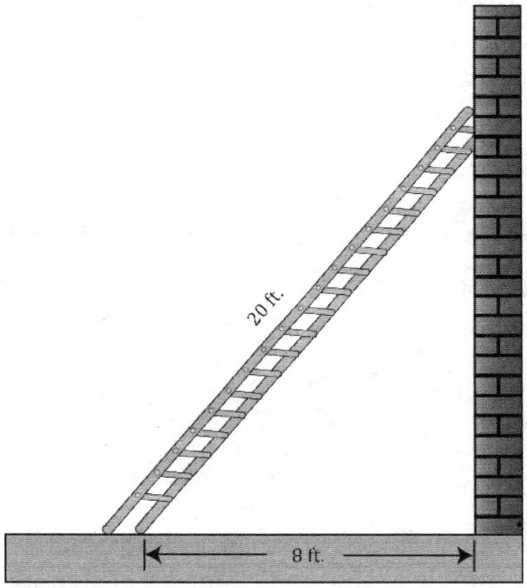


$$a^2 + b^2 = c^2$$
$$(8)^2 + b^2 = (20)^2$$
$$\begin{aligned} 64 + b^2 &= 400 \\ -64 \quad & \quad -64 \end{aligned}$$
$$b^2 = 336$$
$$b = \sqrt{336}$$
$$b \approx 18.3$$

Leg b of the triangle is $\sqrt{336}$ feet long. Round to the nearest tenth to find that the top of the ladder meets the wall about 18.3 feet above the ground.

**Example 3:** Chris lives 16.5 miles due east from the library and works 8 miles due north from the library. Chris rides his bike to the library in a straight line directly from his house. Use the Pythagorean theorem to determine how many miles he must pedal. Draw the diagram representing this situation if needed. Use the Pythagorean theorem to solve for the length of the triangle's hypotenuse.

$$a^2 + b^2 = c^2$$
$$(16.5)^2 + (8)^2 = c^2$$
$$272.25 + 64 = c^2$$
$$c^2 = 336.25$$
$$c = \sqrt{336.25}$$
$$c \approx 18.3$$

Chris must bike approximately 18.3 miles to work.

## Pythagorean Theorem and The Coordinate Plane

The **Pythagorean theorem** states that if a **right triangle** has **legs** of length $a$ and $b$, and **hypotenuse** of length $c$, the sum of the squares of the legs is equal to the square of the hypotenuse: $a^2 + b^2 = c^2$.

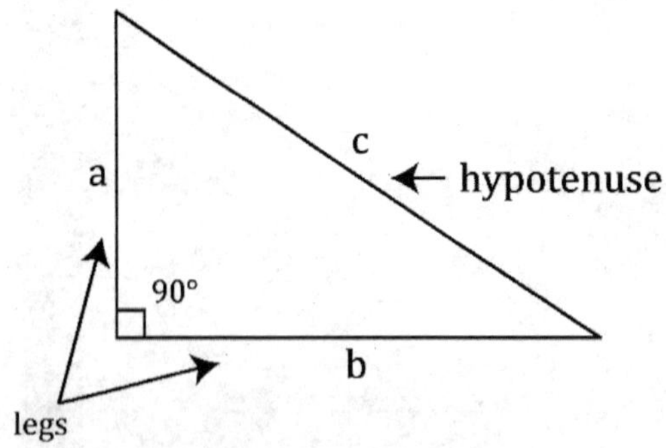


A right triangle is a triangle with one right or 90° angle. The legs of a right triangle are the two sides that meet at a right angle. These are the two shorter sides. The hypotenuse is the side opposite to the right angle, and it is the longest side of the triangle.

Use the Pythagorean theorem to find the **distance between two points** in the coordinate plane. For example, if point A is plotted at $(-6,5)$ in the coordinate plane, and point B is plotted at $(2,4)$, the line connecting A and B is the hypotenuse of a right triangle with legs AC and CB. Point C can be plotted in two different locations to form a right triangle. One way is where point C intersects the vertical line through point A and the horizontal line through point B. Another way to think about this is that point C has the same $x$-coordinate as point A and the same $y$-coordinate as point B. Thus, C is plotted at $(-6,4)$. This is illustrated in the graph below.

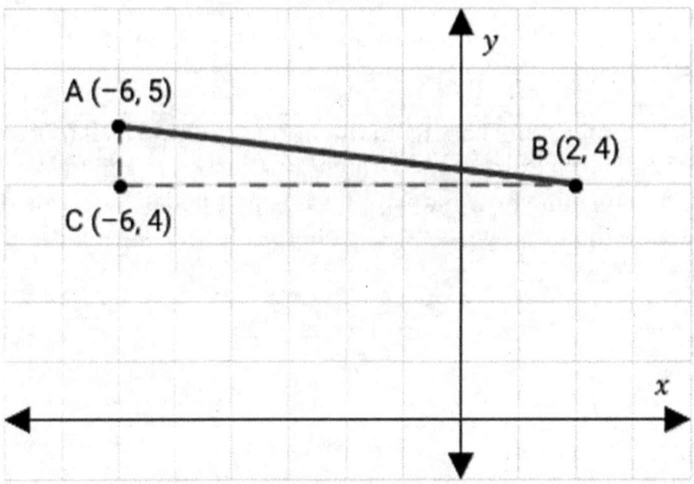

The graph shows the length of AC is equal to one unit, and the length of CB is equal to eight units. Substitute these values into the Pythagorean theorem to find the distance between points A and B in the coordinate plane.

$$\begin{aligned} a^2 + b^2 &= c^2 \\ (1)^2 + (8)^2 &= c^2 \\ 1 + 64 &= c^2 \\ 65 &= c^2 \\ c &= \sqrt{65} \\ c &\approx 8.1 \end{aligned}$$

Rounded to the nearest tenth, point A is about 8.1 units from point B on the coordinate plane.

It is also possible to find the distance between two points plotted in the coordinate plane without using a graph to count the distances of the legs of the right triangle. In general, if point A is plotted at $(x_1, y_1)$ in the coordinate plane, and point B is plotted at $(x_2, y_2)$, point C will be plotted at $(x_1, y_2)$ or $(x_2, y_1)$.

In both cases, to find the hypotenuse of the right triangle ABC, which is also the distance between points A and B, use the Pythagorean theorem. The final formula is called the **distance formula**, where *d* represents the distance between each point on the coordinate plane.

$$\begin{aligned} a^2 + b^2 &= c^2 \\ (x_2 - x_1)^2 + (y_2 - y_1)^2 &= c^2 \\ c &= \sqrt{(x_2 - x_1)^2 + (y_2 - y_1)^2} \\ d &= \sqrt{(x_2 - x_1)^2 + (y_2 - y_1)^2} \end{aligned}$$

**Example 1:** Find the distance, in units, between point A graphed in the coordinate plane at (3,4) and point B graphed at $(1, -5)$ without using a graph. One way to do this is to plot point C at the intersection of the vertical line through point A and the horizontal line through point B: $(x_1, y_2) \rightarrow (3, -5)$. Then, find the length of AC by finding the difference between the *y*-values of each point: $y_2 - y_1 = (-5) - 4 = -9$. Find the length of CB by finding the difference between the *x*-values of each point: $x_2 - x_1 = 1 - 3 = -2$. Substitute these values into the Pythagorean theorem to find the length of the hypotenuse of triangle ABC, which is also the distance between points A and B on the coordinate plane.

$$\begin{aligned} a^2 + b^2 &= c^2 \\ (-2)^2 + (-9)^2 &= c^2 \\ 4 + 81 &= c^2 \\ 85 &= c^2 \\ c &= \sqrt{85} \\ c &\approx 9.2 \end{aligned}$$

Point A is approximately 9.2 units away from point B on the coordinate plane.

## Volume

**Volume** is the measure of how much **space** is contained within a **three-dimensional figure**. Calculating volume is a real-world skill with many applications. For example, volume calculations are involved when determining how much water can be added to a swimming pool, how much lemonade can be contained in a pitcher, or how much soup is contained within a can. There are formulas that make volume calculations efficient and straightforward. For example, consider the three-dimensional solids listed below.

### CYLINDER

A **cylinder** consists of two circular base shapes and a curved rectangular side shape.

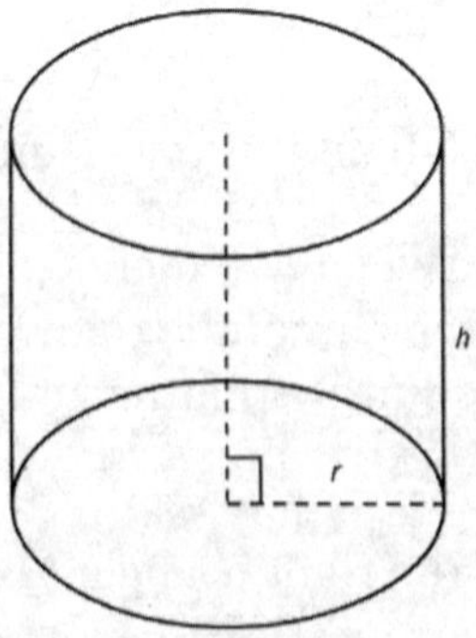


The volume formula for of a cylinder is calculated as $V = \pi r^2 h$, where $V$ represents volume, $\pi$ is approximated as 3.14, $r$ represents radius, and $h$ represents height.

Calculate the volume of a can of soup with a height of 20 centimeters and a radius of 5 centimeters. Use 3.14 as an approximation for pi.

$$V = \pi r^2 h$$
$$V = (3.14)(5)^2(20)$$
$$V = 1{,}570$$

The volume of the cylinder is 1,570 cubic centimeters.

#### *EXAMPLE*

A cylinder has a height of 7 feet and a radius of 5 feet. Calculate the volume of the cylinder. Use 3.14 as an approximation for $\pi$.

$$V = \pi r^2 h$$
$$V = (3.14)(5)^2(7)$$
$$V = 549.5$$

The volume of the cylinder is 549.5 cubic feet.

$$V = 549.5 \text{ ft}^3$$

## CONE

A **cone** consists of a flat circular base joined to a point (vertex) by a curved side.

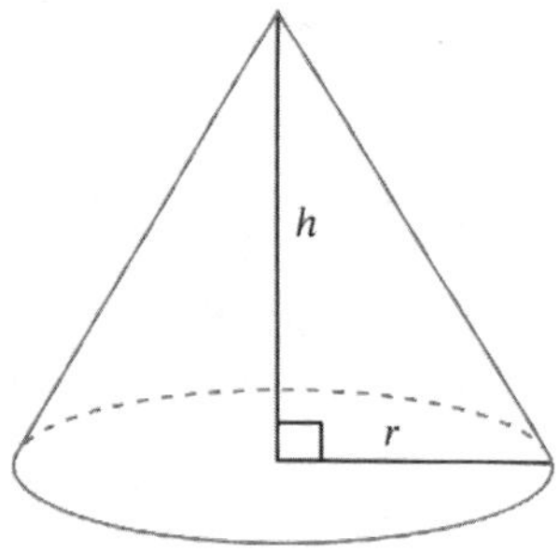


The volume formula for a cone is $V = \frac{1}{3}\pi r^2 h$, where $V$ represents volume, $\pi$ is approximated as 3.14, $r$ represents radius, and $h$ represents height.

Calculate the volume of a cone with a radius of 3 feet and a height of 20 feet. Use 3.14 as an approximation for pi.

$$V = \frac{1}{3}\pi r^2 h$$
$$V = \frac{1}{3}(3.14)(3)^2(20)$$
$$V = 188.4$$

The volume of the cone is 188.4 cubic feet.

**Review Video: Volume and Surface Area of a Right Circular Cone**
Visit mometrix.com/academy and enter code: 573574

## SPHERE

A **sphere** is a round shape. All points on a sphere are at an equal distance from the center.

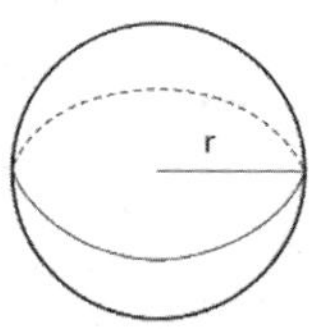


The volume formula for a sphere is $V = \frac{4}{3}\pi r^3$, where $V$ represents volume, $\pi$ is approximated as 3.14, and $r$ represents radius.

Calculate the volume of a sphere with a radius of 24 inches. Use 3.14 as an approximation for pi.

$$V = \frac{4}{3}\pi r^3$$
$$V = \frac{4}{3}(3.14)(24)^3$$
$$V = 57,876.48$$

The volume of the sphere is 57,876.48 cubic inches.

In some scenarios the volume is known and other elements of the formula need to be determined. When this happens, substitute in all the known values, and then solve for the unknown variable. For example, consider the problem below.

Determine the radius of a sphere that has a volume of 72 cubic meters.

Substitute the given value for volume, then solve for the radius, $r$.

$$V = \frac{4}{3}\pi r^3$$
$$72 = \frac{4}{3}\pi r^3$$
$$72 = \left(\frac{4}{3}\right)(3.14)r^3$$
$$72 = (4.187)r^3$$
$$17.196 = r^3$$
$$2.58 \approx r$$

The radius of the sphere is approximately 2.58 meters.

**Review Video: Volume and Surface Area of a Sphere**
Visit mometrix.com/academy and enter code: 786928

### Example

A spherical globe has a radius of 13 inches. Calculate the approximate volume of the globe. Use 3.14 as an approximation for pi.

$$V = \frac{4}{3}\pi r^3$$
$$V = \left(\frac{4}{3}\right)(3.14)(13)^3$$
$$V \approx 9{,}198.1$$

The volume of the sphere is approximately 9,198.1 cubic inches.

$V \approx 9{,}198.1 \text{ in}^3$

## Volume Formula of a Cylinder

A **cylinder** is a solid that consists of two identical flat circular bases and one curved rectangular side. Cylinders are common in the study of geometry as well as many real-world applications. The volume of a cylinder can be calculated using the formula $V = Bh$, where $V$ represents the volume, $B$ represents the area of the base shape, and $h$ represents the height of the cylinder.

Consider the identical cylindrical grain silos below. The formula $V = Bh$ can be applied to determine the volume of grain that each silo can hold (not including the upper region of the cone topper).

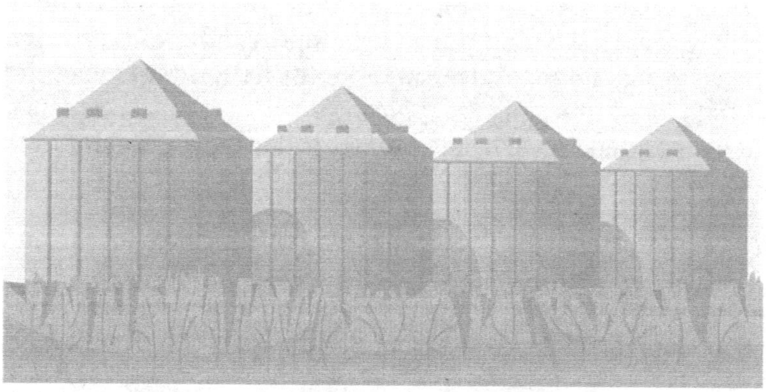

The dimensions of each cylindrical silo without the cone topper:

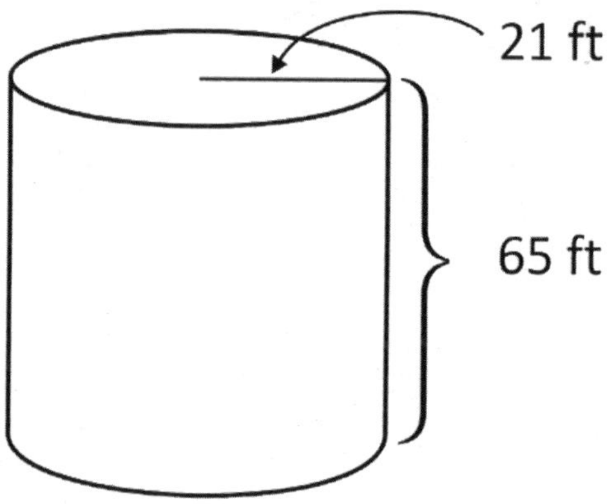


Volume formula for cylinder: $V = Bh$

Start by determining $B$, the area of the base shape. The base shape of a cylinder is a circle, and the area formula for a circle is $A = \pi r^2$. The radius of each silo is 21 feet, and an approximation for $\pi$ is 3.14. Substitute these values into the formula.

$$V = (\pi r^2)h$$
$$V = (3.14)(21)^2 h$$

Now substitute in the value for $h$, height. The height of the silo is 65 feet.

$$V = (3.14)(21)^2(65)$$
$$V = 90{,}008.1$$

This means the volume of each cylindrical silo is 90,008.1 $ft^3$.

**Review Video: Volume and Surface Area of a Right Circular Cylinder**
Visit mometrix.com/academy and enter code: 226463

# Statistics and Probability

**Scatter plots** are visual displays that show the relationship between **bivariate data**. Bivariate data have two variables of interest. The **explanatory variable (or independent variable)** is plotted on the horizontal axis (x-axis), and the **response variable (or dependent variable)** is plotted on the vertical axis (y-axis). Data for scatterplots are typically given in tables or as sets of ordered pairs. Two numbers should be reported for each data point: one for the explanatory variable and one for the response variable.

**Example 1:** Darnell was interested in exploring the relationship between the number of hours 8th-grade students at his school do math homework each week and their average score on math tests. He samples ten students and records the hours they spend on homework each week, $x$, and their average test scores, $y$, in the table below. Construct a scatterplot of Darnell's data.

| Student | A | B | C | D | E | F | G | H | I | J |
|---|---|---|---|---|---|---|---|---|---|---|
| Hrs. of HW per week ($x$) | 2 | 3 | 1 | 4 | 2.5 | 3.5 | 5 | 6 | 7 | 8 |
| Avg. test score ($y$) | 65 | 70 | 60 | 75 | 68 | 72 | 80 | 85 | 90 | 92 |

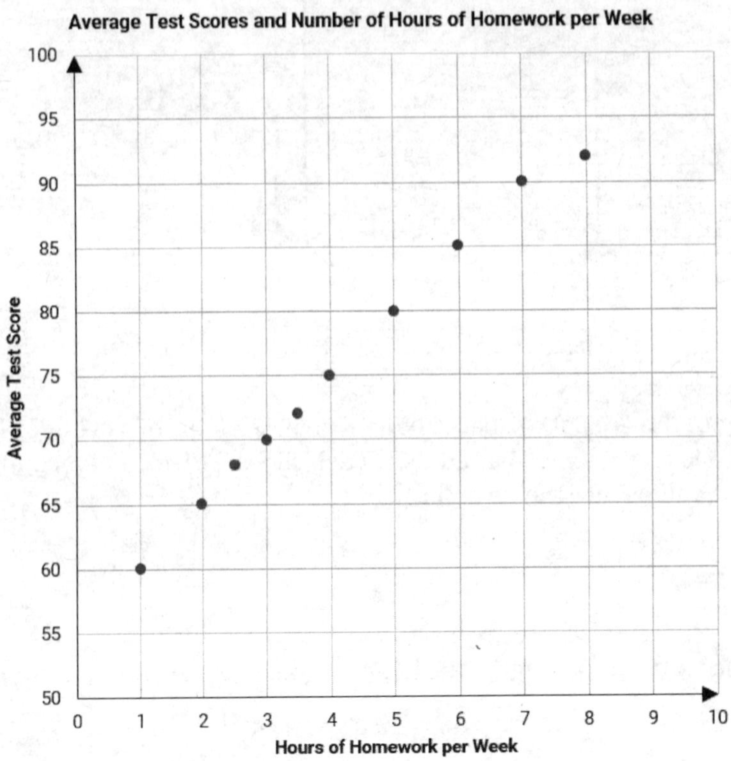


Patterns shown on a scatterplot help explore the relationship of the two quantitative variables on the graph. Suppose a distinct pattern appears on a scatterplot. In that case, the two variables have an **association**, which means they are related, and the explanatory variable can be used to predict the response variable. The two variables have no association if there is no pattern on the scatter plot.

When two variables have an association, the patterns of their plotted data can be further analyzed in the following ways:

**Direction** describes whether the response variable increases or decreases when the explanatory variable increases. **Positive association** means the response variable increases when the explanatory variable increases. **Negative association** means the response variable decreases when the explanatory variable increases.

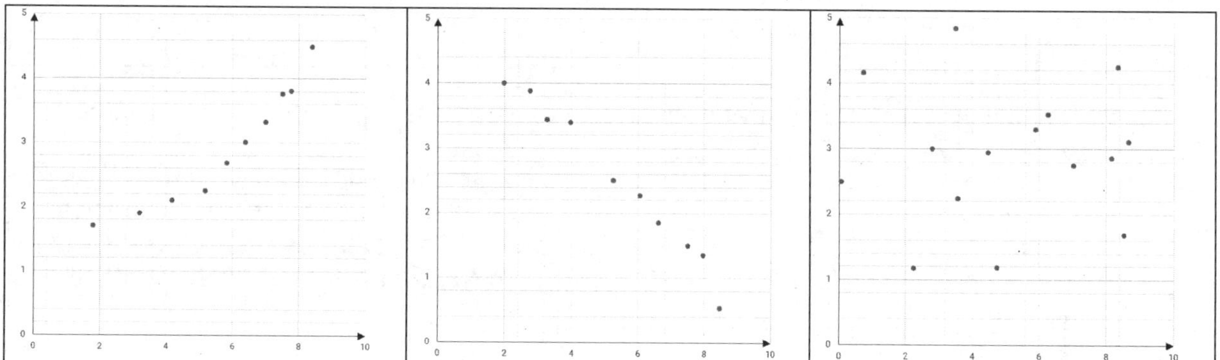

Positive Association | Negative Association | No Association

**Form** describes the overall shape of the pattern. Two different forms to describe bivariate data are **linear association** and **non-linear association.** If a straight line can roughly approximate the points on the scatter plot, there is a linear association. If not, there is likely a curve in the data, so there is a non-linear association.

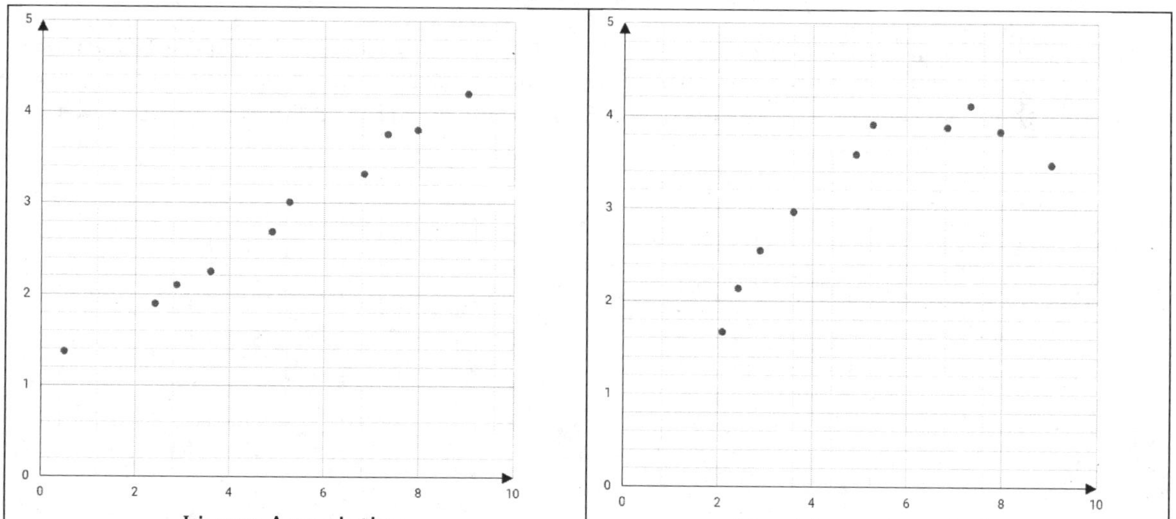

Linear Association | Non-Linear Association

**Clustering** describes data points that are grouped closely together.

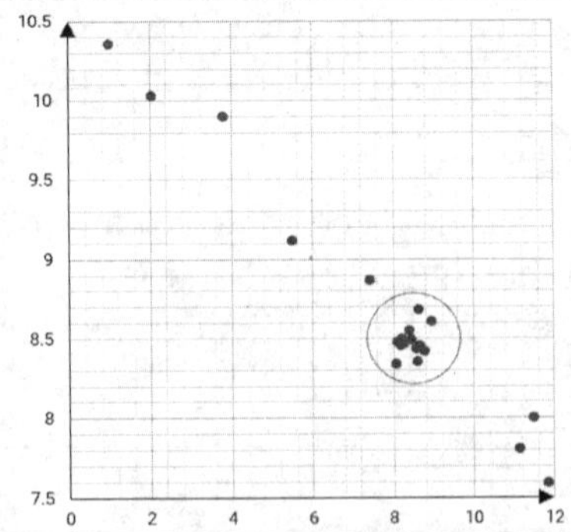


The circled region shows a cluster of data where the explanatory variable is between 8-9 and the response variable is between 8.2 and 8.8.

**Outliers** are data points that drastically deviate from the pattern shown in the rest of the data.

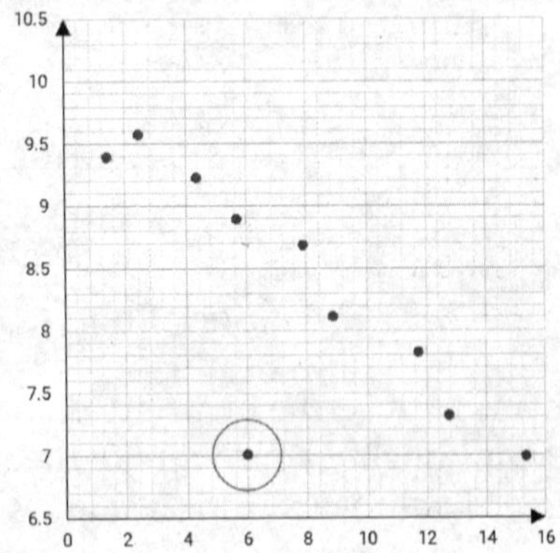


The circled point shows an outlier. When the explanatory variable is 6, the response variable is 7, which is well below the rest of the data, making the point an outlier.

**Example 2**: Health and wellness experts are interested in the effect of healthy habits on stress levels. They asked ten randomly selected adults how many hours of exercise they spent each week and to rate their overall stress level from 1 to 10. They plotted their data on a scatterplot with hours of weekly exercise on the x-axis and self-rated stress levels on the y-axis. Describe the relationship between hours of exercise per week and stress level among the adults sampled. Identify potential outliers in the data set.

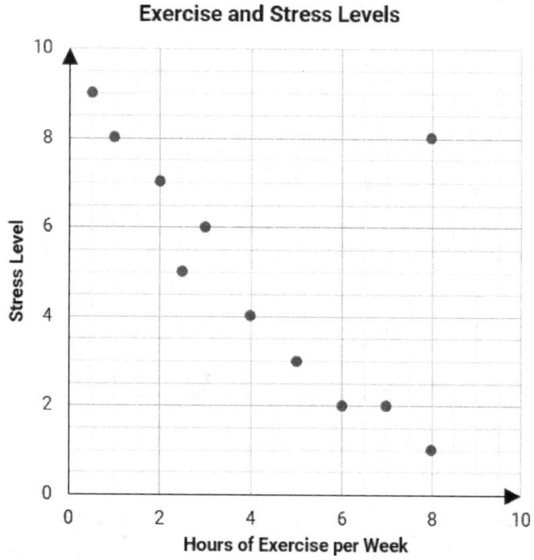


There appears to be a negative linear association between number of hours of exercise per week and stress level. When the number of hours of exercise increases, the stress level tends to decrease, and the data appears to be roughly linear. There is a possible outlier at (8, 8).

**Review Video: Scatter Plot**
Visit mometrix.com/academy and enter code: 596526

## Identifying Linear Relationships

A **linear relationship** describes a relationship between two variables, such as $x$ and $y$, that results in a **straight line** when graphed. When data points are plotted on a scatterplot, a **line of best fit** can be used to determine if the data is linear or not. For example, the scatterplots below both display a linear relationship because the data points trend in the general direction of a straight line. Linear relationships can be **positive**, extending from lower left to upper right, or **negative**, extending from upper left to lower right. If a line of best fit can be drawn over the data points in a way that is consistent with the trend of the data, the relationship is considered linear.

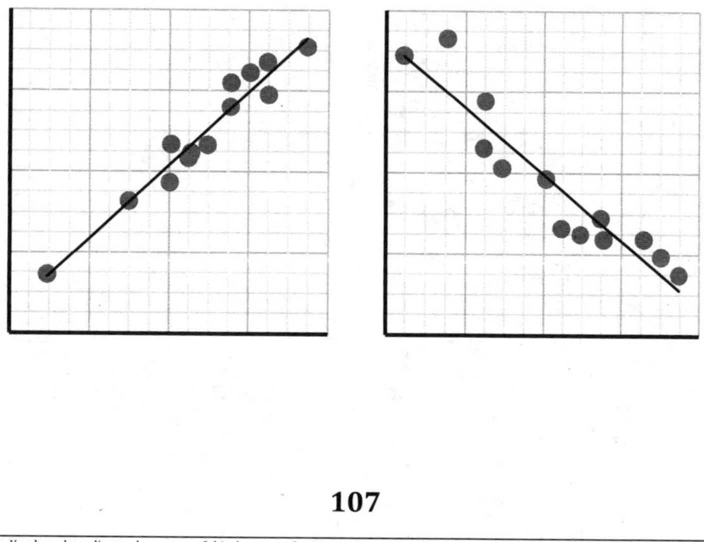

Data that is not considered linear can appear as points with no apparent trend line. For example, the scatterplot below shows no visible trend line, therefore a line of best fit cannot be drawn. The data in this scatterplot is not considered linear.

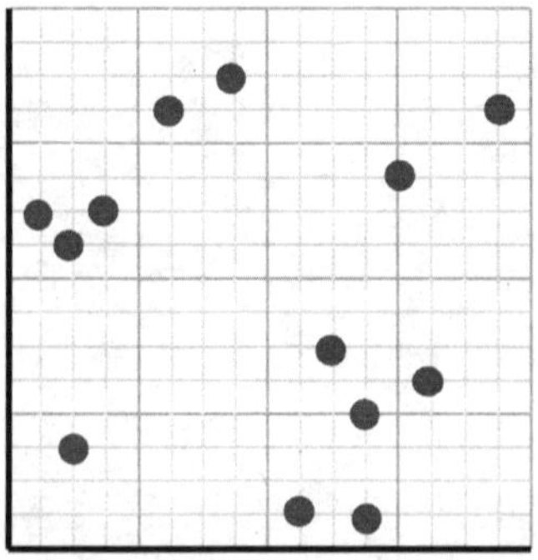

## BIVARIATE DATA

Data is considered **bivariate data** when the primary purpose of the data is to compare the two sets of data (the $x$-variable and the $y$-variable) in order to identify if a relationship exists between the two. For example, consider the bivariate data displayed in the scatter plot below. The $x$-value represents the age of each husband, and the $y$-variable represents the age of each corresponding wife. In this study, there appears to be a correlation between the ages of husbands and their wives. A positive linear relationship is present, and a line of best fit can be drawn over the data points extending from lower left to upper right.

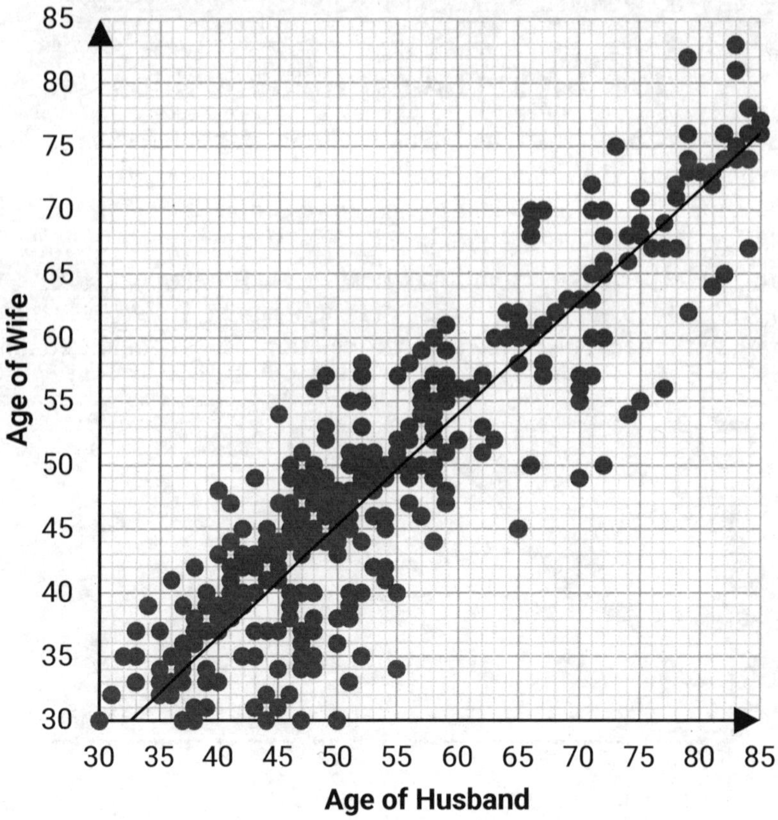

### TREND LINES

When data points on a scatterplot form a line, or the general shape of a line, the data is considered linear. Data points can be somewhat clustered around this line, but in general, the **trend** of the data points need to follow the direction of the line. This line is referred to as a **line of best fit** or a **trend line**. For example, consider the scatterplot below. The number of visitors to the beach appears to be directly related to the average daily temperature. As the temperature increases, the number of visitors also increases. The data points form the general shape of a line, rising from the lower left to the upper right. A trend line can be drawn over the data points to show the general shape and trajectory of the line.

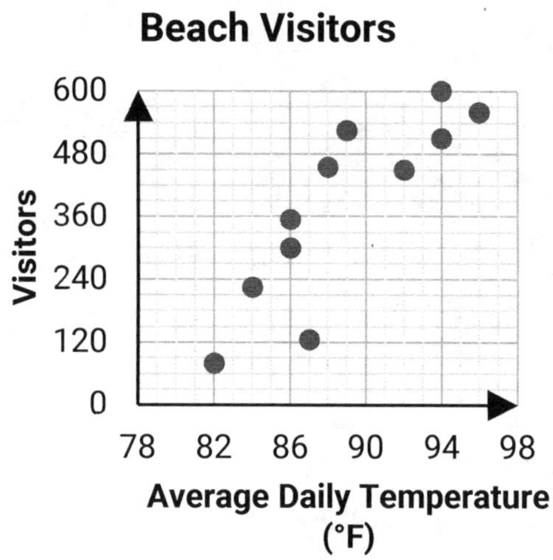


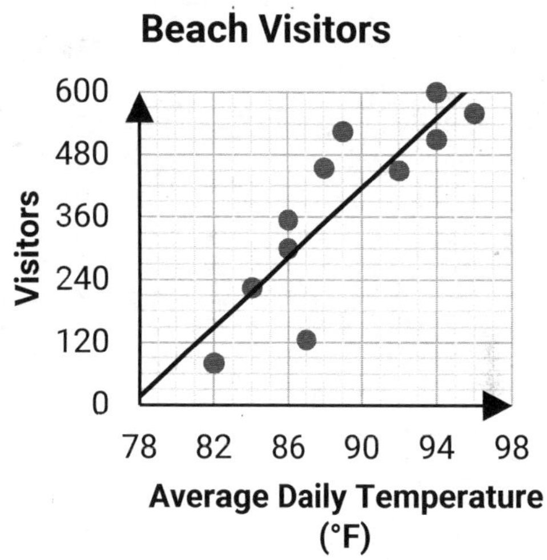


Trend lines are often helpful when determining if there is a correlation between variables and when making predations regarding data. Trend lines can be extended in order to make approximations for $x$- and $y$-values that are not presented within the data set. For example, consider the beach visitors scenario. As the temperature increases, so does the number of visitors to the beach. However, the data stops at 96° and 600 visitors. For example, there are no data points indicating how many visitors would likely be at the beach on a 100° day. However, if the trend line is extended, a prediction can be made.

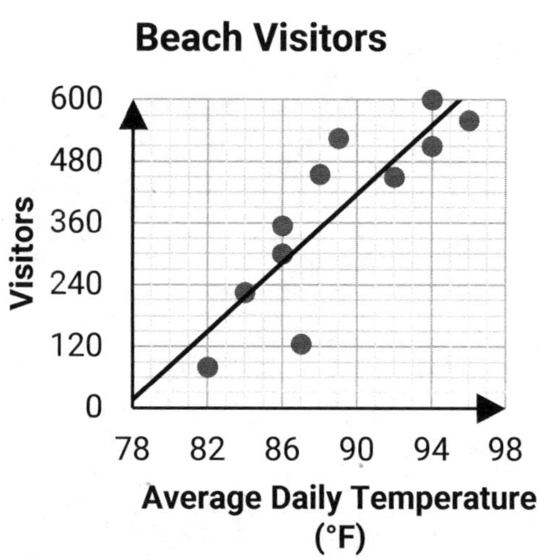


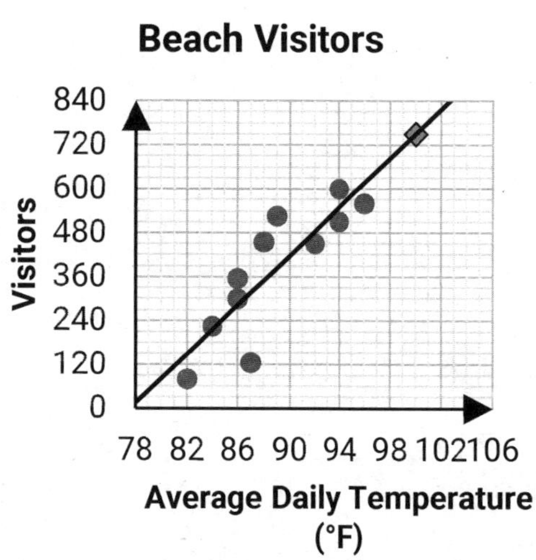

When the trend line is extended, on a 100° day there will be approximately 750 visitors. The data point (100, 750) does not appear in the original data set, but the extended trend line allows predictions to be made based on the consistent linear nature of the data.

Trend lines can also provide valuable information regarding predictions of data points within a scatterplot. For example, there is no specific data point illustrating the number of visitors on a 90° day. However, the trend line can be used to identify a reasonable estimation. For example, place a pencil on the 90° mark on the $x$-axis and move vertically until the pencil contacts the trend line. Now drag the pencil to the left until it contacts the $y$-axis. The pencil should contact the $y$-axis around 415. This means that on a 90° day, there will be approximately 415 visitors to the beach.

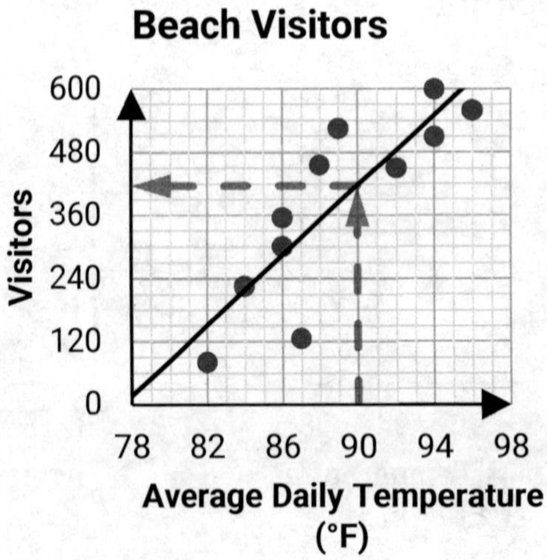

*EXAMPLE*

**The scatterplot below illustrates the cost per ounce of candy sold at a local candy shop.**

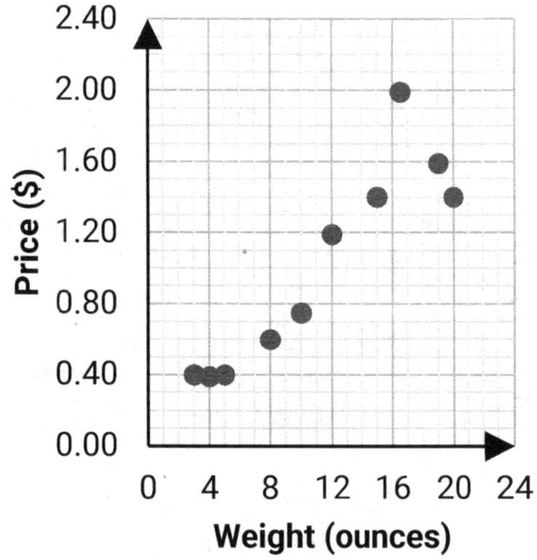


**Based on the scatterplot, which is the best prediction for the price of 11 ounces of candy?**

a. $1.00
b. $1.10
c. $1.15
d. $1.20

A trend line can be drawn though the data points in order to make a prediction. The $x$-value of 11 ounces intersects the trend line at approximately 1.00 on the $y$-axis. This indicates that the cost of 11 ounces of candy is approximately $1.00.

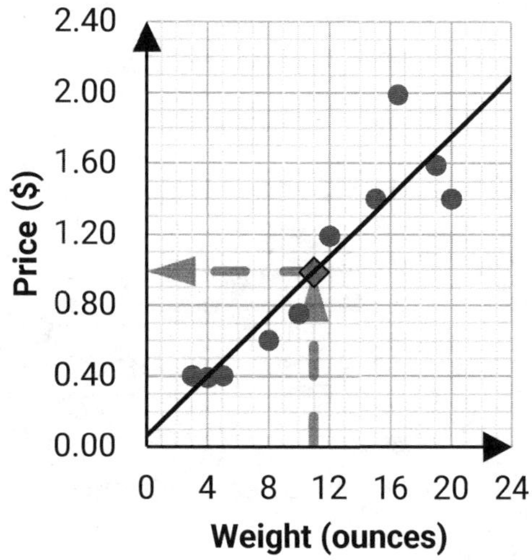


A is the correct answer.

*EXAMPLE*

**Based on the scatterplot, what will the wind chill be with a wind speed of 60 miles per hour?**

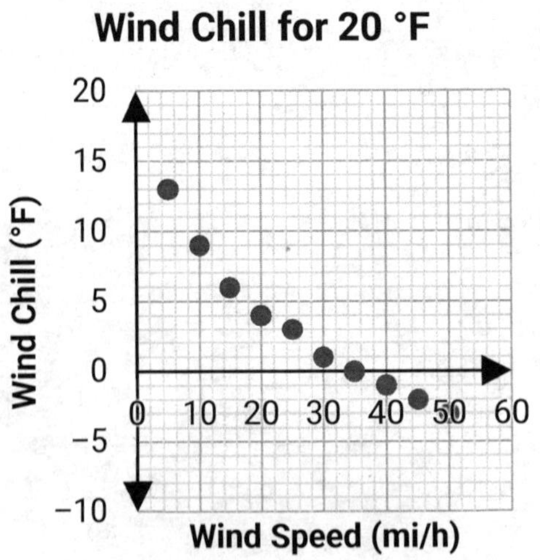


a. -2.5° F
b. -7.5° F
c. -10° F
d. -14° F

A trend line can be drawn though the data points in order to make a prediction. The $x$-value of 60 miles per hour intersects the trend line at approximately -7.5 on the $y$-axis. This indicates that the wind chill will be approximately -7.5 °F when the wind speed is 60 miles per hour.

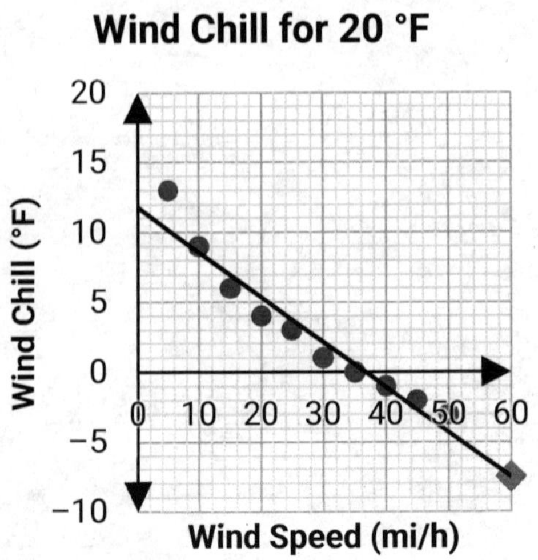


B is the correct answer.

## EQUATIONS WITH BIVARIATE DATA

Lines of best fit are represented by basic linear equations of the form $\boldsymbol{y = mx + b}$, where $y$ represents the dependent variable and $x$ is the independent variable. In this equation, $\boldsymbol{m}$ represents the **slope** of the line of best fit and is used to explain the change in the dependent variable for each change in the independent variable. Furthermore, $\boldsymbol{b}$ represents the **$\boldsymbol{y}$-intercept**, or the **initial value** of the dependent variable, when the independent variable equals zero. When interpreting the slope or $y$-intercept of a linear equation used to model bivariate data, it is essential to understand the data's context and interpret the independent and dependent variables.

**Example 1:** Jason recorded the temperature of a cup of coffee for each minute it was left on the table. The equation $y = -4x + 120$ can be used to model his data, where $y$ is the temperature of the cup of coffee in degrees Fahrenheit, and $x$ is the minutes it was left on the table. Interpret the slope and $y$-intercept of the equation in the context given.

The slope is the coefficient of the independent variable and represents the change in the dependent variable with respect to the change in the independent variable. The dependent variable, $y$, in this context, is the temperature of the cup of coffee in degrees Fahrenheit. The independent variable, $x$, in this context is the number of minutes the cup of coffee was left on the table. The slope is $-4$. This means that, on average, the temperature of the cup of coffee decreased by 4 degrees Fahrenheit for each additional minute it was on the table.

Linear equations used to model bivariate data can also be used to find predicted values for one of the variables (dependent or independent) when given a value of the other. To find the value of the dependent variable when given a specific value of the independent variable, substitute the given value for $x$ and solve for $y$. To find the value of the independent variable when given a specific value of the dependent variable, substitute the value for $y$, then use inverse operations to solve for $x$.

**Example 2:** A biologist was studying the effect of direct sunlight on the height of a budding sunflower. He collected the data and found the line of best fit, $y = 1.5x + 10$, where $y$ is the sunflower's height (in inches), and $x$ is the number of hours of direct sunlight it received on a given day. What would be its predicted height if a sunflower received 6 hours of direct sunlight?

The predicted height of the sunflower is the dependent variable, $y$, and the number of hours of sunlight is the independent variable, $x$. Given 6 hours of sunlight, the predicted height of the sunflower can be found by substituting 6 for $x$ and solving for $y$:

$$\begin{aligned} y &= 1.5x + 10 \\ y &= 1.5(6) + 10 \\ y &= 9 + 10 \\ y &= 19 \end{aligned}$$

The predicted height for a sunflower receiving 6 hours of direct sunlight daily would be 19 inches tall.

**Example 3**: An economist collected data for the salaries earned at a company. The equation $y = 20x + 100$ models his data where $y$ is the amount of money an employee earns in a week and $x$ represents the number of hours worked. If an employee earns $800 in a week, how many hours did he work that week?

In this context, \$800 earned by an employee in a week represents the dependent variable ($y$); the unknown variable is $x$, the number of hours worked. To solve for $x$, substitute the given variable for $y$ and solve for $x$:

$$\begin{aligned} y &= 20x + 100 \\ \begin{matrix} 800 \\ -100 \end{matrix} &= \begin{matrix} 20x + 100 \\ -100 \end{matrix} \\ \frac{700}{20} &= \frac{20x}{20} \\ x &= 35 \end{aligned}$$

An employee who earns \$800 in a week at this company worked 35 hours.

## Direct Variation

**Direct variation** refers to a relationship between two variables such that when one variable increases, the other variable increases or decreases by the same factor. Similarly, if one variable decreases, the other variable increases or decreases by the same factor. In other words, the two variables are in *direct variation*. Two variables show direct variation if $y = kx$, where $k$ is not zero. $x$ and $y$ represent two variables, and $k$ represents the constant of proportionality. In the equation $y = kx$, $x$ and $y$ vary directly. This is because $x$ and $y$ represent a proportional relationship. For example, if tomato plants cost \$12 each, the total cost of purchasing tomato plants will be directly proportional to the number of plants that are purchased. If 5 plants are purchased, then the total cost is $5 \times \$12 = \$60$.

**Review Video: Direct Variation**
Visit mometrix.com/academy and enter code: 547565

### PROPORTIONS

Direct variation problems always represent proportional relationships. This means that a proportion can be set up in order to solve direct variation problems. Consider the tomato plant scenario.

"How much will 7 tomato plants cost?"

Set up a proportion relating the number of tomato plants to total cost.

$$\frac{\text{tomato plants}}{\text{total cost}} = \frac{\text{tomato plants}}{\text{total cost}}$$

Substitute in 3 out of 4 values.

We know that each plant costs \$12. We also know that we want to purchase 7 plants. Let $x$ represent the total cost of 7 plants.

$$\frac{1}{12} = \frac{7}{x}$$

Cross multiply to solve for $x$.

$$1(x) = 7(12)$$
$$x = 84$$

The total cost of 12 tomato plants is $84.

### TABLES

Direct variation problems can also be solved using a table. In the tomato plant scenario, the total cost varies directly based on the number of plants that are purchased. In other words, the $y$-value will always be 12 times the value of $x$. A table of values can be set up in order to solve for the cost of any number of plants. Let the number of plants represent $x$ and the total cost represent $y$.

| Tomato Plants ($x$) | Total Cost in Dollars ($y$) |
|---|---|
| 0 | 0 |
| 5 | 60 |
| 10 | 120 |

The equation $y = kx$ is modeled in the table. The number of plants, $x$, is multiplied by the constant of proportionality, 12, in order to determine the corresponding $y$-value, the total cost, $y = kx$ becomes $y = 12x$. This equation can be used to determine the cost of any number of tomato plants.

## Frequency Tables

**Categorical data** is data that is divided into qualitative categories. You get categorical data if you are taking a survey of favorite foods, or when a company collects data about the sizes of t-shirts they sold. This type of data is categorical data because the data can be divided into categories. One way to describe categorical data is through frequency tables. A **frequency table** is a table that visually divides this categorical data into categories and shows how frequently a category shows up in the data. For example, let's say a food truck is keeping track of how often each menu item is ordered to see which is their most popular item. The food truck sells tacos, sandwiches, salads, and burgers. A frequency table can be created to keep track of this data throughout the day.

| Menu Item | Number Sold |
|---|---|
| Tacos | |
| Sandwiches | |
| Salads | |
| Burgers | |

As items are sold, tallies or marks can be made on the frequency table to keep track of information. Let's say the food truck sold 13 taco plates, 10 sandwiches, 9 salads, and 18 burgers. These frequency tables display the data from the food truck.

| Menu Item | Number Sold |
|---|---|
| Tacos | 𝍸 𝍸 \|\|\| |
| Sandwiches | 𝍸 𝍸 |
| Salads | 𝍸 \|\|\|\| |
| Burgers | 𝍸 𝍸 𝍸 \|\|\| |

| Menu Item | Number Sold |
|---|---|
| Tacos | 13 |
| Sandwiches | 10 |
| Salads | 9 |
| Burgers | 18 |

## Relative Frequency Tables

A **relative frequency table** gives the same data as a frequency table, but also includes the percentages to show what percentage of the data goes with each category. For example, with the food truck, we can use a relative frequency table to identify the percentage of customers that ordered tacos.

To find the relative frequency of a category, we write the relationship between the category and the total as a fraction. Once we have a fraction, we can use division or equivalent fractions to find the percentage. In this example, we would write a fraction to represent the relationship between the number of tacos ordered and the total number of items ordered.

We can find the total number of items ordered by adding up the total number of data items: in this example, the food truck sold a total of 50 items because $13 + 10 + 9 + 18 = 50$.

There are 13 tacos sold and 50 total items, so the relationship can be written as the fraction $\frac{13}{50}$.

Now, to find the percentage of customers that bought tacos, or any menu item, we can use equivalent fractions and convert $\frac{13}{50}$ to a fraction over 100, and then a percentage.

We can also use division and divide 13 by 50 and multiply the quotient by 100% to get a percentage.

In this case, the most efficient process will be using equivalent fractions.

We can complete the relative frequency table to find the percentage of customers that bought each menu item.

| Menu Item | Number Sold | Fraction | Percent |
|---|---|---|---|
| Tacos | 13 | $\frac{13}{50} = \frac{26}{100}$ | 26% |
| Sandwiches | 10 | $\frac{10}{50} = \frac{20}{100}$ | 20% |
| Salads | 9 | $\frac{9}{50} = \frac{18}{100}$ | 18% |
| Burgers | 18 | $\frac{18}{50} = \frac{36}{100}$ | 36% |

There are many ways to interpret data from a frequency table. We know that 26% of customers bought tacos. We know that burgers are the most popular item because 36% of customers bought a burger.

Remember, when converting frequency to a percentage, the total of all percentages will be 100%. 100% of customers recorded purchased an item, so 26% + 20% + 18% + 36% = 100%. It is a good idea to double check your percentages by adding them up to see if they add up to 100%. If they do not add up to 100%, you may need to double check your calculations.

### *Percent Bar Graphs*

The information on a relative frequency table can also be illustrated by a percent bar graph. A **percent bar graph** is a graph that shows percent frequencies of each category in a bar labeled by percentages from 0% to 100%.

We can convert the data from the relative frequency table to a percent bar graph.

26% of customers bought tacos. 20% of customers bought sandwiches. 18% of customers bought salads. 36% of customers bought burgers. Which means that 100% of customers bought something off the food truck menu.

This information can be shown using a percent bar graph. A percent bar graph can be horizontal or vertical.

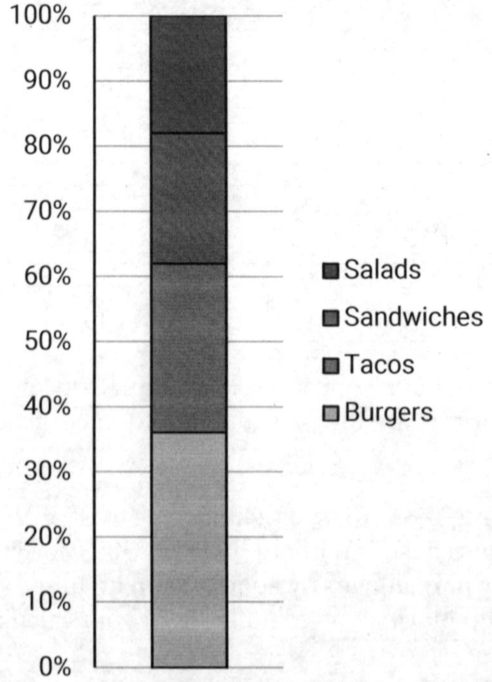


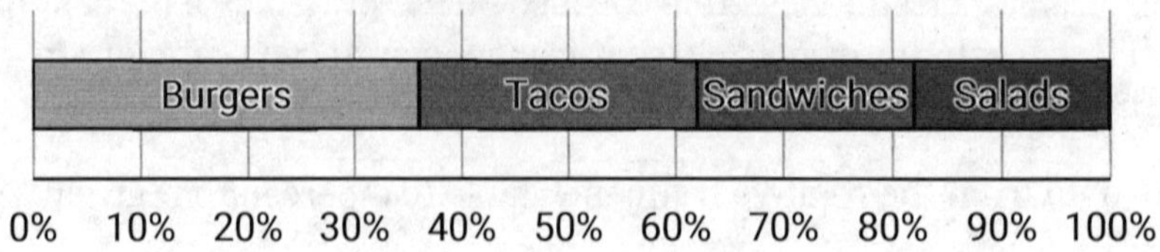


A percent bar graph will be labeled from 0 to 100, sometimes with whole number values and sometimes with percentages. Each part of the bar represents a different data category. In this example, there are four: burgers, tacos, sandwiches, and salads.

Typically, a percent bar graph will show data from greatest to least, where the category with the highest frequency starts at 0% and the category with the least frequency ends the 100%. In this example, burgers is the highest frequency category with 36%, so the burger section goes from 0% to 36%. Salads is the lowest frequency category with 18%, so the salads section goes from 82% to 100%.

Sometimes each category will be labeled with words; other times it will be labeled by color with a key. Each category will show the percent frequency, and the total percent frequency will add up to 100%.

*EXAMPLE*

**A middle school is changing their mascot and asked students to vote for their choice. The table shows the number of votes each mascot received.**

| Mascot | Votes | Key for Bar Graph |
|---|---|---|
| Lion | 58 | |
| Tiger | 120 | |
| Bear | 22 | |

**Which percent bar graph best represents the data?**

a.

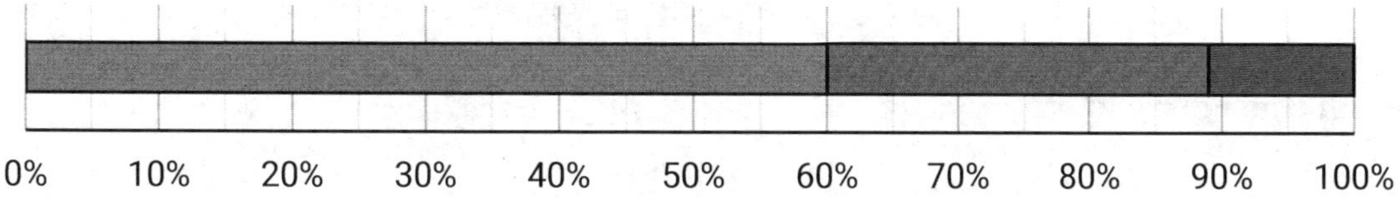


b.

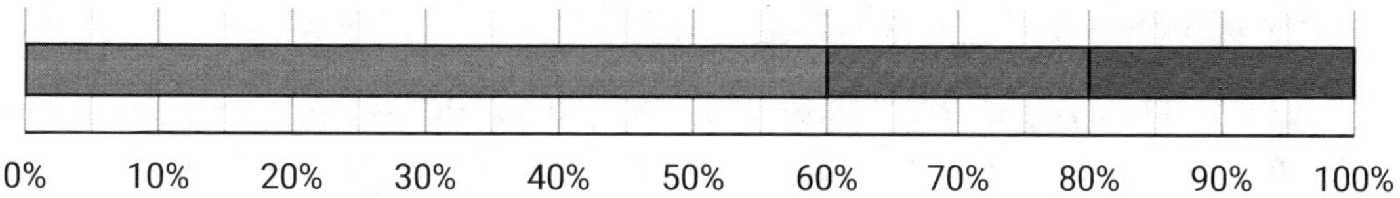


c.

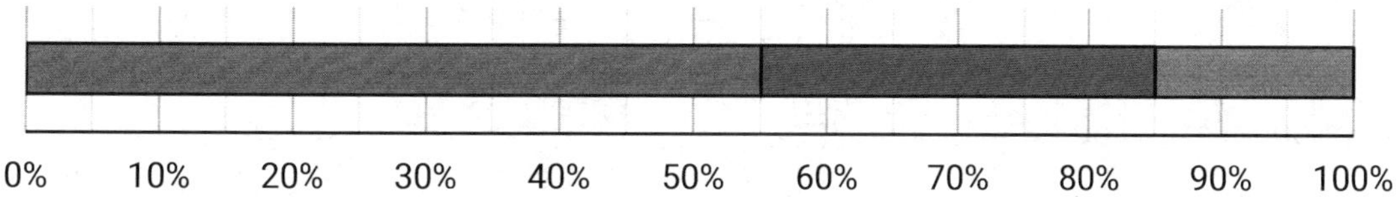


d.

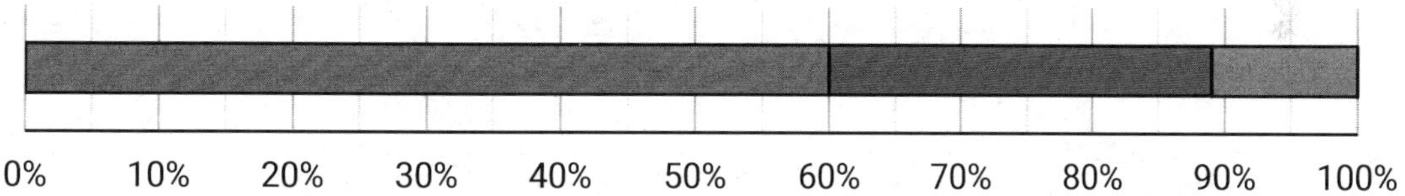


In this problem, we are given a frequency table that shows the number of votes each mascot received and we need to choose the percent bar graph that best represents the data.

To approach this problem, we need to first identify the percentage of the votes each mascot received. To find the percentage, we need to divide the number of votes for each mascot by the total number of votes.

We can find the total number of votes by adding the number of votes for each mascot.

$$58 + 120 + 22 = 200$$

The total number of votes cast was 200.

Now, we can find the percentages for each mascot.

The lion mascot got 58 votes, or $\frac{58}{200}$ of the votes. We can convert this to a percentage by using division or equivalent fractions.

Using division:

$$\begin{array}{r} 0.29 \\ 200\overline{)58.00} \\ \underline{40\,0} \\ 18\,00 \end{array}$$

$$0.29 \times 100 = 29\%$$

Using equivalent fractions:

$$\frac{58}{200} \div \frac{2}{2} = \frac{29}{100} = 29\%$$

Lion got 29% of the votes.

The tiger mascot got 120 votes, or $\frac{120}{200}$ of the votes. We can find the percentage by using division or equivalent fractions. Using equivalent fractions is a little faster because it is simple to convert fractions out of 200 to fractions out of 100.

$$\frac{120}{200} \div \frac{2}{2} = \frac{60}{100} = 60\%$$

Tiger got 60% of the votes.

The bear mascot got 22 votes, or $\frac{22}{200}$ of the votes.

$$\frac{22}{200} \div \frac{2}{2} = \frac{11}{100} = 11\%$$

Bear got 11% of the votes.

Now that we know the percentage of the total votes each mascot received, we can compare these values to our choices.

Choice A matches the percentages we found and matches the given key for the data.

# Practice Test #1

**1. A company is hosting a banquet for 200 guests that will be seated at four person tables, $x$, and six person tables, $y$. If there are 45 tables in all, how many of each type of table will there be?**

a. $x = 20, y = 25$
b. $x = 35, y = 10$
c. $x = 25, y = 20$
d. $x = 10, y = 35$

**2. Part A: Draw a dot on the number line that corresponds to $\sqrt{8}$.**

**Part B: What category does $\sqrt{8}$ fit best under?**

a. Integer
b. Repeating Decimal
c. Terminating Decimal
d. Irrational Number

**3. If a cube has a volume of 27 cubic inches, what is the length of one edge of the cube?**

a. $x = -9$
b. $x = 9$
c. $x = -3$
d. $x = 3$

**4. Solve the equation:**

$$\frac{6x + 2}{3} = 2x + 1$$

a. $\frac{1}{4}$
b. 4
c. Infinitely many solutions
d. No solution

**5. The graph below represents the number of pages Jim can read for a certain time in minutes. Find the slope of the graph and interpret what it means in the context of Jim reading his book.**

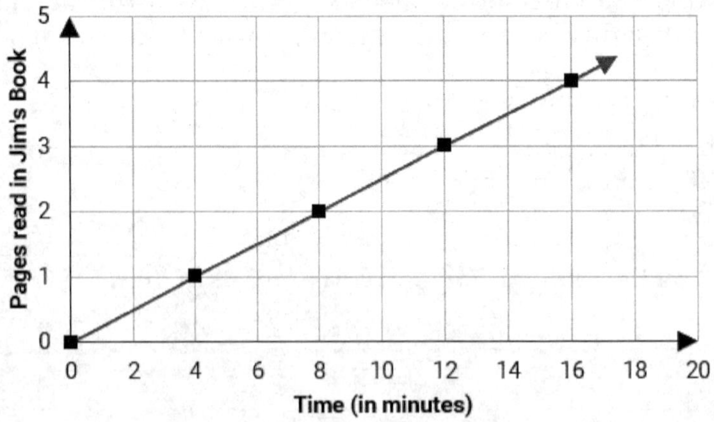


a. 0.25 pages per minute
b. 0.25 pages total
c. 4 pages per minute
d. 4 pages total

**6. Solve for $x$:**

$$x^3 = 64$$

a. 4
b. 8
c. 21
d. 192

**7. A photo album has 50 pages in it. Some pages hold 9 photos, $x$, while other pages hold 12 photos, $y$. When it is full, the album holds 540 photos. How many pages hold 9 photos and how many hold 12 photos in the album?**

a. $x = 24, y = 26$
b. $x = 30, y = 20$
c. $x = 20, y = 30$
d. $x = 26, y = 24$

**8. Which of the following equations have infinitely many solutions?**

a. $3(2x - 5) = 6x - 15$
b. $4x - 8 = 12$
c. $5 = 10x - 15$
d. $7x = 2x + 35$

**9. Solve the equation for $x$.**

$$3(x-1) = 2(3x-9)$$

a. $x = 2$
b. $x = \frac{8}{3}$
c. $x = -5$
d. $x = 5$

**10. Solve the equation:**

$$-\frac{5}{2}(2x-4) = \frac{1}{7}(49x+70)$$

a. $x = 5$
b. $x = 0$
c. $x = 25$
d. $x = -10$

**11. In 2023, The National Park Service reported $3.2 \times 10^7$ people visited Joshua Tree National Park and $4 \times 10^4$ people visited North Cascades National Park. How many times as many visitors were there to Joshua Tree National Park as there were to North Cascades National Park?**

a. 800
b. 8,000
c. 80
d. 8

**12. Which point represents the solution to the system of linear equations graphed below?**

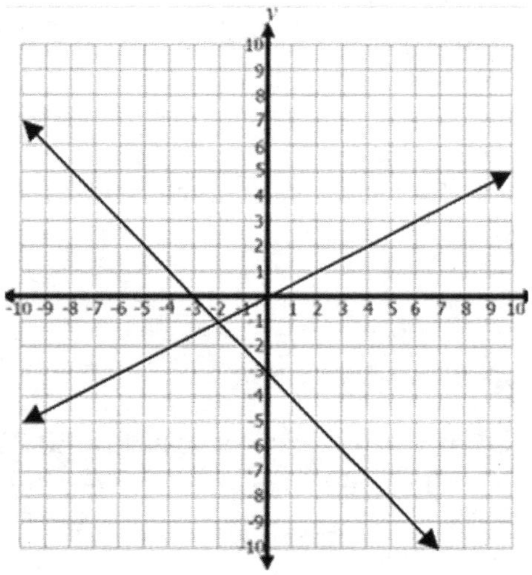

a. $(0, 0)$
b. $(0, -3)$
c. $(-2, -1)$
d. $(-3, 0)$

**13. Solve the system of linear equations.** $\begin{cases} 3x - 2y = -10 \\ y = 2x + 5 \end{cases}$

a. $(0, 5)$
b. $(-2, 1)$
c. $(1, 2)$
d. $(-3, -4)$

**14. Solve the system of linear equations.** $\begin{cases} 5x - y = -41 \\ 3x + y = -15 \end{cases}$

a. $(1, -18)$
b. $(-6, 3)$
c. $(-8, 1)$
d. $(-7, 6)$

**15. An average honeybee egg weighs 0.000006 ounces. Express the average weight of a honeybee egg in scientific notation.**

a. $6 \times 10^{-5}$
b. $6 \times 10^{6}$
c. $6 \times 10^{-6}$
d. $6 \times 10^{5}$

**16. The area of a patio is given by the expression $\left(\frac{5}{2}\right)^4$ square feet. Simplify the area to an integer or fraction.**

a. $\frac{20}{8}$ ft$^2$
b. $\frac{625}{16}$ ft$^2$
c. $\frac{625}{8}$ ft$^2$
d. $\frac{20}{16}$ ft$^2$

**17. Find the quotient and express the result in scientific notation: $\frac{38{,}000{,}000{,}000}{5 \times 10^{-2}}$.**

a. $7.6 \times 10^{11}$
b. $7.6 \times 10^{7}$
c. $7.6 \times 10^{10}$
d. $7.6 \times 10^{8}$

**18. At a grocery store, 5 granola bars and 3 apples cost \$10.80. With the same prices, 1 granola bars and 3 apples cost \$4.80. Find the cost of one granola bar, $g$, and one apple, $a$.**

a. $g = \$1.10, a = \$1.50$
b. $g = \$0.90, a = \$1.44$
c. $g = \$1.44, a = \$0.90$
d. $g = \$1.50, a = \$1.10$

**19. Which function has the greater rate of change?**

**Function 1**

| $x$ | $y$ |
|---|---|
| 2 | 4 |
| 3 | 6 |
| 4 | 8 |

**Function 2**

$y = 5x - 1$

a. Function I
b. Function II
c. They have the same rate of change.
d. Cannot be determined

**20. Part A: Using the triangle below, which equation would be used to solve for the missing side?**

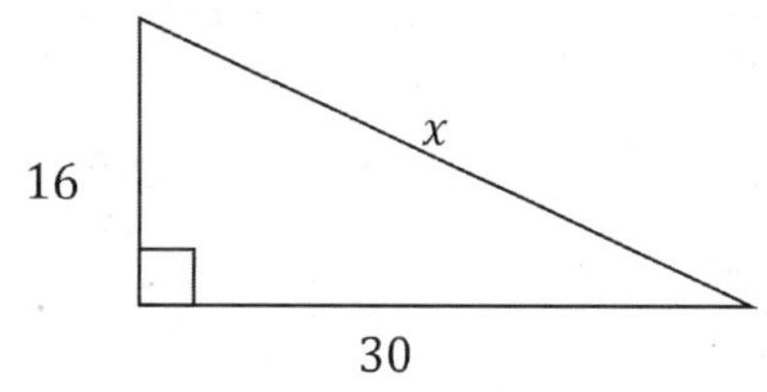


a. $x = \sqrt{16^2 + 30^2}$
b. $x = \sqrt{30^2 - 16^2}$
c. $16 = \sqrt{30^2 - x^2}$
d. $16 = \sqrt{30^2 + x^2}$

**Part B: Solve for the missing length of the triangle above.**

a. 25.4
b. 15
c. 34
d. 46

**21. Which linear function represents the values in the table?**

| $x$ | 0 | 1 | 2 | 3 |
|---|---|---|---|---|
| $y$ | 3 | 1 | −1 | −3 |

a. $y = -2x + 1$
b. $y = 2x + 3$
c. $y = 3x + 1$
d. $y = -2x + 3$

**22. Look at the graph below. Which equation represents a function with a greater slope?**

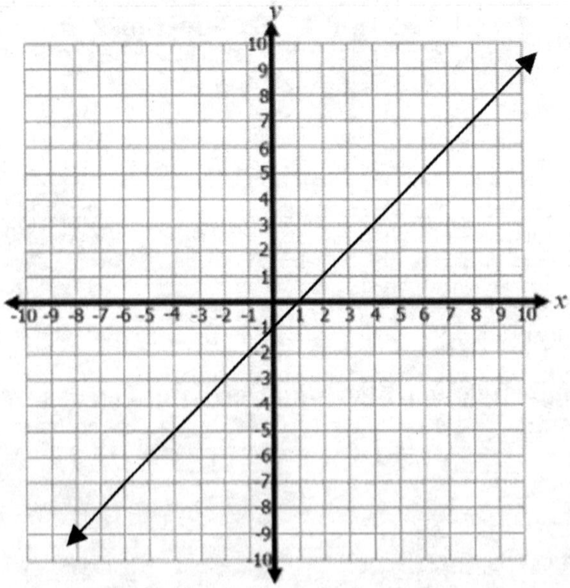


a. $y = x - 2$
b. $y = 2x - 2$
c. $y = \frac{1}{2}x - 1$
d. $y = x - 4$

**23. Simplify the numerical exponential expression to an integer or fraction:**

$$\frac{3^2}{3^{-3}}$$

a. $-\frac{2}{3}$
b. 162
c. 243
d. $-\frac{1}{3}$

**24. Which preimage and image represent a reflection?**

a. 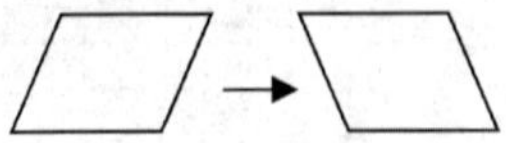

b. 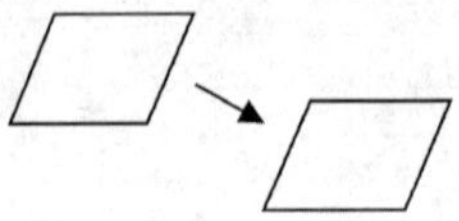

c. 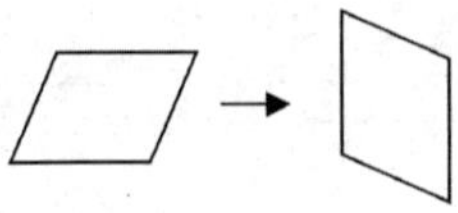

d. 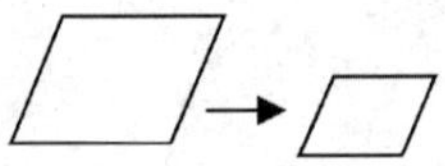

**25. Given the image below, what transformation did it undergo?**

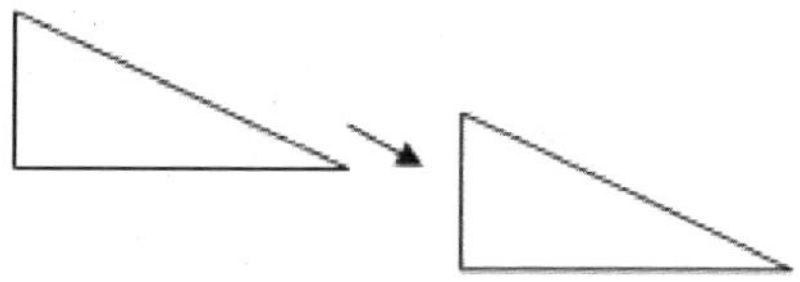

a. Translation
b. Dilation
c. Reflection
d. Rotation

**26. Between which two numbers does $-\sqrt{42}$ fall between on a number line?**

a. 6 and 7
b. $-8$ and $-7$
c. 7 and 8
d. $-7$ and $-6$

**27. If $\Delta ABC$ is reflected across the $x$-axis what ordered pair would point $C$ map onto?**

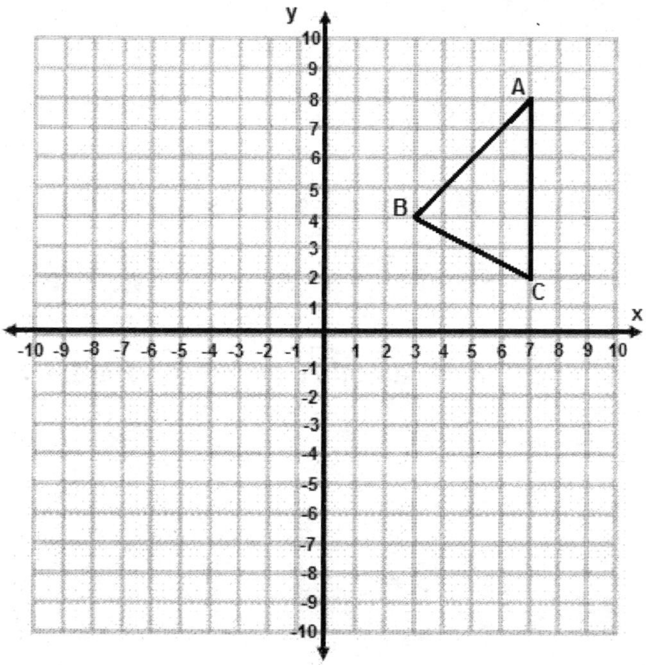


a. $(-7, 2)$
b. $(2, 7)$
c. $(7, -2)$
d. $(-2, 7)$

**28. What two transformations will map figure *A* onto figure *B*?**

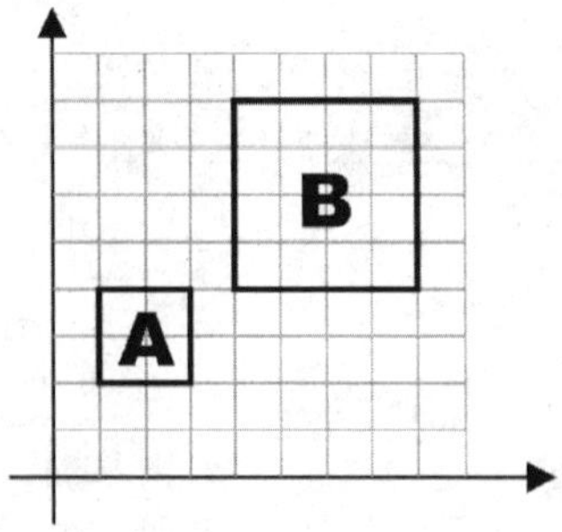


a. Rotation and Translation
b. Translation and Reflection
c. Translation and Dilation
d. Reflection and Rotation

**29. What category does $-\frac{13}{11}$ fit best under?**

a. Whole Number
b. Integer
c. Rational Number
d. Irrational Number

**30. Which of the following equations is <u>not</u> a function?**

a. $x = 2y^2 + 4y - 1$
b. $y = \frac{1}{4}x + 2$
c. $f(x) = x^2 + 2x - 3$
d. $g(x) = x - 5$

**31. How many cubic feet of grain will fill the silo if the silo is completely full?**

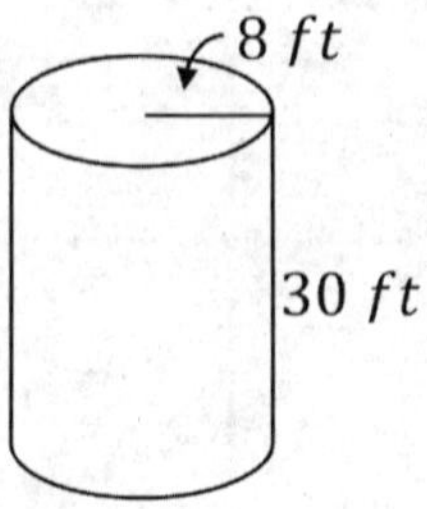


a. 753.6 $ft^3$
b. 6028.8 $ft^3$
c. 1920 $ft^3$
d. 22608 $ft^3$

**32. What kind of association does the scatter plot show?**

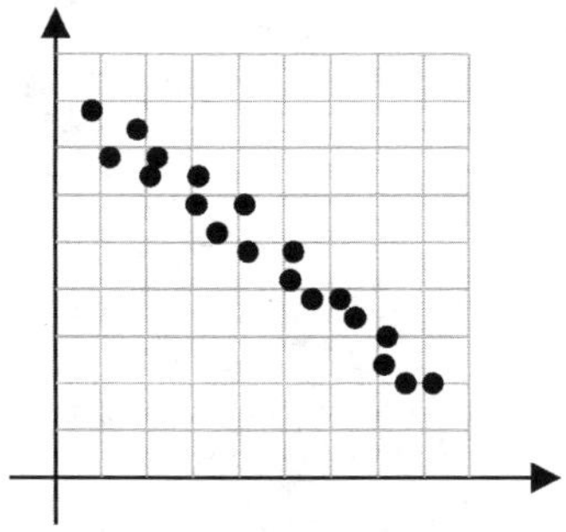

a. Positive, Linear Association
b. Negative, Linear Association
c. Non-linear Association
d. No association can be determined

**33. Part A: What category does $-\sqrt{7}$ fit best under?**

a. Integer
b. Repeating Decimal
c. Terminating Decimal
d. Irrational Number

**Part B: What is the best approximation for $-\sqrt{7}$ when rounded to the nearest hundredth?**

a. $-1.78$
b. $-3.23$
c. $-2.65$
d. $-4.59$

**34. Which graph represents a function that is nonlinear and decreasing?**

a.

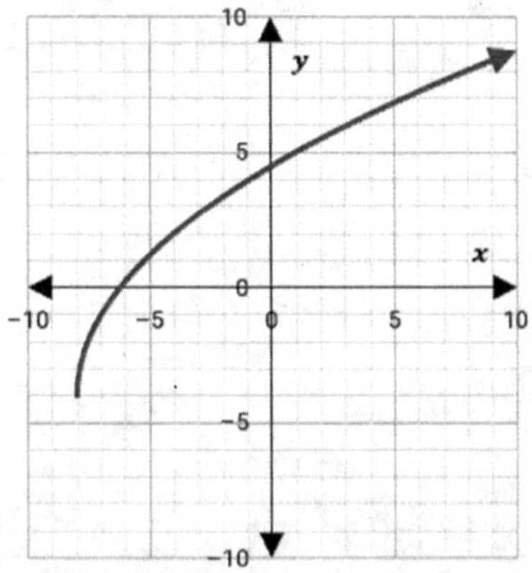


b.

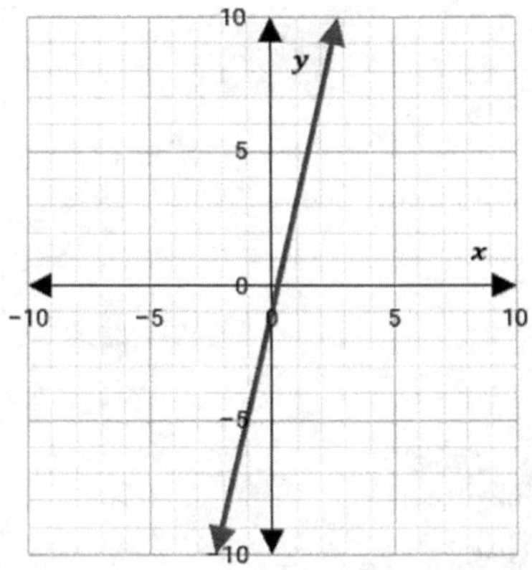


c.

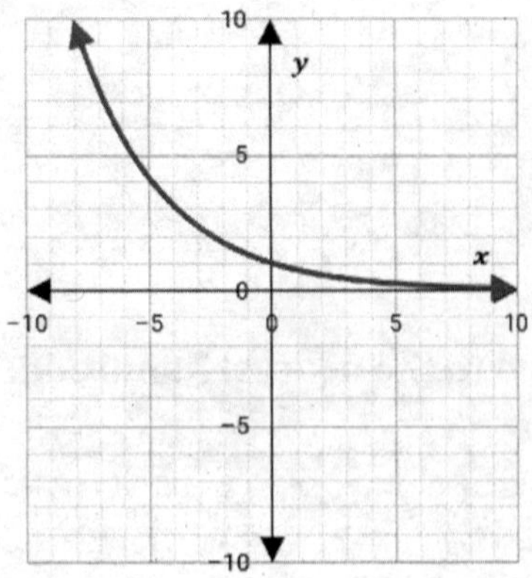


d.

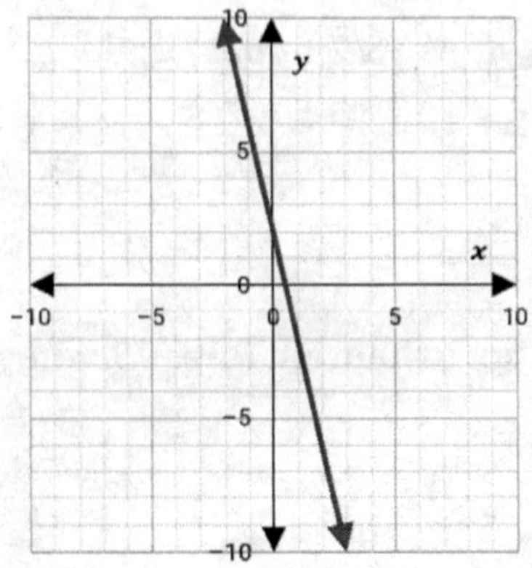


**35. Which of the following tables is <u>not</u> a function? Select all that apply.**

a.

| Input | Output |
|---|---|
| 0 | 5 |
| 4 | 1 |
| 0 | -2 |
| 1 | -7 |

b.

| x | y |
|---|---|
| 8 | 12 |
| 14 | 24 |
| 20 | 36 |
| 26 | 48 |

c.

| x | y |
|---|---|
| 1 | −4 |
| 2 | −2 |
| 3 | 0 |
| 2 | 2 |

d.

| Input | Output |
|---|---|
| −10 | 3 |
| −6 | 4 |
| −2 | 5 |
| 2 | 6 |

**36. The length of the hypotenuse of a triangle was calculated to be $\sqrt{25}$. Classify the length.**

a. Rational Number
b. Integer
c. Irrational Number
d. Whole Number

**37. A sphere and a cylinder have the same volume. Each figure has a radius of 4 inches. What is the height of the cylinder?**

a. $5\frac{1}{2}$
b. $5\frac{1}{3}$
c. $3\frac{1}{5}$
d. $3\frac{1}{2}$

**38. This set of ordered pairs represents a relation that is not a function:**

$$\{(-3,1),(8,1),(9,0),(-3,5),(-2,1),(4,-6)\}$$

**Which ordered pair, if it were removed from the set, would make the relation a function?**

a. (8,1)
b. (−3,5)
c. (9,0)
d. (4,−6)

**39. Which of the following equations does NOT define a linear function?**

a. $3x - 2y = 6$
b. $y = \frac{3}{x}$
c. $y = 3$
d. $x = 2(y - 1)$

**40. Polygon ABCD is reflected over the line $y = 2$ to form A'B'C'D'. If the distance between AB and the line of reflection is five units, what is the distance between the A'B' and the line of reflection?**

a. 2 units
b. 7 units
c. 5 units
d. 3 units

**41. Parallel lines cut by a transversal form consecutive interior angles with measures $3x + 10$ and $7x - 30$. Find the value of x.**

a. $x = 10$
b. $x = 20$
c. $x = 35$
d. $x = 55$

**42. Describe the transformation sequence that mapped preimage ABC to intermediate image A'B'C' to image A"B"C" in the figure below.**

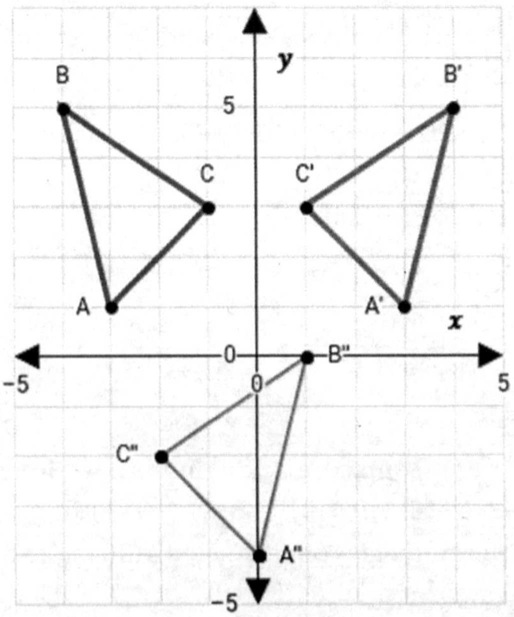


a. Reflection over the *y*-axis, translation down 5 units, translation left 3 units
b. Rotation around the origin, translation up 1 unit, translation right 1 unit
c. Reflection over the *x*-axis, translation up 5 units, translation right 3 units
d. Rotation around the origin, translation down 1 unit, translation left 1 unit

**43. Find the distance, in units, between points D and E on the coordinate plane. Round to the nearest tenth if necessary.**

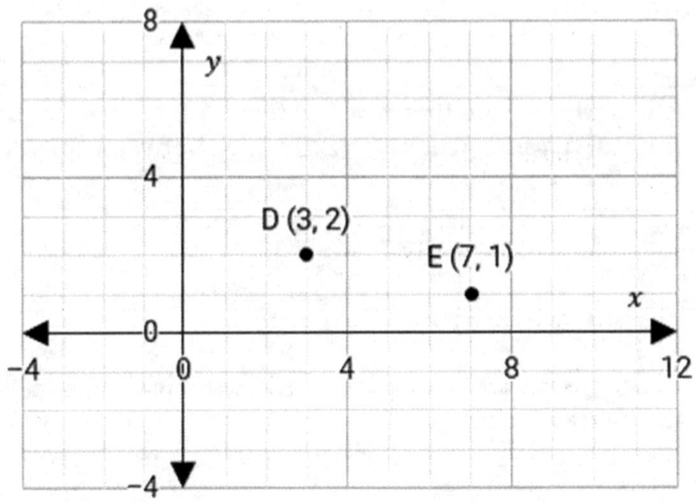


a. 4.0 units
b. 3.9 units
c. 4.1 units
d. 4.2 units

**44. In the image below, triangle ABC is rotated about point S to create triangle A'B'C'. What is the measure of $\angle A'$?**

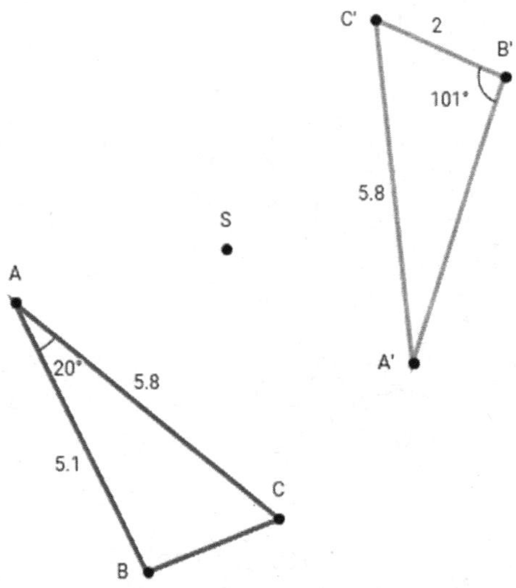


a. 101°
b. 121°
c. 59°
d. 20°

**45. Avery purchases a new bag of dog food once a month for her golden retriever. The graph below represents the linear relationship between the number of days after opening the bag of dog food and the number of cups remaining in the bag.**

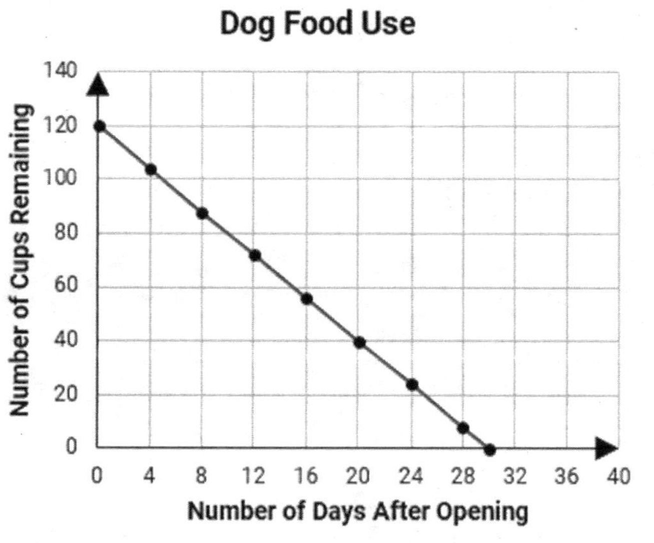


**What equation represents this linear function?**

a. $y = -4x + 120$
b. $y = 4x + 120$
c. $y = -5x + 30$
d. $y = -30x + 120$

**46. What is the measure of the exterior angle below?**

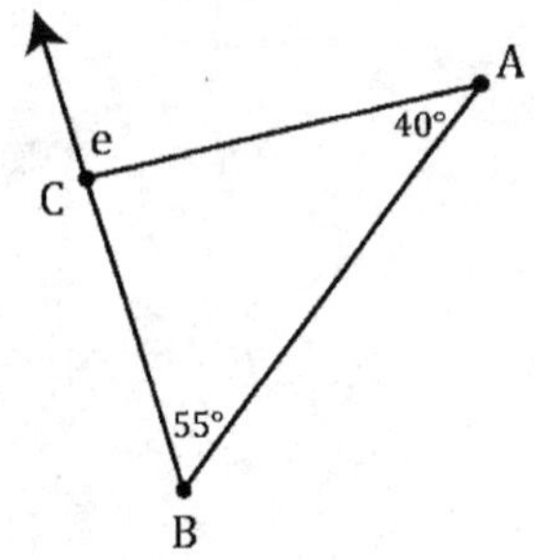


a. 85°
b. 95°
c. 90°
d. 125°

**47. A school leader was interested in analyzing the relationship between the number of hours spent studying for a math test and the student scores on the test. She plotted the data on a scatterplot and found the line of best fit to be $y = 8.75x + 65$. Based on this model, what is the expected score for a student who studies for 4 hours?**

a. 73.75
b. 82.5
c. 91.25
d. 100

**48. If a triangle has side lengths of 11, 12, and 16 units, is it a right triangle? How do you know?**

a. Yes, using the converse of the Pythagorean theorem.
b. Yes, using SSS.
c. No, using the converse of the Pythagorean theorem.
d. No, using SSS.

**49. An ecologist studied the relationship between the amount of rainfall in inches and the growth of a certain type of grass (type A) in inches per month. Her data can be modeled by the equation $y = 0.3x + 2$, where $y$ is the growth of the grass and $x$ is the amount of rainfall in the given month. If the grass grew 5.6 inches in a month, what would the predicted amount of rainfall be?**

a. 12 inches
b. 3.3 inches
c. 10 inches
d. 8 inches

**50. Which statement correctly describes the graph of the function below on a given interval?**

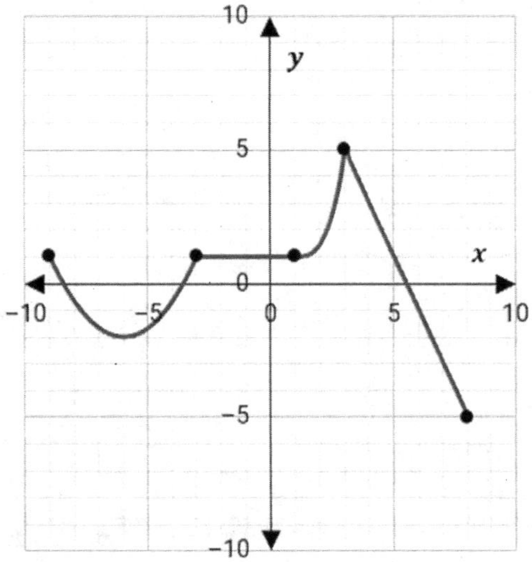


a. From $x = -10$ to $x = -3$ the function is nonlinear and increasing.
b. From $x = -3$ to $x = 1$ the function is linear and increasing.
c. From $x = 1$ to $x = 3$ the function is nonlinear and decreasing.
d. From $x = 3$ to $x = 8$ the function is linear and decreasing.

**51. A scatterplot of bivariate data is shown below. Which of the following answer choices best shows a graph with the line of best fit?**

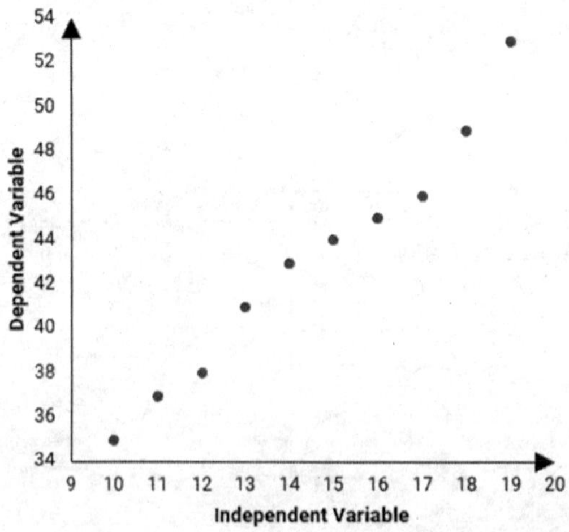


a.

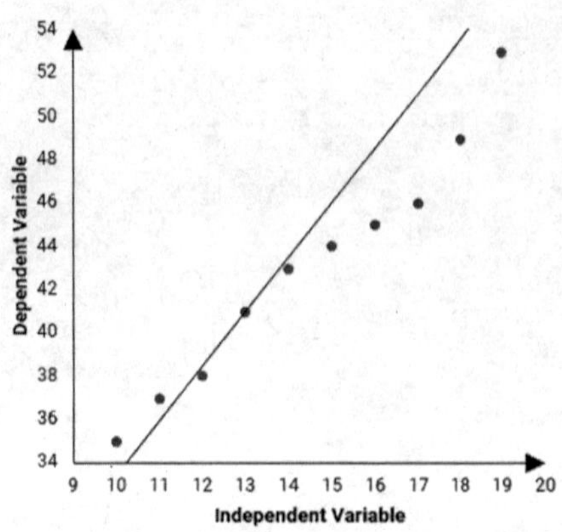


b.

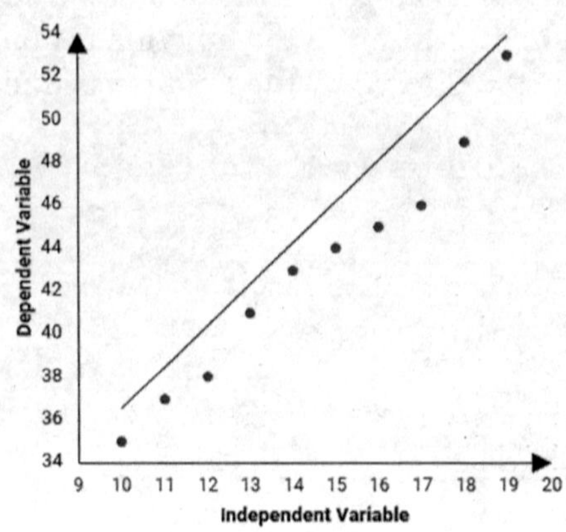


c.

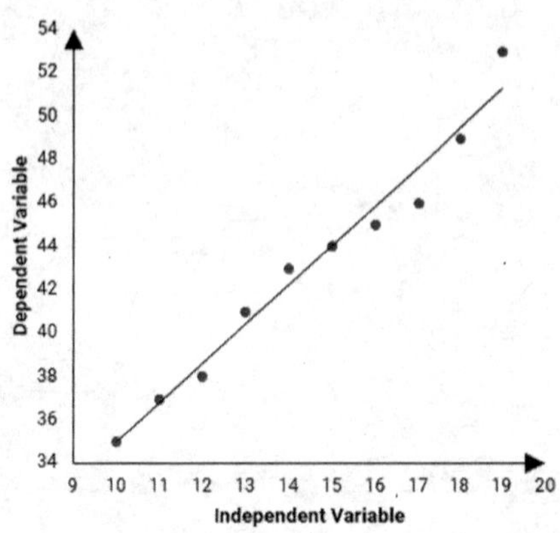


d.

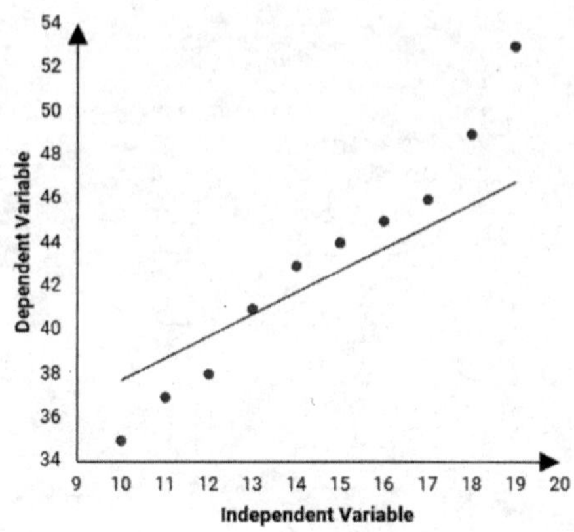

52. **A movie streaming site has a monthly base price of \$16 plus \$7 for each additional household added beyond the primary account holder. Write a linear function to model the monthly cost, *y*, for a plan on this streaming site with *x* additional households added.**

a. $y = 16x + 7$
b. $x = 7y + 16$
c. $y = 7x + 16$
d. $x = 16y + 7$

53. **If quadrilateral FGHI, with coordinate H plotted at $(4, -2)$ is reflected over the *x*-axis and translated three units right describe the resulting figure.**

a. F'G'H'I' is a similar quadrilateral to FGHI, and H' is plotted at (7,2)
b. F'G'H'I' is a similar quadrilateral to FGHI, and H' is plotted at $(-1, -2)$
c. F'G'H'I' is a congruent quadrilateral to FGHI, and H' is plotted at (7,2)
d. F'G'H'I' is a congruent quadrilateral to FGHI, and H' is plotted at $(-1, -2)$

54. **Triangle EFG has angle measures $m\angle F = 45°, m\angle G = 90°$. What is the measure of angle E?**

a. 45°
b. 135°
c. 90°
d. 100°

55. **Is the function represented by the graph below increasing, decreasing, or constant?**

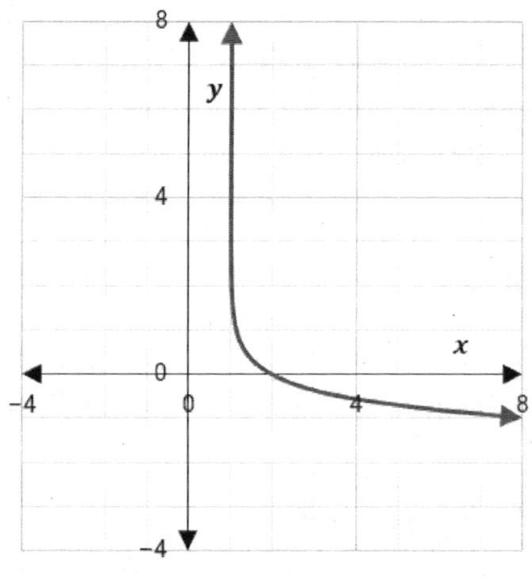


a. Increasing
b. Decreasing
c. Constant
d. Cannot be determined

# Answers and Explanations for Test #1

**1. B:** Let $x$ represent the number of four-person tables and $y$ represent the number of six-person tables. The two totals given are 200 guests and 45 tables. In the equation equaling 200, each variable must be multiplied by the number of guests at each table to give the number of guests because the variables represent number of tables not number of guests. The first equation is $4x + 6y = 200$. The sum of the variables is the total amount of tables, so the second equation is $x + y = 45$. To solve by eliminating $x$, multiply the second equation by $-4$.

**2. Part A:** The square root of 8 is approximately 2.83. The dot should be placed like so:

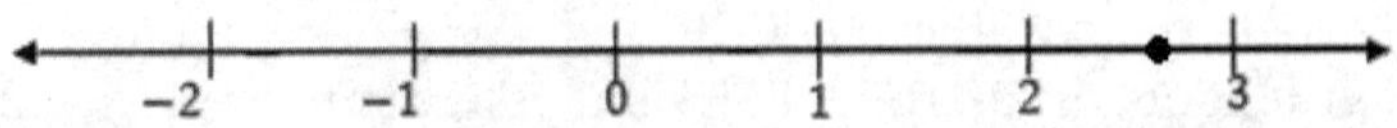


**Part B: D:** The square root of 8 does not simplify to an integer, so it cannot be expressed as a rational number in the form of a terminating or repeating decimal. All radicals that do not simplify to an integer are irrational.

**3. D:** The volume of a cube is found by cubing the length of one edge of the cube. So given a volume and asked to find the length of the edge of a cube simply take the cube root of the volume.

$$x^3 = 27$$

$$\sqrt[3]{x^3} = \sqrt[3]{27}$$

$$x = 3$$

**4. D:** Multiply by 3 on both sides to eliminate the division on the left side. After multiplying, the equation is a false statement because $6x + 2$ cannot equal $6x + 3$. When solving for the variable results in a false statement, there is no solution. If you continue solving, the same conclusion will be reached because the variable terms cancel out, and the equation becomes $2 = 3$, another false statement.

$$3\left(\frac{6x+2}{3}\right) = (2x+1)3$$

$$\begin{array}{ccc} 6x+2 & = & 6x+3 \\ -6x & & -6x \end{array}$$

$$2 = 3$$

**5. A:** The graph shows a proportional relationship because it passes through the origin. The slope of the graph of a proportional relationship is the same as the unit rate. The unit rate can be found using a point on the graph such as (4,1) and dividing the $y$ value by the $x$ value. Dividing 1 by 4 results in 0.25; therefore, the slope is 0.25. The $y$-values are the number of pages and $x$-values are the number of minutes. The slope gives the pages per minute Jim reads.

**6. A:** Use the cube root to undo the power of 3 on the variable. 64 is a perfect cube. $64 = 4^3$, so $\sqrt[3]{64}$ simplifies to 4.

$$x^3 = 64$$
$$\sqrt[3]{x} = \sqrt[3]{64}$$
$$x = 4$$

**7. C:** Let $x$ represent the number of pages holding 9 photos and $y$ represent the number of pages holding 12 photos. The two totals given are 50 pages and 540 photos. With the variables representing the number of pages, the sum of the variables equals the total number of pages. The first equation is $x + y = 50$. For the total photos, the variables are multiplied by the number of photos each page holds so that each side of the equation gives the total photos. The second equation is $9x + 12y = 540$. To solve using substitution, solve for $x$ in the first equation which results in $x = 50 - y$.

$$9(50 - y) + 12y = 540$$
$$450 - 9y + 12y = 540$$
$$\begin{matrix} 450 + 3y \\ -450 \end{matrix} = \begin{matrix} 540 \\ -450 \end{matrix}$$
$$\frac{3y}{3} = \frac{90}{3}$$
$$y = 30$$

To find $x$, plug in 30 for $y$ into $x = 50 - y$. $x = 50 - 30 = 20$

**8. A:** A is the only one that has infinitely many solutions because when the 3 is distributed across the parentheses, the resulting equation is $6x - 15 = 6x - 15$. Because each side of the equation is identical to the other side, any value of $x$ will make a true statement, so there are infinitely many solutions.

**9. D:**

$3(x - 1) = 2(3x - 9)$

| | |
|---|---|
| $3x - 3 = 6x - 18$ | Distribute |
| $-3 = 3x - 18$ | Subtract $3x$ from both sides |
| $15 = 3x$ | Add 18 to both sides |
| $5 = x$ | Divide both sides by 3 |

**10. B:** While the equation does have fractions that can be cleared by multiplying by the LCD, it is not necessary. There will no longer be fractions if the distributive property is applied first.

$$-\frac{5}{2}(2x-4)=\frac{1}{7}(49x+70)$$
$$\begin{aligned} -5x+10 &= 7x+10 \\ -7x \quad & \quad -7x \\ -12x+10 &= 10 \\ -10 \quad & \quad -10 \\ \frac{-12x}{-12} &= \frac{0}{-12} \\ x &= 0 \end{aligned}$$

**11. A:** To determine how many times as many Joshua Tree's visitors there were as compared to North Cascade's visitors, compare each part of the number in scientific notation. The smaller park's non-exponential number is 4 compared to the larger park's value of 3.2. 4 times 0.8 is 3.2. The smaller park has a power of 3 on the base of 10 whereas the larger park has a power of 7. The powers differ by three powers of 10 which is the same as 1000 ($10^3 = 1000$). Combining these differences, 0.8 times 1000 results in the number of visitors to Joshua Tree being 800 times as many as North Cascade's number of visitors.

**12. C:** Given the graph of a system of linear equations, the solution is the point of intersection of the two lines. In this graph, the two lines intersect at $(-2,-1)$.

**13. A:** $3x-2(2x+5)=-10$ Substitute the expression for y into the other equation

| | |
|---|---|
| $3x-4x-10=-$ | Distribute the $-2$ across the parentheses |
| $-x-10=-10$ | Combine like terms |
| $-x=0$ | Add 10 to both sides |
| $x=0$ | Divide by $-1$ |
| $y=20+5=5$ | Substitute the value of $x$ into the original equation and simplify. |
| 0,5 | Write your final answer as an ordered pair $(x,y)$ |

**14. D:**

| | |
|---|---|
| $5x-y=-413x+y=-15$ | Add the two equations together to get this equation |
| $8x=-56$ | Divide both sides by 8 |
| $x=-7$ | Substitute the value of $x$ into one of the original |
| $3-7+y=-15$ | equations |
| $-21+y=-15$ | Multiply |
| $y=6$ | Add 21 to both sides |
| $-7, 6$ | Write your final answer as an ordered pair $(x,y)$ |

**15. C:** To find the scientific notation form of the egg's weight, the decimal moves to the right 6 times before having the single digit of 6 in front of it. The zero digits before 6 are dropped and accounted for in the power of 10. 10 is raised to the power of $-6$ showing the decimal moved 6 places to the right.

$$0.000006 = 0.\underbrace{0}\underbrace{0}\underbrace{0}\underbrace{0}\underbrace{0}\underbrace{6}. = 6 \times 10^{-6}$$

**16. B:** Because the bases are different, the terms cannot be combined using the properties of exponents. The value for each is calculated separately.

$$\left(\frac{5}{2}\right)^4 = \frac{5^4}{2^4} = \frac{625}{16}$$

**17. A:** Before dividing, re-write 38,000,000,000 as $3.8 \times 10^{10}$. To find the quotient, divide the non-exponential terms and the exponential terms separately. When dividing the exponential terms, subtract the exponents.

$$\frac{3.8 \times 10^{10}}{5 \times 10^{-2}} = \left(\frac{3.8}{5}\right) \times \left(\frac{10^{10}}{10^{-2}}\right) = 0.76 \times 10^{12}$$

The result is not in scientific notation because there is not a non-zero digit in front of the decimal. Re-write 0.76 as $7.6 \times 10^{-1}$. Two powers of 10 now exist in the result and can be combined by adding exponents.

$$0.76 \times 10^{12} = (7.6 \times 10^{-1}) \times 10^{12} = 7.6 \times (10^{-1} \times 10^{12}) = 7.6 \times 10^{11}$$

**18. D:** Let $g$ represent the cost of one granola bar and $a$ represent the cost of one apple. The two totals given are \$10.80 and \$4.80. In each equation, the variables need to be multiplied by the number of each item accounted for in the total cost because the variable represents the cost of only one item. The first equation is $5g + 3a = 10.80$ and the second equation is $g + 3a = 4.80$. The coefficients on $y$ are the same in each equation. By multiplying the first equation by $-1$, $a$ will be eliminated when the equations are added together.

$$\begin{cases} 5g + 3a = 10.80 \\ -g - 3a = -4.80 \end{cases}$$
$$\frac{4g}{4} = \frac{6}{4}$$
$$g = 1.50$$

To find $a$, plug in 1.5 for $g$ into either equation.

$$5(1.5) + 3a = 10.8$$
$$\frac{7.5 + 3a}{-7.5} = \frac{10.8}{-7.5}$$
$$\frac{3a}{3} = \frac{3.3}{3}$$
$$a = 1.10$$

**19. B:** The rate of change is also the slope of the linear function, that is, the vertical change over horizontal change. The rate of change for Function I is 2, because the y-value increases 2 for every 1 the input increases. The rate of change for Function II is 5. Function II is written in slope-intercept form and the number that corresponds to the slope is 5. Since 5 is greater than 2, Function II has the greater rate of change.

**20. Part A: A:** The Pythagorean Theorem, $a^2 + b^2 = c^2$, states that the sum of the squares of the legs equals the square of the hypotenuse. Therefore, the hypotenuse is equal to the square root of the sum of the squares of the legs. The legs of the triangle are 16 and 30. The hypotenuse is $x$. The equation solved for the value of the hypotenuse will be $x = \sqrt{16^2 + 30^2}$.

**Part B: C:** Simplify the following equation to find the missing side of the triangle.

$$x = \sqrt{16^2 + 30^2}$$
$$x = \sqrt{256 + 900}$$
$$x = \sqrt{1156}$$
$$x = 34$$

**21. D:** Based on the table, the rate of change is -2 and the y-intercept is $(0, 3)$. Plugging this information into the slope-intercept form $y = mx + b$, the equation is $y = -2x + 3$.

**22. B:** The y-intercept of the line is $(0, -1)$. Another point on the line is $(1,0)$. Slope is the vertical change over horizontal change which is $\frac{1}{1} = 1$. The answer choices are already given in slope-intercept form, so you just have to pick the one with a greater slope than 1. The only one that has a greater slope is $2x - 2$.

**23. C:** Use the quotient of powers rule to divide. To divide exponents with the same base, subtract the exponents.

$$\frac{3^2}{3^{-3}} = 3^{2-(-3)} = 3^{2+3} = 3^5 = 243$$

**24. A:** Answer A is the only one that represents a reflection or "flip." Answer B represents a translation or "slide." Answer C represents a rotation or turn. Answer D represents a dilation or changing size.

**25. A:** Answer A is the only one that represents a translation or "slide." Answer B represents a reflection or "flip." Answer C is a dilation. Answer D is a rotation or "turn."

**26. D:** $-\sqrt{42}$ is an irrational number and must be estimated using the perfect squares it is closest to on the number line. 42 lies between the perfect squares of 36 and 49 whose square roots are 6 and 7. Based on this, $-7 < -\sqrt{42} < -6$.

**27. C:** Point $C$ starts at the ordered pair $(7, 2)$. If it is reflected across the x-axis it would end up at the ordered pair (7-2).

**28. C:** Since the size of B is different from the size of A, a dilation must occur. The only option that has a dilation is C.

**29. C:** $-\frac{13}{11}$ is given as a quotient in fraction form, so it is a rational number. A rational number can also be expressed as a terminating or repeating decimal. Long division converts a fraction to a decimal and must be carried out to determine whether it is a terminating or repeating decimal.

Ignore the negative sign to divide. The numerator of 13 is the dividend and the denominator of 11 is the divisor. After dividing, the digits 1 and 8 repeat indefinitely, so $-\frac{13}{11}$ is the repeating decimal $-1.\overline{18}$. Terminating or repeating decimals fall under the category of rational numbers.

$$\begin{array}{r} 1.1818 \\ 11\overline{)13.0000} \\ -\underline{11}\phantom{.0000} \\ 20\phantom{000} \\ -\underline{11}\phantom{000} \\ 90\phantom{00} \\ -\underline{88}\phantom{00} \\ 20\phantom{0} \\ -\underline{11}\phantom{0} \\ 90 \\ -\underline{88} \\ 2 \end{array}$$

**30. A:** A function cannot map a single input to more than one output. In the equation $x = 2y^2 + 4y - 1$, the $x$-value can be paired with both a positive and negative $y$-value. Therefore, it cannot be a function.

**31. B:** The formula for the volume of a cylinder is $V = \pi r^2 h$. All values are placed into the formula and simplified. The work is shown below:

$$V = (3.14)(8\,ft)^2(30\,ft)$$

$$V = (3.14)(64\,ft^2)(30\,ft)$$

$$V = 6028.8\,ft^3$$

**32. B:** A single straight line can be drawn that is close to many of the points. The slope of that line would be negative, so the points have a negative, linear association.

**33. Part A: D:** The square root of 7 does not simplify to an integer, so it cannot be expressed as a rational number in the form of a terminating or repeating decimal. All radicals that do not simplify to an integer are irrational.

**Part B:** Since this is an irrational number, the decimal sequence will never terminate or repeat. It must be estimated using the perfect squares it is closest to on the number line. 7 lies between the perfect squares of 4 and 9 whose square roots are 2 and 3. Based on this, $-3 < -\sqrt{7} < -2$. Since 7 is closer to 9 than it is to 4, it can also be determined, that the square root has to be closer to $-3$ than $-2$.

**34. C:** The graph of a function that is nonlinear is not a straight line. The graph of a function that is decreasing falls from left to right. Answer choice C is the only graph that is not a straight line and is falling. Answer choice A is nonlinear but increasing. Answer choice B is linear and increasing. Answer choice D is decreasing but linear.

**35. A, C:** A function cannot map a single input to more than one output. Therefore, there can only be one $y$-value for each $x$-value.

**36. A:** The square root of 25 simplifies to 5, an integer. All integers are rational numbers because they can be expressed as a quotient of two integers. Also, the decimal expansion of an integer is terminating. It is important to be aware that radicals do not automatically make a number irrational.

$$\sqrt{25} = 5 = \frac{5}{1}$$

**37. B:** The volume of a sphere is, $V = \frac{4}{3}\pi r^3$, and the volume of a cylinder is, $V = \pi r^2 h$. Since we know the radius we can solve for the volume of the sphere and we get $V = \frac{4}{3}\pi(4)^3 = 268.08257$cubic inches. Then, begin to solve for the volume of the cylinder $V = \pi(4)^2 h = 268.08257$. So, $50.26548h = 268.08257$, and $h = 5\frac{1}{3}$.

**38. B:** The relation given is not a function because the input $-3$ is paired with two different outputs: 1 and 5. If either $(-3,1)$ or $(-3,5)$ is removed from the set, the relation would be a function because every input would have exactly one output. Of those two points, $(-3,5)$ is answer choice B. The ordered pairs $(8,1)$ and $(-2,1)$ have the same output value, but it is possible for a function to have two different inputs with the same output.

**39. B:** To identify an equation of a linear function not written in slope-intercept form, the exponents on both variables cannot be larger than 1. Neither variable can be inside an operation such as a root, an absolute value, or be in the denominator of a fraction. Also, the variables cannot be multiplied by one another. Answer choice B has the variable $x$ in the denominator which makes the function nonlinear. Despite not being in the form $y = mx + b$, all the other answer choices are linear and could be re-written in slope-intercept form, though it is not necessary to do that in order to classify it as linear.

**40. C:** Reflections do not change the size or shape of the figure. Further, the line of reflection is a perpendicular bisector of AA', making the distance between AB and the line of reflection equal to the distance between A'B' and the line of reflection.

**41. B:** Consecutive interior angles are supplementary, so $(3x + 10) + (7x - 30) = 180$. Combine like terms and isolate the variable term to solve for x:

$$\begin{aligned} (3x + 10) + (7x - 30) &= 180 \\ 10x - 20 &= 180 \\ +20 \quad & \quad +20 \\ \frac{10x}{10} &= \frac{200}{10} \\ x &= 20 \end{aligned}$$

**42. A:** Triangle ABC has been reflected over the $y$-axis to create triangle A'B'C'. This is true because the orientation of the triangle has changed between the preimage and the image, and the $y$-axis is the perpendicular bisector of line segments AA', BB', and CC'. Triangle A'B'C' has been translated down 5 units and left 3 units to create triangle A"B"C". This is true because each vertex of A'B'C' changed from $(x, y)$ to $(x - 3, y - 5)$. For example, point A'(3,1) mapped to A"(0,−4): $(3,1) \rightarrow (3 - 3, 1 - 5) \rightarrow (0, -4)$.

**43. C:** Plot point C at (7,2). Find the difference between the y-values of points E and C: $1 - 2 = -1$, and find the difference between the $x$-values of points C and D: $7 - 3 = 4$. Substitute these values into the Pythagorean theorem to find the length of the hypotenuse of triangle DCE, which is also the distance between points D and E in the plane.

$$a^2 + b^2 = c^2$$
$$(-1)^2 + (4)^2 = c^2$$
$$1 + 16 = c^2$$
$$17 = c^2$$
$$c = \sqrt{17}$$
$$c \approx 4.1$$

**44. D:** Rotations preserve angle measures, so $\angle A \cong \angle A'$. Since $\angle A = 20°$, $\angle A' = 20°$.

**45. A:** To write a linear function in the form of $y = mx + b$, the slope, or rate of change, and the $y$-intercept, or initial value in this real-world situation, must be found. To find the slope, identify any two points on the graph and divide the difference in outputs by the difference in inputs. Be careful to choose two points whose coordinates can be clearly known from the graph. Use (0,120) and (20,40) to calculate the slope.

$$m = \frac{y_2 - y_1}{x_2 - x_1} = \frac{40 - 120}{20 - 0} = \frac{-80}{20} = -4$$

The $y$-intercept is located at (0,120) on the graph, so the value of $b$ in the equation is 120. With $m = -4$ and $b = 120$, the equation representing this linear function is $y = -4x + 120$.

**46. B:** Use the Exterior Angle Sum Theorem, which states that the measure of an exterior angle is the sum of the opposite interior angles. Substitute the given angles and solve for angle $e$.

$$m\angle e = m\angle A + m\angle B$$
$$m\angle e = 40 + 55$$
$$m\angle e = 95°$$

**47. D**: For this model, the independent variable, $x$, represents the hours a student spends studying for a math test, and the dependent variable, $y$, represents the expected student score on a math test. To find the expected score of a student who spends 4 hours studying for a test, substitute 4 for $x$ in the given equation and solve for $y$.

$$y = 8.75x + 65$$
$$y = 8.75(4) + 65$$
$$y = 35 + 65$$
$$y = 100$$

The expected score for a student who spends 4 hours studying for a math test is 100.

**48. C:** Use the converse of the Pythagorean theorem: if given side lengths a, b, and c: $a^2 + b^2 = c^2$, then the triangle is a right triangle. Substitute 11, 12, and 16. Use the two smaller sides for a and b and the longest side for c.

$$a^2 + b^2 = c^2$$
$$(11)^2 + (12)^2 = (16)^2$$
$$121 + 144 = 256$$
$$265 \neq 256$$

**49. A:** Substitute the given value, 5.6 inches, for the dependent variable, y, and solve for x.

$$\begin{aligned} 5.6 &= 0.3x + 2 \\ -2 &\quad\quad -2 \\ \frac{3.6}{0.3} &= \frac{0.3x}{0.3} \\ 12 &= x \end{aligned}$$

If type A grass grew 5.6 inches in a month, the predicted rainfall would be 12 inches.

**50. D:** Answer choice A describes the interval from $x = -10$ to $x = -3$ as nonlinear and increasing. It is nonlinear, but it is not increasing on the entire interval. It is only increasing from $x = -6$ to $x = -3$. Answer choice B describes the interval from $x = -3$ to $x = 1$ as linear and increasing. It is linear, but it is not increasing. The graph is constant between those $x$ values because it is a horizontal line. Answer choice C describes the interval from $x = 1$ to $x = 3$ as nonlinear and decreasing. It is nonlinear, but it is not decreasing. The graph is rising between those $x$ values, so it is increasing. Answer choice D describes the interval from $x = 3$ to $x = 8$ as linear and decreasing which correctly describes this interval on the graph. The graph is a straight line and falls. Answer choice D is the only statement that correctly describes the given interval.

**51. C:** The line of best fit should be as close to as many points as possible and fit the overall trend of the data. The line on the graph for answer choice C does this best. The line on answer choice A has a slope steeper than the overall trend in the data. Answer choice B has a line above the data. Answer choice D has a line with a slope less steep than the trend of the data.

**52. C:** The base price of $16 is a fixed cost that does not depend on the number of additional households, so it is the constant $b$ in the linear function, $y = mx + b$. The price increases at a rate of $7 per additional household, so 7 is the rate of change, $m$. The linear function is $y = 7x + 16$.

**53. C:** F'G'H'I' is a congruent quadrilateral to FGHI. Point H' is plotted at (7,2). Reflections and transformations in the plane preserve the size and shape of a figure but change its orientation. Therefore, the corresponding side lengths and angle measures of FGHI and F'G'H'I' are congruent. Thus, the figures themselves are congruent. To find the coordinates of H', first reflect H over the x-axis: $(4, -2) \rightarrow (4,2)$, then translate it three units right: $(4,2) \rightarrow (4 + 3,2) \rightarrow (7,2)$. Point H' is plotted at (7,2).

**54. A:** Use the Angle-Sum Theorem, which states that in any triangle, the sum of the three interior angles is equal to 180 degrees. Substitute the given angle measures and solve for angle E.

$$m\angle E + m\angle F + m\angle G = 180$$
$$m\angle E + 45 + 90 = 180$$
$$\begin{array}{rcl} m\angle E + 135 & = & 180 \\ -135 & & -135 \end{array}$$
$$m\angle E = 45°$$

**55. B:** The graph is falling over its entire domain, therefore it is decreasing. The outputs decrease as the inputs increase.

# Practice Test #2

**1. Which point represents the solution to the system of linear equations graphed below?**

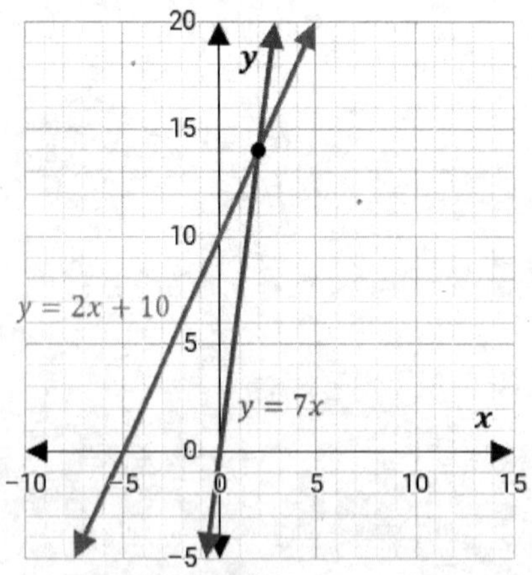


a. (0,10 )
b. (0,0 )
c. (2, 14)
d. (−5,0 )

**2. $2\sqrt{5}$ is between which two numbers?**

a. 4 and 5
b. 2 and 3
c. 3 and 4
d. 10 and 11

**3. A square has an area of 64 square units. What is the length of one side square?**

a. 7
b. 6
c. 10
d. 8

**4. The total length of the world's coastlines is about 315,000 miles. Which answer expresses this in scientific notation?**

a. $3.15 \times 10^{-6}$
b. $3.15 \times 10^{-5}$
c. $3.15 \times 10^{6}$
d. $3.15 \times 10^{5}$

**5. Solve the equation:**

$$\frac{3}{4}x + 12 = 4 - \frac{1}{8}x$$

a. $x = -24$
b. $x = -\frac{64}{7}$
c. $x = -32$
d. $x = -\frac{64}{5}$

**6. The equation $y = 24x$ represents the total calories a certain dog breed needs each day given its weight in pounds, $x$. The graph below shows the total calories a certain cat breed needs each day according to its weight. Which animal breed needs more calories per pound each day and how many more calories per pound does it need?**

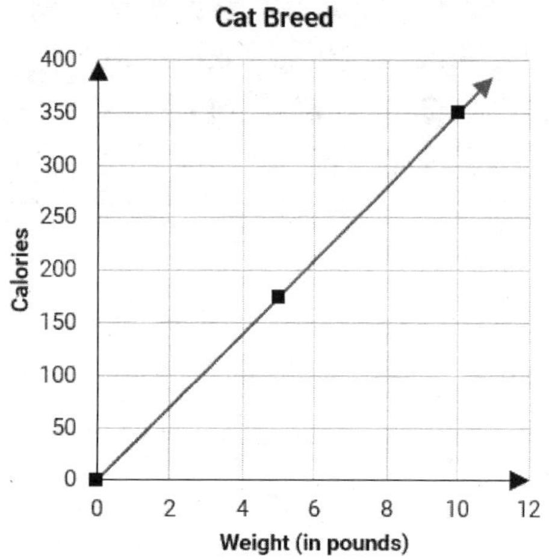


a. The dog breed needs 11 more calories per pound.
b. The dog breed needs 14 more calories per pound.
c. The cat breed needs 11 more calories per pound.
d. The cat breed needs 14 more calories per pound.

**7. Solve for $x$:**

$$x^2 = \frac{121}{49}$$

a. $\pm\frac{12}{7}$
b. $\pm\frac{11}{7}$
c. $\pm\frac{12}{5}$
d. $\pm\frac{11}{5}$

**8. Mike ordered a pizza and bread sticks for dinner. The pizza, $p$, was 3 times the cost of the breadsticks, $b$. If both items cost a total of \$18, how much did each item cost?**

a. $b = \$4.50, p = \$13.50$
b. $b = \$6.00, p = \$12.00$
c. $b = \$13.50, p = \$4.50$
d. $b = \$12.00, p = \$6.00$

**9. Given the equation, create an equation with infinitely many solutions. Select all that apply.**

$$6x + 1 = \_x + \_$$

a. $6x + 1 = 6x + 3$
b. $6x + 1 = 6x + 1$
c. $6x + 1 = 3(2x) + 1$
d. $6x + 1 = 4x + 9$
e. $6x + 1 = 2x + 10$

**10. How many solutions does the equation below have?**

$$2(7x - 5) = 14x - 8$$

a. None
b. One
c. Two
d. Infinitely many solutions

**11. Solve the equation for $x$.**

$$\frac{1}{2}(x - 7) = \frac{3}{5}(5x + 15)$$

a. $x = -\frac{16}{5}$
b. $x = \frac{16}{5}$
c. $x = 5$
d. $x = -5$

**12. Which point is a solution to the system of equations?**

$$\begin{cases} 2x + y = 7 \\ x - y = 2 \end{cases}$$

a. $(4, -1)$
b. $(2, 3)$
c. $(3, 1)$
d. $(5, 3)$

**13. Solve the system of linear equations.**

$$\begin{cases} y = -x + 3 \\ y = \frac{1}{2}x + 9 \end{cases}$$

a. $(1, 2)$
b. $(-4, 7)$
c. $(4, -1)$
d. $(6, 12)$

**14. The size of a white blood cell that measures $6 \times 10^{-4}$ inches is larger than the size of a red blood cell that measures $3 \times 10^{-4}$ inches. How many times as large is this white blood cell as the red blood cell?**

a. $\frac{1}{2}$
b. 3
c. 2
d. $\frac{1}{3}$

**15. A school auditorium has 600 seats total on the main floor and balcony combined. There are 5 times as many seats on the main floor than there are in the balcony. Based on this information how many seats are in each section?**

a. $m = 500, b = 100$
b. $m = 150, b = 450$
c. $m = 100, b = 500$
d. $m = 450, b = 150$

**16. Which of the following graphs is <u>not</u> a function?**

a.
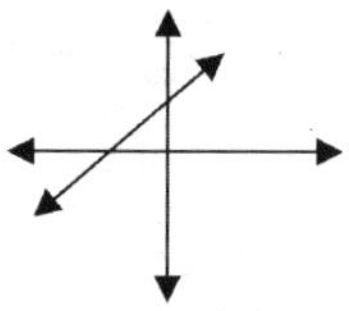
b.
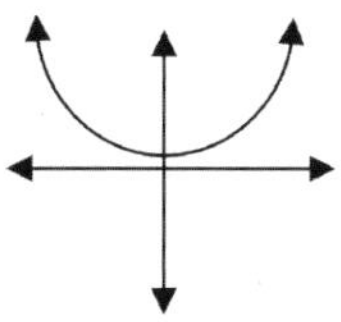
c.
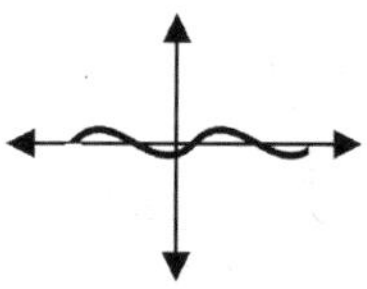
d.
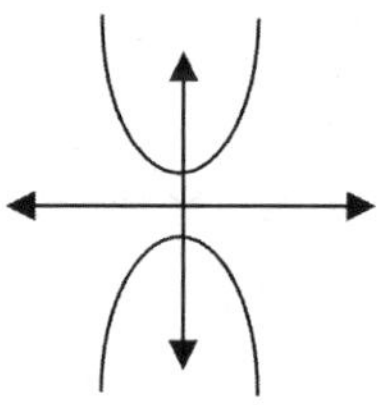

**17. Which transformations can be done to image *A* to produce image *B*? Select all that apply.**

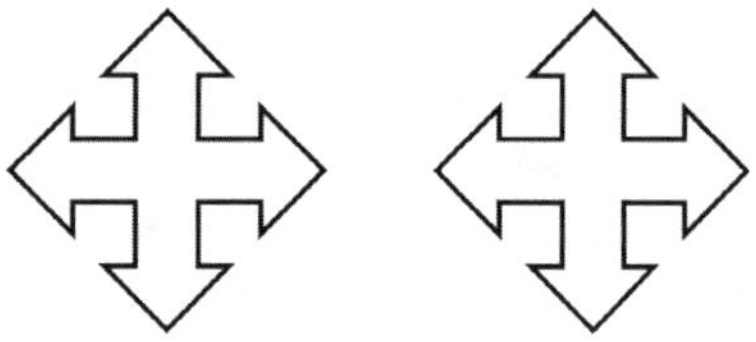

*A* *B*

a. Translation
b. Rotation
c. Reflection
d. Dilation

**18. Which function has the smaller range?**

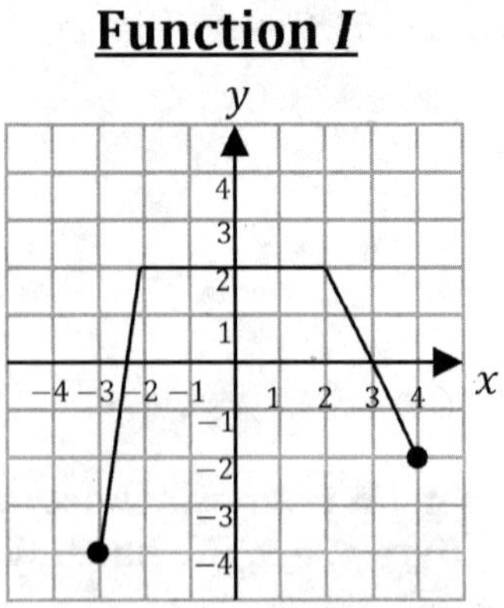


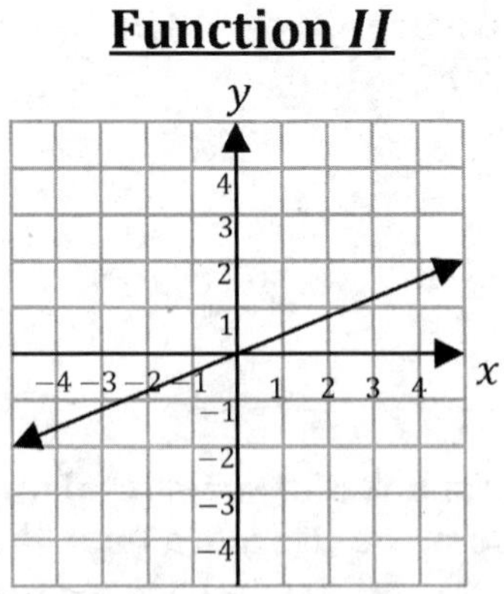


a. Function I
b. Functions II
c. They have the same y-intercept
d. Cannot be determined

**19. Which function below is <u>not</u> linear?**

a. $4y + 3x = -1$
b. $2x - y = 5$
c. $y = 3x - 9$
d. $y = \sqrt{x} + 2$

**20. What function represents the table values in slope-intercept form?**

| $x$ | 0 | 2 | 4 | 5 |
|---|---|---|---|---|
| $y$ | −2 | 8 | 18 | 23 |

a. $y = \frac{1}{5}x - 2$
b. $x = 5y - 2$
c. $y = 5x - 2$
d. $x = \frac{1}{5}y - 2$

**21. Which function represents the graph?**

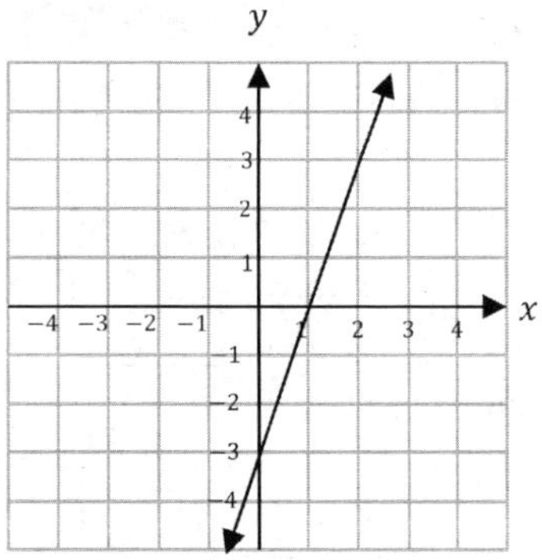


a. $y = 3x + 1$
b. $y = 3x - 3$
c. $y = -3x + 1$
d. $y = -3x - 3$

**22. Part A: On which interval is the function increasing?**

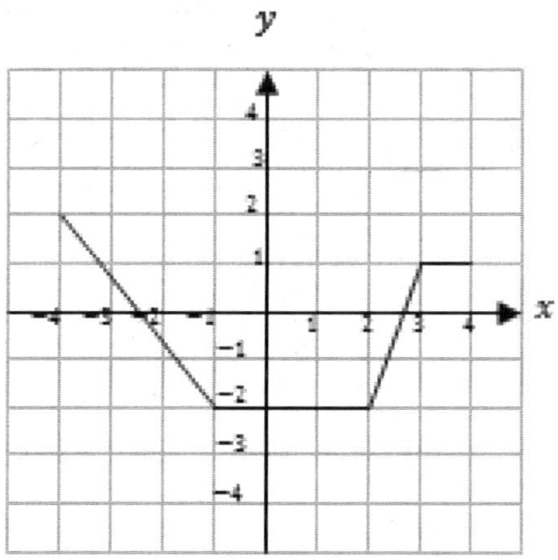


a. $2 < x < 3$
b. $3 < x < 4$
c. $-1 < x < 2$
d. $-4 < x < -1$

**Part B: On which interval is the function decreasing?**

a. $2 < x < 3$
b. $-4 < x < -1$
c. $-1 < x < 2$
d. $-4 < x < -1$

**23. A child is saving one-dollar bills, *x*, and five-dollar bills, *y*, and currently has a total of \$102. He has 6 more five-dollar bills than one-dollar bills. How many of each kind of bill does the child have?**

a. $x = 12, y = 18$
b. $x = 18, y = 12$
c. $x = 11, y = 15$
d. $x = 15, y = 11$

**24. Which two shapes represent a rotation?**

a.
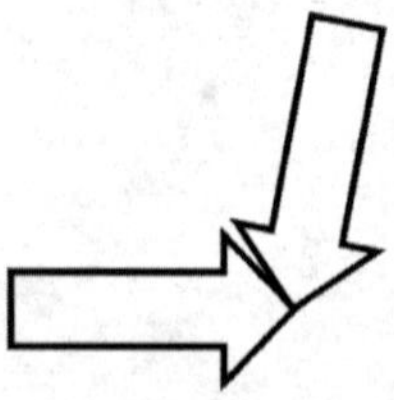

b.
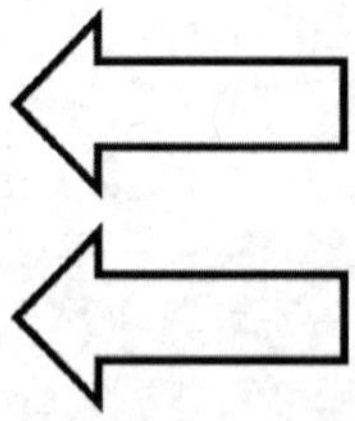

c.

d.
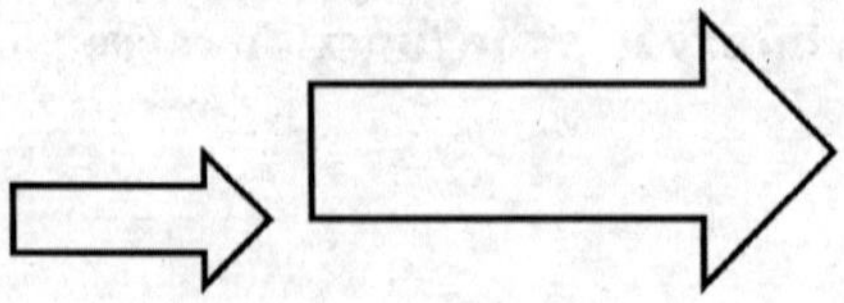

**25. What transformation do the two shapes below represent?**

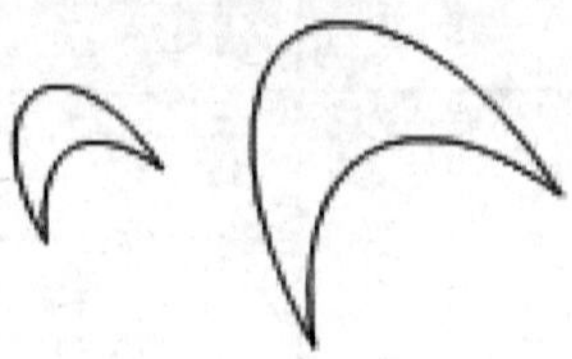

a. Reflection
b. Translation
c. Dilation
d. Rotation

**26. If $\Delta ABC$ is dilated by a factor of 3, what is the new measure of $\overline{AB}$?**

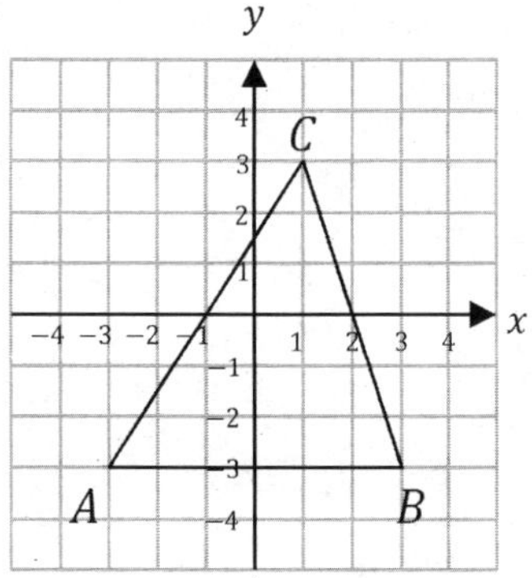


a. 2
b. 6
c. 9
d. 18

**27. What two transformations will map figure *A* onto figure *B*?**

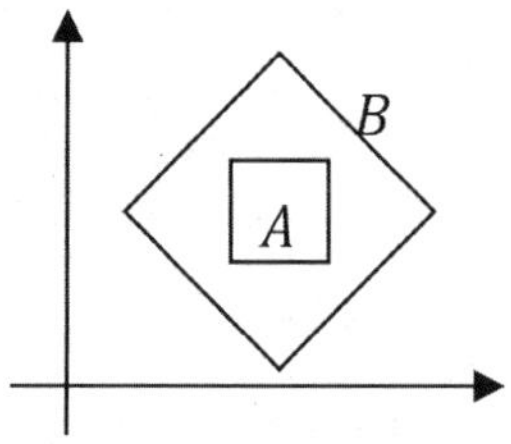


a. Rotation and Translation
b. Reflection and Translation
c. Rotation and Dilation
d. Translation and Dilation

**28. Given triangle $\Delta ABC$, with the $m\angle C$ is 60°, and the $m\angle B$ is $\frac{2}{3}$ of $m\angle C$. What is the $m\angle A$?**

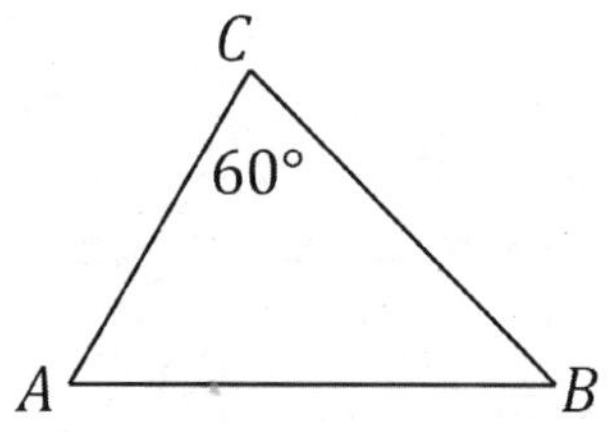


a. 45°
b. 105°
c. 60°
d. 80°

**29. How much more is $AB + BC$ than $AC$?**

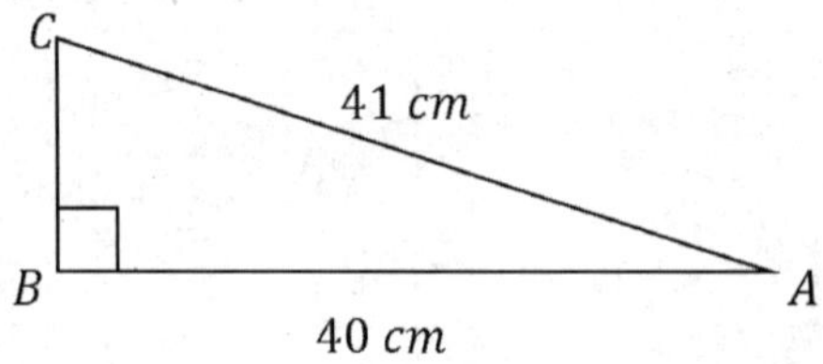


a. 8 cm
b. 9 cm
c. 10 cm
d. 11 cm

**30. Given the two points on the graph below, what is the approximate distance between them in units?**

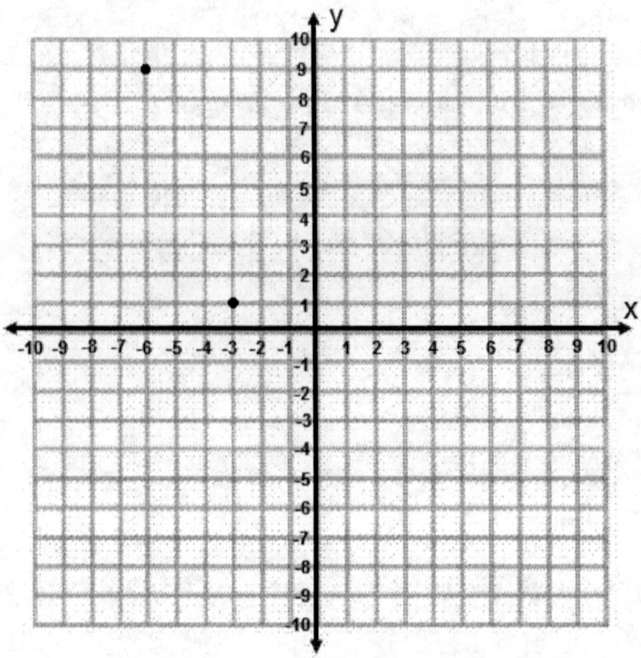

a. 7.42
b. 9.49
c. 8.54
d. 8.94

**31. The side of a square measures $2^3$ feet. Write a simplified exponential expression for the area of the square and then use the expression to find the area.**

a. $2^6$; 64 square feet
b. $2^6$; 12 square feet
c. $2^5$; 32 square feet
d. $2^5$; 10 square feet

**32. What is the volume of the sphere?**

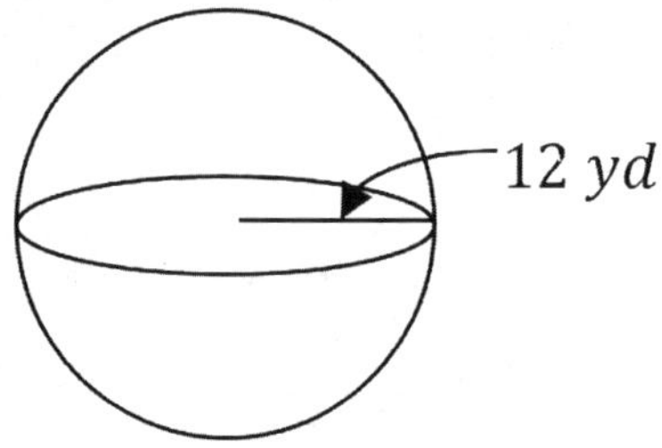


a. 904.32 cubic yard
b. 7234.56 cubic yards
c. 602.88 cubic yards
d. 57876.48 cubic yards

**33. Which line best represents the line-of-fit for the data?**

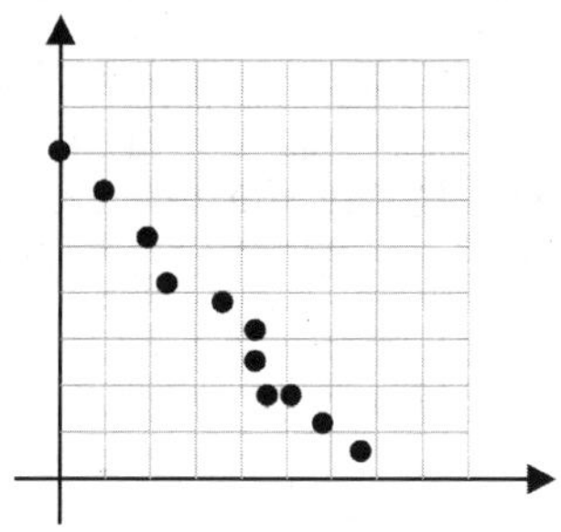

a. $y = -7x + 1$
b. $y = 7x - 1$
c. $y = -x + 7$
d. $y = x - 7$

**34. Using the data at the right, what statement best describes the rate of change?**

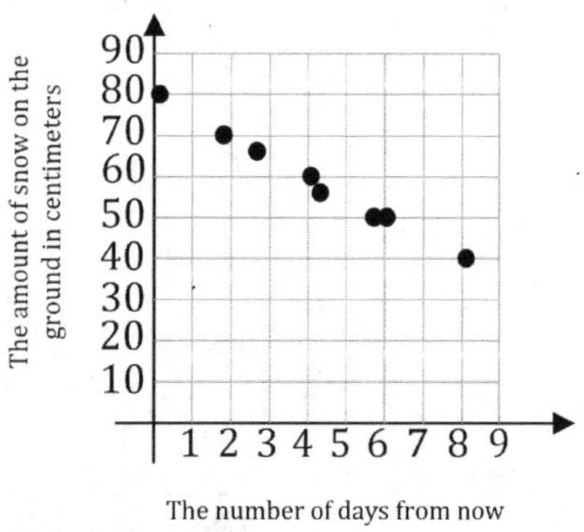


a. Every day, the snow melts 10 centimeters.
b. Every day, the snow melts 5 centimeters.
c. Every day, the snow increases by 10 centimeters.
d. Every day, the snow increases by 5 centimeters.

**35. Simplify the numerical exponential expression to an integer or fraction:**

$$\frac{6^3 \cdot 6^{-2}}{6^4}$$

a. $-9$
b. $\frac{1}{16}$
c. $-6$
d. $\frac{1}{216}$

**36. 50 containers each weighing $1.1 \times 10^4$ pounds are loaded onto a ship for transport. How much total weight, in pounds, was added to the ship when the containers were loaded? Express the weight in scientific notation.**

a. $5.5 \times 10^4$ pounds
b. $5.5 \times 10^5$ pounds
c. $5.1 \times 10^5$ pounds
d. $5.1 \times 10^4$ pounds

**37. Between which two numbers does $\sqrt{58}$ fall between on a number line?**

a. 7 and 8
b. 6 and 7
c. 8 and 9
d. 9 and 10

**38. What category does $-\sqrt[3]{64}$ fit best under?**

a. Natural Number
b. Whole Number
c. Rational Number
d. Irrational Number

**39. Which of the following tables is <u>not</u> a function? Select all that apply.**

a.

| Input | Output |
|---|---|
| 20 | 12 |
| 40 | 16 |
| 60 | 20 |
| 80 | 24 |

b.

| x | y |
|---|---|
| 3 | 12 |
| 6 | 5 |
| 3 | −12 |
| 0 | −5 |

c.

| x | y |
|---|---|
| 14 | −3 |
| 7 | −2 |
| 0 | −1 |
| 7 | 0 |

d.

| Input | Output |
|---|---|
| −10 | 1 |
| −6 | 2 |
| −10 | 3 |
| −14 | 4 |

**40. Two linear functions describing the total cost of renting two different event centers are described below. Each event center has a one-time base fee and an hourly rate.**

**Function A: An event center costs $100 to rent the facility plus an additional $25 per hour, $x$, that it is rented for the total cost $y$.**

**Function B:**

| Time (hours) | 1 | 2 | 3 | 4 |
|---|---|---|---|---|
| Total Cost | $160 | $170 | $180 | $190 |

**Which statement about the two event centers is true?**

a. Event Center A charges $85 more per hour than Event Center B.
b. Event Center B charges $85 more per hour than Event Center A.
c. Event Center A's base fee is $50 more than Event Center B's base fee.
d. Event Center B's base fee is $50 more than Event Center A's base fee.

**41. Line segment AB is reflected over the line $y = 2$ to create line segment A'B'. Use the graph below to find the coordinates of B'.**

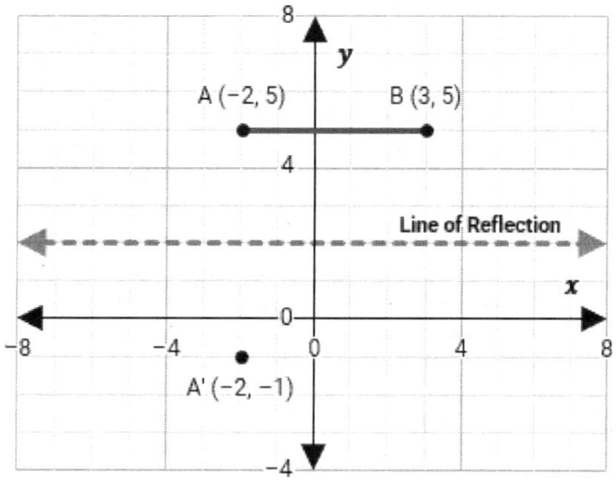


a. $(3, -1)$
b. $(3, -5)$
c. $(-1, 3)$
d. $(-5, 3)$

**42. Find the value of *y* in the triangle below.**

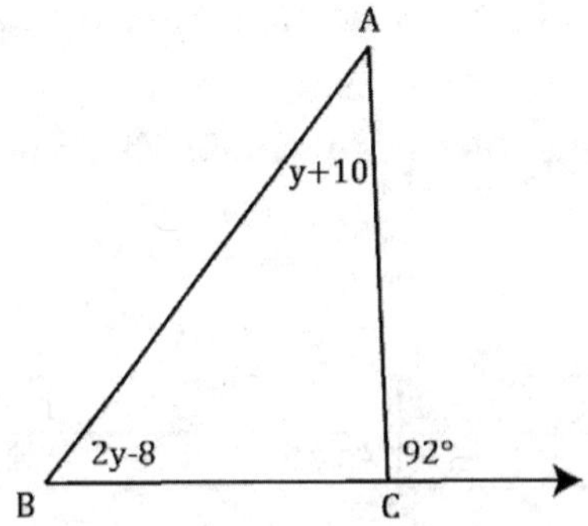


a. $y = 30$
b. $y = 88$
c. $y = 92$
d. $y = 25$

**43. Describe a sequence of transformations mapping triangle XYZ to triangle X'Y'Z' in the figure below.**

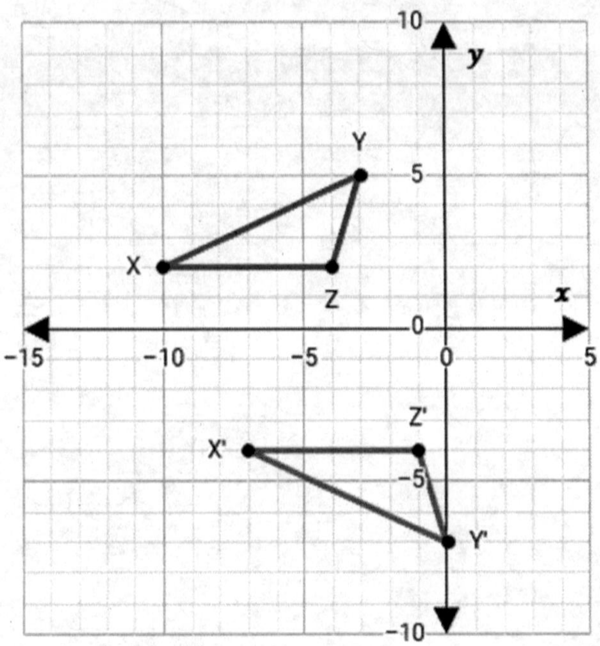


a. Reflection over the *y*-axis, translation two units down, three units right
b. Reflection over the *x*-axis, translation two units up, three units left
c. Reflection over the *y*-axis, translation two units up, three units left
d. Reflection over the *x*-axis, translation two units down, three units right

**44. What category does $\pi$ belong in?**

a. Integer
b. Irrational Number
c. Whole Number
d. Rational Number

**45. Which of the following graphs is NOT a function?**

a.

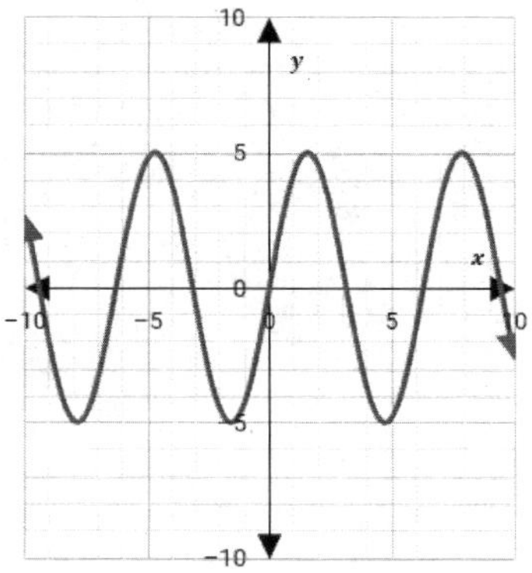


b.

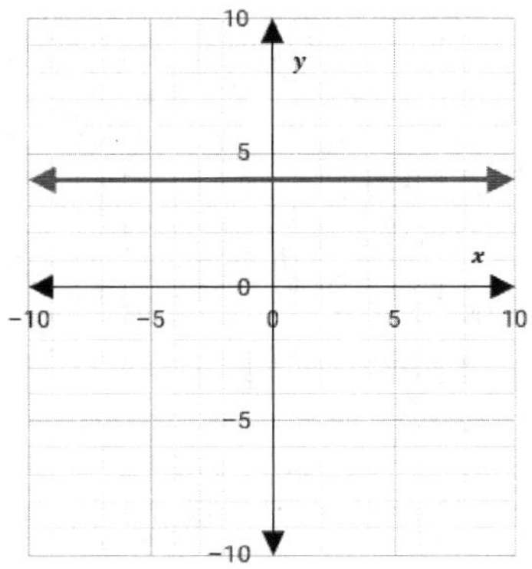


c.

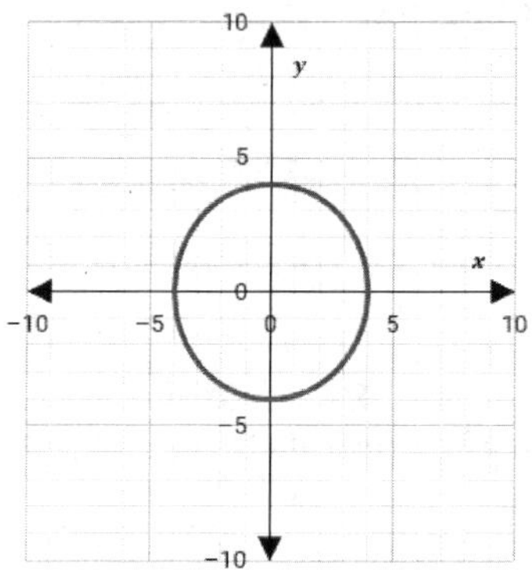


d.

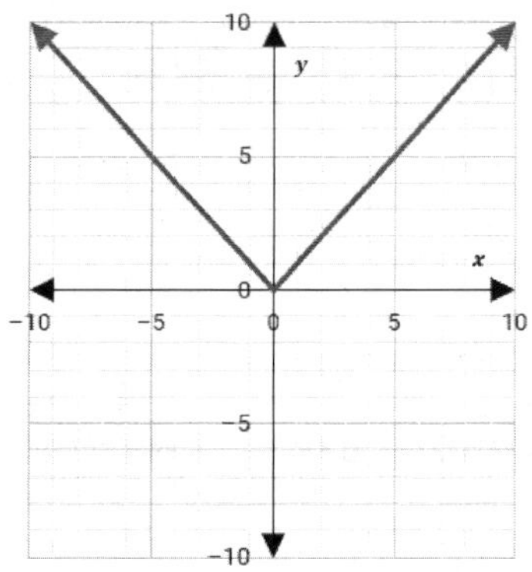

**46. Is the function represented by the graph below increasing, decreasing, or constant?**

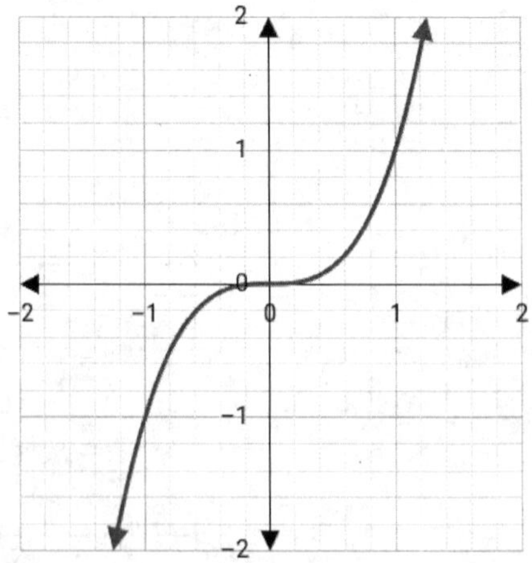


a. Increasing
b. Decreasing
c. Constant
d. Cannot be determined

**47. Triangle ABC is rotated 90° clockwise about the origin and translated down two units. If $\angle A = 23°, \angle B = 46°$, what is the measure of $\angle C'$?**

a. 111°
b. 69°
c. 23°
d. 46°

**48. If a right triangle has a leg 5 units long and a hypotenuse 11 units long, find the area of the square with a side length equal to the remaining leg of the right triangle.**

a. 27.5 $\text{units}^2$
b. 25 $\text{units}^2$
c. 96 $\text{units}^2$
d. 146 $\text{units}^2$

**49. Part A: Scientists wanted to explore the association between the altitude of various locations and the average temperature recorded at those sites in December. They collected a random sample of 16 locations in North America and plotted the data on the scatterplot shown below.**

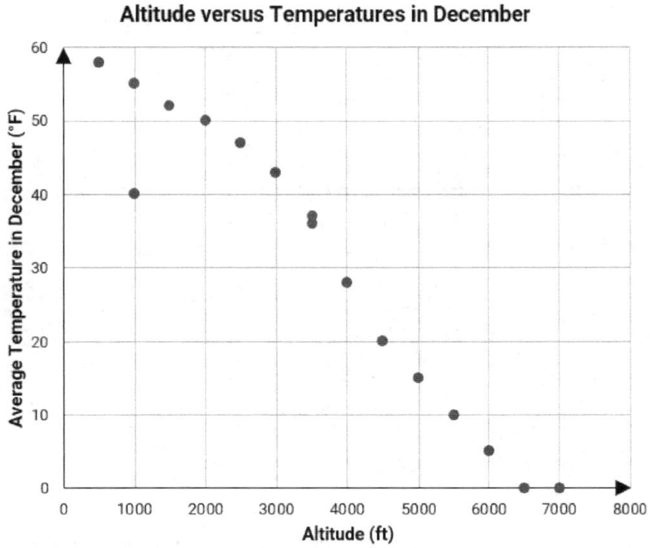


**What is the outlier in the data set?**

a. (1000,40)
b. (500,58)
c. (7000,0)
d. There are no outliers.

**Part B: What kind of association does the scatterplot have?**

a. Positive, nonlinear
b. Positive, linear
c. Negative, nonlinear
d. Negative, linear

**50. Function M is represented by the graph below:**

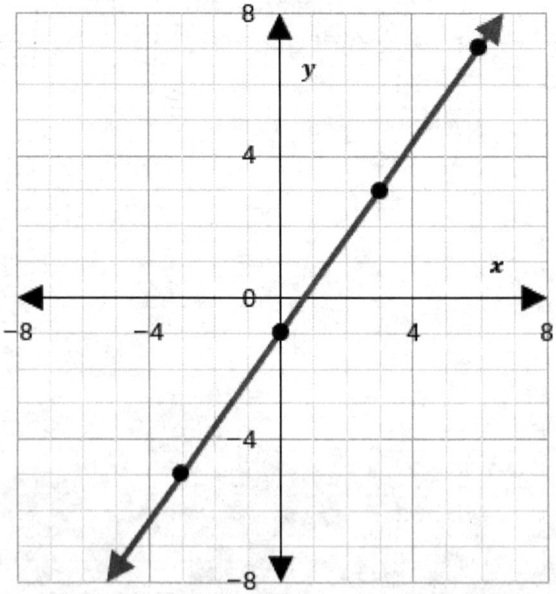


**If Function N is also a linear function whose rate of change is 1 less than the rate of change of Function M, which of the following could be an equation for Function N?**

a. $y = -\frac{1}{3}x - 1$
b. $y = \frac{1}{3}x + 4$
c. $y = \frac{4}{3}x - 2$
d. $y = -x - 1$

**51. An ecologist studied the relationship between the amount of rainfall in inches and the growth of a certain type of grass (type A) in inches per month. Her data can be modeled by the equation $y = 0.3x + 2$, where $y$ is the growth of the grass and $x$ is the amount of rainfall in the given month. If it rained 5.5 inches in a month, what would be the predicted growth in the grass that month?**

a. 1.5 inches
b. 0.8 inches
c. 3.65 inches
d. 7.5 inches

**52. Find the volume, in cubic feet, of the sphere given below. Use $\pi = 3.14$ and round to the nearest tenth.**

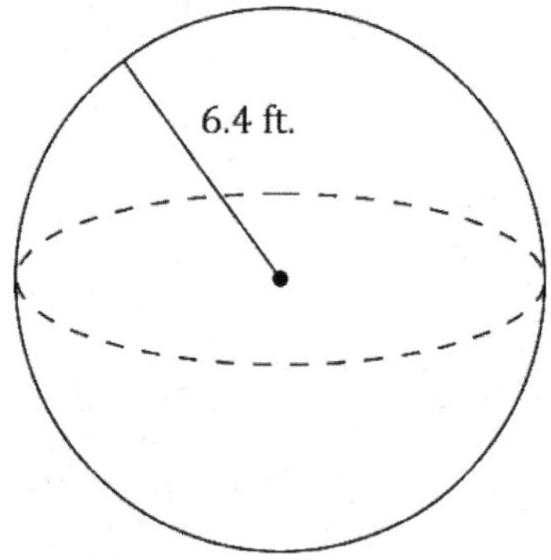


a. 171.5 $ft^3$
b. 617.3 $ft^3$
c. 1097.5 $ft^3$
d. 96.5 $ft^3$

**53. In the figure below, lines *a* and *b* are parallel. Find the value of *x*.**

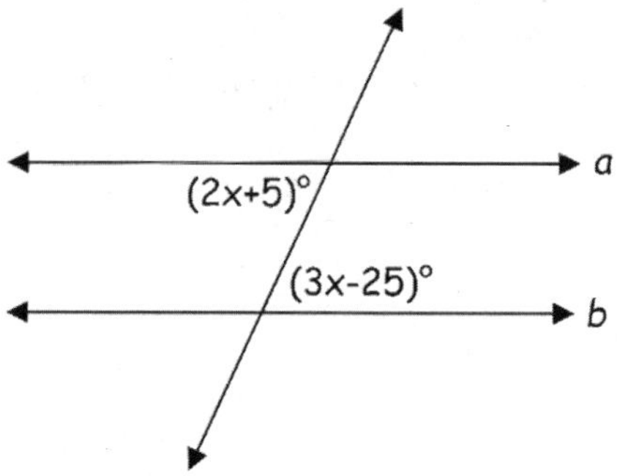


a. $x = 22$
b. $x = 30$
c. $x = 40$
d. $x = 55$

**54. Describe the intervals where the function represented on the graph below is increasing, decreasing, and constant.**

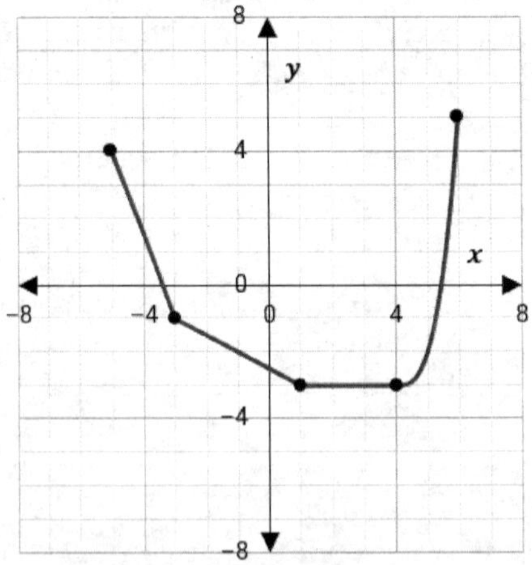


a. Increasing from $x = 4$ to $x = 6$, Decreasing from $x = -5$ to $x = 1$, Constant from $x = 1$ to $x = 4$
b. Constant from $x = 4$ to $x = 6$, Decreasing from $x = -5$ to $x = 1$, Increasing from $x = 1$ to $x = 4$
c. Decreasing from $x = 4$ to $x = 6$, Increasing from $x = -5$ to $x = 1$, Constant from $x = 1$ to $x = 4$
d. Constant from $x = 4$ to $x = 6$, Increasing from $x = -5$ to $x = 1$, Decreasing from $x = 1$ to $x = 4$

**55. What category does $\frac{170}{99}$ fit best under?**

a. Integer
b. Repeating Decimal
c. Terminating Decimal
d. Irrational Number

# Answers and Explanations for Test #2

**1. C:** Given the graph of a system of linear equations, the solution is the point of intersection of the two lines. In this graph, the two lines intersect at $(2, 14)$.

**2. A:** Compare the square of $2\sqrt{5}$ to the square of the whole numbers. $(2\sqrt{5})^2 = 2^2\sqrt{5}^2 = 4 \times 5 = 20$. See that 20 is between 16 and 25, or $4^2$ and $5^2$, so $2\sqrt{5}$ is between 4 and 5. Checking with a calculator, $2\sqrt{5} \approx 4.472$.

**3. D:** The formula for the area of a square is $A = s^2$, where s is the length of one side of the square. In this case, $64 = s^2$. To solve for $s$, just square root both sides of the equation and s=8.

**4. D:** To write a number in scientific notation, the form is $a \times 10^n$, where $1 \leq a < 10$. The decimal need to move 5 spaces to the left so it is immediately to the right of the 3. Because it moved 5 spaces to the left, $n = 5$, so the answer is $3.15 \times 10^5$

**5. B:** To get rid of the fractions, multiply both sides by the LCD of 4 and 8, which is 8.

$$\frac{3}{4}x + 12 = 4 - \frac{1}{8}x$$

$$8(\frac{3}{4}x + 12) = \left(4 - \frac{1}{8}x\right)8$$

$$\begin{aligned} 6x + 96 &= 32 - x \\ +x \quad &\quad\; +x \\ 7x + 96 &= 32 \\ -96 &\quad -96 \\ \frac{7x}{7} &= \frac{-64}{7} \\ x &= -\frac{64}{7} \end{aligned}$$

**6. C:** The equation for the dog breed shows the unit rate as 24 calories per pound. For the cat breed, a point on the graph that can be used to determine the unit rate is $(10, 350)$. Dividing 350 by 10 gives a unit rate of 35 calories per pound which is $35 - 24 = 11$ more calories per pound than the dog breed.

**7. B:** Use the square root to undo the power of 2 on the variable. When taking the square root of a number to solve an equation, a plus or minus sign must be used to indicate both the positive and negative values of the solution. When taking the square root of a fraction, take the square root of both the numerator and denominator. 121 is a perfect square. $121 = 11^2$, so $\sqrt{121}$ simplifies to 11. 49 is a perfect square. $49 = 7^2$, so $\sqrt{49} = 7$.

$$x^2 = \frac{121}{49}$$

$$\sqrt{x^2} = \pm\sqrt{\frac{121}{49}}$$

$$x = \pm\frac{\sqrt{121}}{\sqrt{49}}$$

$$x = \pm\frac{11}{7}$$

**8. A:** Let $p$ represent the cost of the pizza and $b$ represent the cost of the breadsticks. The one total given is $18 which is the cost of both items, so the first equation is $p + b = 18$. The second equation can be written using the fact that the pizza was 3 times the cost of the breadsticks, so $p = 3b$. Solving using substitution, $3b$ is plugged in for $p$ in the first equation.

$$(3b) + b = 18$$

$$\frac{4b}{4} = \frac{18}{4}$$

$$b = 4.50$$

To find $p$, plug in 4.5 for $b$ into $p = 3b$. $p = 3(4.50) = 13.50$

**9. B, C:** The equation $6x + 1 = 6x + 1$ has infinitely many solutions. For any value of $x$ that is plugged in each side will always equal the other side.

An example of an equation with no solutions is $6x + 1 = 6x + 3$. To solve this equation, $6x$ can be subtracted from both sides of the equation. This leaves 3=1 which is not true so there is no solution to this equation.

An example of an equation with one solution is $6x + 1 = 4x + 9$. The equation is solved below:

$$6x + 1 = 4x + 9$$

$$2x + 1 = 9$$

$$2x = 8$$

$$x = 4$$

**10. A:** The equation is solved below:

| | |
|---|---|
| $2(7x - 5) = 14x - 8$ | Distribute 2 across the parentheses |
| $14x - 10 = 14x - 8$ | Subtract $14x$ from both sides of the equation |
| $-10 = -8$ | |

Because $-10 \neq -8$, no solution exists for the equation.

**11. D: The equation is solved below:**

$$\frac{1}{2}(x-7) = \frac{3}{5}(5x+15)$$

| | |
|---|---|
| $x - 7 = \frac{6}{5}(5x+15)$ | Clear the fraction $\frac{1}{2}$ on the left by multiplying both sides by 2 |
| $x - 7 = 6x + 18$ | Distribute $\frac{6}{5}$ across the parentheses |
| $-7 = 5x + 18$ | Subtract $x$ from both sides |
| $-25 = 5x$ | Subtract 18 from both sides |
| $-5 = x$ | Divide both sides by 5 |

**12. C:** The problem is solved below

$$\begin{cases} 2x + y = 7 \\ x - y = 2 \end{cases}$$

| | |
|---|---|
| $3x = 9$ | Because the two equations had opposite terms, add them vertically |
| $x = 3$ | Divide both sides by 3 |
| $2(3) + y = 7$ | Substitute 3 into one of the original equations |
| $6 + y = 7$ | Multiply |
| $y = 1$ | Subtract 6 from both sides |
| $(3,1)$ | Write the final answer as an ordered pair $(x, y)$ |

**13. B:** The answer is solved below:

$$\begin{cases} y = -x + 3 \\ y = \frac{1}{2}x + 9 \end{cases}$$

Since both expressions are equal to $y$, set the expressions equal to each other: $-x + 3 = \frac{1}{2}x + 9$.

| | |
|---|---|
| $3 = \frac{3}{2}x + 9$ | Add $x$ to both sides of the equation |
| $-6 = \frac{3}{2}x$ | Subtract 9 from both sides of the equation |
| $-4 = x$ | Multiply both sides by $\frac{2}{3}$ |
| $y = -(-4) + 3 = 7$ | Substitute the value for x into one of the original equations |
| $(-4, 7)$ | Write the final answer as an ordered pair $(x, y)$ |

**14. C:** Comparing each part of the numbers in scientific notation, the size only differs in the non-exponential numbers. The power of 10 is the same for each type of blood cell. The red blood cell's non-exponential number is 3 compared to the white blood cell's non-exponential number of 6. 3 times 2 equals 6, so the size of the white blood cell is two times the size of the red blood cell.

**15. A:** The system of linear equations that can be formed from the problem is $\begin{cases} m+b=600 \\ m=5b \end{cases}$. The solution to the system is below:

| | |
|---|---|
| $(5b)+b=600$ | Substitute the expression for $m$ into the other equation |
| $5b+b=600$ | Remove parentheses |
| $6b=600$ | Combine like terms |
| $b=100$ | Divide by 6 on both sides |
| $m=5(100)=500$ | Substitute the value for $b$ into the expression for m and evaluate. |

So, the final equation would be $500+100=600$

**16. D:** A function cannot map a single input to more than one output. The vertical line test states that if a vertical line touches a graph in more than one point, then it is not a function. The graph from answer D does not pass the vertical line test so it is not a function.

**17. A, B, C:** Image A could be translated, rotated, or reflected to form image B. It cannot be dilated to form image B. A translation is just "sliding" an image to a new location. A reflection makes a mirror image on the other side of a line of reflection. A rotation just turns the image. It cannot be dilated because that would change the size of the image.

**18. A:** The range of the function is the set of all outputs, or y-values. The range of Function I is from$-4$ to 2, and the range of Function II is the set of all real numbers. Therefore, the range of Function I is smaller than the range of Function II.

**19. D:** A function is linear if the powers of the x and y variables are 1. In answer D, the $\sqrt{x}=x^{1/2}$, so its exponent is not 1, thus answer D is not linear.

**20. C:** First find the y-intercept, which is where $x=0$. In this case it is $-2$. Next, find the slope of the line. Slope is equal to rise over run, or in this case $\frac{10}{2}=5$. So, the equation in slope intercept form is $y=5x-2$.

**21. B:** The equations are in slope-intercept form. The y-intercept, b, is the point where the graph touches the y-axis. The y-intercept of this graph is $(0,-3)$. The slope, m, is the vertical change over the horizontal change. The vertical change is 3 and the horizontal change is 1 so the slope is $\frac{3}{1}=3$. Substituting these numbers into the slope-intercept form you will get $y=3x-3$.

**22. Part A: A:** On a graph, a function is increasing if the line is sloping up as it is moving from left to right. The only interval on the graph with positive slope is $2<x<3$.

**Part B: D:** On a graph, a function is decreasing if the line is sloping down as it is moving from left to right. The only interval on the graph with negative slope is $-4<x<-1$.

**23. A:** Let $x$ represent the number of one-dollar bills and $y$ represent the number of five-dollar bills. The total given is \$102. The variables do not represent the value of the bills, so each variable is multiplied by the value of the bill in the equation equaling 102. The first equation is $1x+5y=102$. The second equation is created using the fact that there are 6 more five-dollar bills than one-dollar bills, so 6 is added to the number of one-dollar bills to equal the number of five-dollar bills. This gives the second equation as $y = x + 6$. Solving using substitution, plug $x + 6$ in for $y$ in the first equation.

$$\begin{aligned} 1x + 5(x+6) &= 102 \\ 1x + 5x + 30 &= 102 \\ 6x + 30 &= 102 \\ -30 &\quad -30 \\ \frac{6x}{6} &= \frac{72}{6} \\ x &= 12 \end{aligned}$$

To find $y$, plug in 12 for $x$ into $y = x + 6$. $y = 12 + 6 = 18$

**24. A:** A rotation, or turn, is only seen in answer A. Answer B shows a translation, or slide; answer C shows a dilation; and answer C shows a reflection or translation.

**25. C:** They represent a dilation. The shapes are congruent, one is just bigger than the other.

**26. D:** If a dilation has a scale factor if 3, then the length of each side is multiplied by 3 to get the new length. The measure of $\overline{AB}$ is 6, so when it is multiplied by 3 it becomes 18.

**27. C:** Because the two figures are different sizes, one of the transformations is a dilation. Also, the figures are turned which is a rotation. Answer C gives those two answers.

**28. D:** The Triangle Sum Theorem says the three angles of a triangle must add up to **180°.**

$60° + 40° + m\angle A = 180°$

$100° + m\angle A = 180°$ Combine like terms

$m\angle A = 80°$ Subtract 105 from both sides

**29. A:** First solve for $BC$. By use of the Pythagorean Theorem $a^2 + b^2 = c^2$ and substituting the appropriate values, the equation becomes

$BC^2 + 40^2 = 41^2$

$BC^2 + 1600 = 1681$ Evaluate the exponents

$BC^2 = 81$ Subtract 1600 from both sides

$BC = 9$ Take the square root of both sides

To find how much more $AB + BC$ is compared to $AC$ evaluate the expression $(AB + BC) - AC$. This yields $(40 + 9) - 41 = 8$.

**30. C:** Using Pythagorean theorem, the distance between the two points can be determined. The points are 8 units away vertically and 3 units away horizontally. Therefore, the legs of the imaginary right triangle are 8 units and 3 units.

$$8^2 + 3^2 = c^2$$
$$64 + 9 = c^2$$
$$73 = c^2$$
$$\sqrt{73} = \text{c}$$
$$8.54 \approx \text{c}$$

**31. A:** The area of a square is the length of its side squared which is $(2^3)^2$. Applying the power of a power rule, multiply the exponents to find the simplified exponential expression and calculate the value of the area.

$$\text{Area} = (2^3)^2 = 2^{3 \cdot 2} = 2^6 = 64$$

**32. B:** The volume formula for a sphere is $V = \frac{4}{3}\pi r^3$. Plugging in the value of the radius then evaluating will yield the final answer:

$$V = \frac{4}{3}(3.14)(12\ yd)^3$$

$$V = 7234.56\ yd^3$$

**33. C:** If a line is drawn as close to the points as possible, the y-intercept would be 7 and the slope would be -1. From this information, the line is $y = -x + 7$.

**34. B:** If a line-of-fit is drawn through the points, the slope will be $-\frac{1}{5}$ so the snow melts 5 centimeters every day.

**35. D:** Use the product of powers rule to multiply. To multiply exponents with the same base, add the exponents.

$$\frac{6^3 \cdot 6^{-2}}{6^4} = \frac{6^{3+(-2)}}{6^4} = \frac{6^1}{6^4}$$

Use the quotient of powers rule to divide. To divide exponents with the same base, subtract the exponents. The result is an expression with a negative exponent. Applying the negative power rule to change the exponent to a positive power by putting the base and power in the denominator.

$$\frac{6^1}{6^4} = 6^{1-4} = 6^{-3} = \frac{1}{6^3} = \frac{1}{216}$$

**36. B:** The total weight of the containers is found by multiplying the weight of one container times the total amount of containers. With one container weighing $1.1 \times 10^4$ pounds and 50 containers in all, the expression $(1.1 \times 10^4) \times 50$ gives the total weight added to the ship. Since 50 is not in scientific notation, re-write it as $5 \times 10^1$. To find the product, multiply the non-exponential numbers and the exponential numbers separately. When multiplying the exponential numbers, add the exponents.

$$(1.1 \times 10^4)(5 \times 10^1) = (1.1 \times 5) \times (10^4 \times 10^1) = 5.5 \times 10^5$$

**37. A:** $\sqrt{58}$ is an irrational number and must be estimated using the perfect squares it is closest to on the number line. 58 lies between the perfect squares of 49 and 64 whose square roots are 7 and 8. Based on this, $7 < \sqrt{58} < 8$.

**38. C:** The cube root of 64 simplifies to 4, an integer. All integers are rational numbers because they can be expressed as a quotient of two integers. Also, the decimal expansion of an integer is terminating. It is important to be aware that radicals do not automatically make a number irrational.

$$-\sqrt{64} = -4 = \frac{-4}{1}$$

**39. B, C, D:** A function cannot map a single input to more than one output. Therefore, there can only be one $y$-value for each $x$-value.

**40. D:** The answer choices are statements comparing the hourly rate and the base fee of the event centers. Function A's verbal description explicitly states the hourly rate at $25 per hour and the base fee at $100. Stating this as an equation in slope-intercept form gives us $y = 25x + 100$. The table for Function B can be used to find both the hourly rate and base fee. For each point in the table, the total cost increases by $10 for every 1 hour resulting in an hourly rate of $10 per hour. The base fee is the total cost for 0 hours. For a time of 0 hours which is 1 hour less than the first point in the table, the total cost would be $10 less than $160 resulting in a base fee of $150. Stating this as an equation in slope-intercept form gives us $y = 10x + 150$. Comparing the hourly rates, Event Center A charges $15 more per hour than Event Center B which is not an answer choice. Comparing the base fees, Event Center B charges $50 more than Event Center A which is answer choice D.

**41. A:** In a reflection, the length of a line segment is preserved. Therefore, the length of AB must be equal to the length of A'B'. Therefore, B' must be 5 horizontal units away from A' at $(3, -1)$.

**42. A:** Use the Exterior Angle Sum Theorem, which states that the measure of an exterior angle is the sum of the opposite interior angles. Substitute the given angles and solve for angle ACD.

$$m\angle ACD = m\angle A + m\angle B$$
$$92 = (y + 10) + (2y - 8)$$
$$\frac{92}{-2} = \frac{3y + 2}{-2}$$
$$\frac{90}{3} = \frac{3y}{3}$$
$$y = 30$$

**43. D:** The orientation of triangle XYZ changed to result in triangle X'Y'Z', so triangle XYZ was reflected over the $x$-axis first, changing each coordinate point from $(x, y)$ to $(x, -y)$. Next, the triangle was translated two units down and three units right. This can be seen by looking at the coordinates of each vertex as the points changed from $(x, -y)$ to $(x+3, -y-2)$. For example, point X(−10,2) mapped to X'(−7,−4): $(-10,2) \rightarrow (-10+3, -2-2) \rightarrow (-7,-4)$.

**44. B:** Pi is an irrational number. It has no fractional form, and it cannot be expressed as a repeating or terminating decimal. While it is often rounded to 3.14, the decimal expansion sequence is never ending, and it also does not form a repeating pattern. Therefore, it cannot be a rational number.

**45. C:** The vertical line test states that a graph is a function if no vertical line intersects the graph at more than one point. If a vertical line intersects the graph at more than one point anywhere on the graph, it is not a function. When a vertical line is drawn on the graph of answer choice C at any point between $x = -4$ to $x = 4$, it will intersect the graph in more than one place; therefore, the graph is not a function. All the other graphs pass the vertical line test.

**46. A:** The graph is rising over its entire domain, therefore it is increasing. The outputs increase as the inputs increase.

**47. A:** Rotations and translations in the plane preserve angle measures. Therefore, $\angle A \cong \angle A'$, $\angle B \cong \angle B'$, and $\angle C \cong \angle C'$. The sum of the three interior angles of a triangle is 180°.

$$\begin{aligned} \angle A + \angle B + \angle C &= 180 \\ 23 + 46 + \angle C &= 180 \\ 69 + \angle C &= 180 \\ -69 \quad\quad &\phantom{=} -69 \\ \angle C &= 111° \end{aligned}$$

Since $\angle C \cong \angle C'$, $\angle C' = 111°$.

**48. C:** The sum of the areas of the squares with side lengths equal to the legs of the triangle must be equal to the area of the square with side lengths equal to the hypotenuse. Thus, it must be true that $5^2 + x = 11^2$, where $x$ is the area of the square with a side length equal to the remaining leg of the right triangle. Solve for $x$.

$$\begin{aligned} 5^2 + x &= 11^2 \\ 25 + x &= 121 \\ -25 \quad &\phantom{=} -25 \\ x &= 96 \end{aligned}$$

**49. Part A: A:** Outliers are data points that drastically deviate from the pattern shown in the rest of the data. This point is lower than the rest of the data in the pattern.

**Part B: D:** This scatterplot depicts a downward trend. One variable increases while the other decreases. Thus, this is a negative association. Majority of the data is clustered around a line sloping from the top left to the bottom right. Therefore, it is a linear association.

**50. B:** Function N is linear and all answer choices are written in the form of $y = mx + b$. Function N's rate of change is 1 less than Function M's rate of change. Find the rate of change for Function M. Beginning at $(0, -1)$, the graph of Function M rises 4 and runs right 3 to the point $(3,3)$, therefore the rate of change is $\frac{4}{3}$ for Function M. Since Function N's rate of change is 1 less than Function M's rate of change, subtract 1 from $\frac{4}{3}$ to find the rate of change of Function N. A common denominator of 3 will need to be found to subtract.

$$\frac{4}{3} - 1 = \frac{4}{3} - \frac{3}{3} = \frac{1}{3}$$

Answer choice B is the only equation with a rate of change of $\frac{1}{3}$.

**51. C:** Substitute the given value, 5.5 inches, for the independent variable *x*, and solve for *y*.

$$y = 0.3(5.5) + 2$$
$$y = 1.65 + 2$$
$$y = 3.65$$

If it rained 5.5 inches in a month, the predicted growth for type A grass would be 3.65 inches.

**52. C:** Use the formula for the volume of a sphere. Substitute the given radius to solve for volume.

$$V = \frac{4}{3}\pi r^3$$
$$V = \frac{4}{3}(3.14)(6.4)^3$$
$$V = 1097.5\,ft^3$$

**53. B:** The given angles are alternate interior angles. According to the alternate interior angles theorem, when a transversal cuts across parallel lines, the alternate interior angles are congruent. Since lines $a$ and $b$ are parallel, it means that the two given angles are congruent. Solve the following equation for $x$.

$$2x + 5 = 3x - 25$$
$$2x + 30 = 3x$$
$$30 = x$$

Therefore, the value of $x$ is 30.

**54. A:** From left to right, the function begins by decreasing from $x = -5$ to $x = 1$ because the graph is falling. Even though the "piece" from $x = -5$ to $x = -3$ and the "piece" from $x = -3$ to $x = 1$ have different slopes, the function is still decreasing. There is no need to differentiate between the two segments since it continues to decrease. It is then constant from $x = 1$ to $x = 4$ because the interval is a horizontal line. The outputs are the same between $x = 1$ and $x = 4$. The last part of the graph is increasing because the graph is rising from $x = 4$ to $x = 6$.

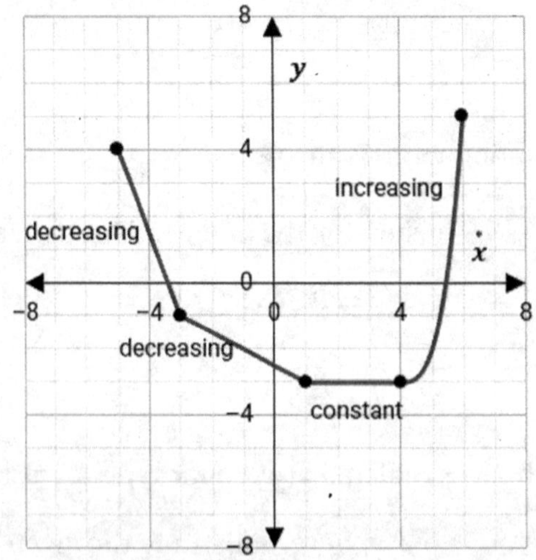


**55. D:** $\frac{170}{99}$ is given as a quotient in fraction form, so it is a rational number. A rational number can also be expressed as a terminating or repeating decimal. Long division converts a fraction to a decimal and must be carried out to determine whether it is a terminating or repeating decimal. Ignore the negative sign to divide. The numerator of 170 is the dividend and the denominator of 99 is the divisor. After dividing, the digits 7 and 1 repeat indefinitely, so $\frac{170}{99}$ is the repeating decimal $1.\overline{71}$. Terminating or repeating decimals fall under the category of rational numbers.

$$
\begin{array}{r}
1.7171 \\
99\overline{)170.000} \\
-99 \\
\hline
710 \\
-693 \\
\hline
170 \\
-99 \\
\hline
710 \\
-693 \\
\hline
170 \\
-99 \\
\hline
71
\end{array}
$$

# How to Overcome Test Anxiety

Just the thought of taking a test is enough to make most people a little nervous. A test is an important event that can have a long-term impact on your future, so it's important to take it seriously and it's natural to feel anxious about performing well. But just because anxiety is normal, that doesn't mean that it's helpful in test taking, or that you should simply accept it as part of your life. Anxiety can have a variety of effects. These effects can be mild, like making you feel slightly nervous, or severe, like blocking your ability to focus or remember even a simple detail.

If you experience test anxiety—whether severe or mild—it's important to know how to beat it. To discover this, first you need to understand what causes test anxiety.

## Causes of Test Anxiety

While we often think of anxiety as an uncontrollable emotional state, it can actually be caused by simple, practical things. One of the most common causes of test anxiety is that a person does not feel adequately prepared for their test. This feeling can be the result of many different issues such as poor study habits or lack of organization, but the most common culprit is time management. Starting to study too late, failing to organize your study time to cover all of the material, or being distracted while you study will mean that you're not well prepared for the test. This may lead to cramming the night before, which will cause you to be physically and mentally exhausted for the test. Poor time management also contributes to feelings of stress, fear, and hopelessness as you realize you are not well prepared but don't know what to do about it.

Other times, test anxiety is not related to your preparation for the test but comes from unresolved fear. This may be a past failure on a test, or poor performance on tests in general. It may come from comparing yourself to others who seem to be performing better or from the stress of living up to expectations. Anxiety may be driven by fears of the future—how failure on this test would affect your educational and career goals. These fears are often completely irrational, but they can still negatively impact your test performance.

## Elements of Test Anxiety

As mentioned earlier, test anxiety is considered to be an emotional state, but it has physical and mental components as well. Sometimes you may not even realize that you are suffering from test anxiety until you notice the physical symptoms. These can include trembling hands, rapid heartbeat, sweating, nausea, and tense muscles. Extreme anxiety may lead to fainting or vomiting. Obviously, any of these symptoms can have a negative impact on testing. It is important to recognize them as soon as they begin to occur so that you can address the problem before it damages your performance.

The mental components of test anxiety include trouble focusing and inability to remember learned information. During a test, your mind is on high alert, which can help you recall information and stay focused for an extended period of time. However, anxiety interferes with your mind's natural processes, causing you to blank out, even on the questions you know well. The strain of testing during anxiety makes it difficult to stay focused, especially on a test that may take several hours. Extreme anxiety can take a huge mental toll, making it difficult not only to recall test information but even to understand the test questions or pull your thoughts together.

## Effects of Test Anxiety

Test anxiety is like a disease—if left untreated, it will get progressively worse. Anxiety leads to poor performance, and this reinforces the feelings of fear and failure, which in turn lead to poor performances on subsequent tests. It can grow from a mild nervousness to a crippling condition. If allowed to progress, test anxiety can have a big impact on your schooling, and consequently on your future.

Test anxiety can spread to other parts of your life. Anxiety on tests can become anxiety in any stressful situation, and blanking on a test can turn into panicking in a job situation. But fortunately, you don't have to let anxiety rule your testing and determine your grades. There are a number of relatively simple steps you can take to move past anxiety and function normally on a test and in the rest of life.

## Physical Steps for Beating Test Anxiety

While test anxiety is a serious problem, the good news is that it can be overcome. It doesn't have to control your ability to think and remember information. While it may take time, you can begin taking steps today to beat anxiety.

Just as your first hint that you may be struggling with anxiety comes from the physical symptoms, the first step to treating it is also physical. Rest is crucial for having a clear, strong mind. If you are tired, it is much easier to give in to anxiety. But if you establish good sleep habits, your body and mind will be ready to perform optimally, without the strain of exhaustion. Additionally, sleeping well helps you to retain information better, so you're more likely to recall the answers when you see the test questions.

Getting good sleep means more than going to bed on time. It's important to allow your brain time to relax. Take study breaks from time to time so it doesn't get overworked, and don't study right before bed. Take time to rest your mind before trying to rest your body, or you may find it difficult to fall asleep.

Along with sleep, other aspects of physical health are important in preparing for a test. Good nutrition is vital for good brain function. Sugary foods and drinks may give a burst of energy but this burst is followed by a crash, both physically and emotionally. Instead, fuel your body with protein and vitamin-rich foods.

Also, drink plenty of water. Dehydration can lead to headaches and exhaustion, especially if your brain is already under stress from the rigors of the test. Particularly if your test is a long one, drink water during the breaks. And if possible, take an energy-boosting snack to eat between sections.

Along with sleep and diet, a third important part of physical health is exercise. Maintaining a steady workout schedule is helpful, but even taking 5-minute study breaks to walk can help get your blood pumping faster and clear your head. Exercise also releases endorphins, which contribute to a positive feeling and can help combat test anxiety.

When you nurture your physical health, you are also contributing to your mental health. If your body is healthy, your mind is much more likely to be healthy as well. So take time to rest, nourish your body with healthy food and water, and get moving as much as possible. Taking these physical steps will make you stronger and more able to take the mental steps necessary to overcome test anxiety.

## Mental Steps for Beating Test Anxiety

Working on the mental side of test anxiety can be more challenging, but as with the physical side, there are clear steps you can take to overcome it. As mentioned earlier, test anxiety often stems from lack of preparation, so the obvious solution is to prepare for the test. Effective studying may be the most important weapon you have for beating test anxiety, but you can and should employ several other mental tools to combat fear.

First, boost your confidence by reminding yourself of past success—tests or projects that you aced. If you're putting as much effort into preparing for this test as you did for those, there's no reason you should expect to fail here. Work hard to prepare; then trust your preparation.

Second, surround yourself with encouraging people. It can be helpful to find a study group, but be sure that the people you're around will encourage a positive attitude. If you spend time with others who are anxious or cynical, this will only contribute to your own anxiety. Look for others who are motivated to study hard from a desire to succeed, not from a fear of failure.

Third, reward yourself. A test is physically and mentally tiring, even without anxiety, and it can be helpful to have something to look forward to. Plan an activity following the test, regardless of the outcome, such as going to a movie or getting ice cream.

When you are taking the test, if you find yourself beginning to feel anxious, remind yourself that you know the material. Visualize successfully completing the test. Then take a few deep, relaxing breaths and return to it. Work through the questions carefully but with confidence, knowing that you are capable of succeeding.

Developing a healthy mental approach to test taking will also aid in other areas of life. Test anxiety affects more than just the actual test—it can be damaging to your mental health and even contribute to depression. It's important to beat test anxiety before it becomes a problem for more than testing.

## Study Strategy

Being prepared for the test is necessary to combat anxiety, but what does being prepared look like? You may study for hours on end and still not feel prepared. What you need is a strategy for test prep. The next few pages outline our recommended steps to help you plan out and conquer the challenge of preparation.

### Step 1: Scope Out the Test

Learn everything you can about the format (multiple choice, essay, etc.) and what will be on the test. Gather any study materials, course outlines, or sample exams that may be available. Not only will this help you to prepare, but knowing what to expect can help to alleviate test anxiety.

### Step 2: Map Out the Material

Look through the textbook or study guide and make note of how many chapters or sections it has. Then divide these over the time you have. For example, if a book has 15 chapters and you have five days to study, you need to cover three chapters each day. Even better, if you have the time, leave an extra day at the end for overall review after you have gone through the material in depth.

If time is limited, you may need to prioritize the material. Look through it and make note of which sections you think you already have a good grasp on, and which need review. While you are studying, skim quickly through the familiar sections and take more time on the challenging parts.

Write out your plan so you don't get lost as you go. Having a written plan also helps you feel more in control of the study, so anxiety is less likely to arise from feeling overwhelmed at the amount to cover.

## Step 3: Gather Your Tools

Decide what study method works best for you. Do you prefer to highlight in the book as you study and then go back over the highlighted portions? Or do you type out notes of the important information? Or is it helpful to make flashcards that you can carry with you? Assemble the pens, index cards, highlighters, post-it notes, and any other materials you may need so you won't be distracted by getting up to find things while you study.

If you're having a hard time retaining the information or organizing your notes, experiment with different methods. For example, try color-coding by subject with colored pens, highlighters, or post-it notes. If you learn better by hearing, try recording yourself reading your notes so you can listen while in the car, working out, or simply sitting at your desk. Ask a friend to quiz you from your flashcards, or try teaching someone the material to solidify it in your mind.

## Step 4: Create Your Environment

It's important to avoid distractions while you study. This includes both the obvious distractions like visitors and the subtle distractions like an uncomfortable chair (or a too-comfortable couch that makes you want to fall asleep). Set up the best study environment possible: good lighting and a comfortable work area. If background music helps you focus, you may want to turn it on, but otherwise keep the room quiet. If you are using a computer to take notes, be sure you don't have any other windows open, especially applications like social media, games, or anything else that could distract you. Silence your phone and turn off notifications. Be sure to keep water close by so you stay hydrated while you study (but avoid unhealthy drinks and snacks).

Also, take into account the best time of day to study. Are you freshest first thing in the morning? Try to set aside some time then to work through the material. Is your mind clearer in the afternoon or evening? Schedule your study session then. Another method is to study at the same time of day that you will take the test, so that your brain gets used to working on the material at that time and will be ready to focus at test time.

## Step 5: Study!

Once you have done all the study preparation, it's time to settle into the actual studying. Sit down, take a few moments to settle your mind so you can focus, and begin to follow your study plan. Don't give in to distractions or let yourself procrastinate. This is your time to prepare so you'll be ready to fearlessly approach the test. Make the most of the time and stay focused.

Of course, you don't want to burn out. If you study too long you may find that you're not retaining the information very well. Take regular study breaks. For example, taking five minutes out of every hour to walk briskly, breathing deeply and swinging your arms, can help your mind stay fresh.

As you get to the end of each chapter or section, it's a good idea to do a quick review. Remind yourself of what you learned and work on any difficult parts. When you feel that you've mastered the material, move on to the next part. At the end of your study session, briefly skim through your notes again.

But while review is helpful, cramming last minute is NOT. If at all possible, work ahead so that you won't need to fit all your study into the last day. Cramming overloads your brain with more information than it can process and retain, and your tired mind may struggle to recall even previously learned information when it is overwhelmed with last-minute study. Also, the urgent nature of cramming and the stress placed on your brain contribute to anxiety. You'll be more likely to go to the test feeling unprepared and having trouble thinking clearly.

So don't cram, and don't stay up late before the test, even just to review your notes at a leisurely pace. Your brain needs rest more than it needs to go over the information again. In fact, plan to finish your studies by noon or early afternoon the day before the test. Give your brain the rest of the day to relax or focus on other things, and get a good night's sleep. Then you will be fresh for the test and better able to recall what you've studied.

### Step 6: Take a Practice Test

Many courses offer sample tests, either online or in the study materials. This is an excellent resource to check whether you have mastered the material, as well as to prepare for the test format and environment.

Check the test format ahead of time: the number of questions, the type (multiple choice, free response, etc.), and the time limit. Then create a plan for working through them. For example, if you have 30 minutes to take a 60-question test, your limit is 30 seconds per question. Spend less time on the questions you know well so that you can take more time on the difficult ones.

If you have time to take several practice tests, take the first one open book, with no time limit. Work through the questions at your own pace and make sure you fully understand them. Gradually work up to taking a test under test conditions: sit at a desk with all study materials put away and set a timer. Pace yourself to make sure you finish the test with time to spare and go back to check your answers if you have time.

After each test, check your answers. On the questions you missed, be sure you understand why you missed them. Did you misread the question (tests can use tricky wording)? Did you forget the information? Or was it something you hadn't learned? Go back and study any shaky areas that the practice tests reveal.

Taking these tests not only helps with your grade, but also aids in combating test anxiety. If you're already used to the test conditions, you're less likely to worry about it, and working through tests until you're scoring well gives you a confidence boost. Go through the practice tests until you feel comfortable, and then you can go into the test knowing that you're ready for it.

## Test Tips

On test day, you should be confident, knowing that you've prepared well and are ready to answer the questions. But aside from preparation, there are several test day strategies you can employ to maximize your performance.

First, as stated before, get a good night's sleep the night before the test (and for several nights before that, if possible). Go into the test with a fresh, alert mind rather than staying up late to study.

Try not to change too much about your normal routine on the day of the test. It's important to eat a nutritious breakfast, but if you normally don't eat breakfast at all, consider eating just a protein bar. If you're a coffee drinker, go ahead and have your normal coffee. Just make sure you time it so that the caffeine doesn't wear off right in the middle of your test. Avoid sugary beverages, and drink enough water to stay hydrated but not so much that you need a restroom break 10 minutes into the test. If your test isn't first thing in the morning, consider going for a walk or doing a light workout before the test to get your blood flowing.

Allow yourself enough time to get ready, and leave for the test with plenty of time to spare so you won't have the anxiety of scrambling to arrive in time. Another reason to be early is to select a good seat. It's helpful to sit away from doors and windows, which can be distracting. Find a good seat, get out your supplies, and settle your mind before the test begins.

When the test begins, start by going over the instructions carefully, even if you already know what to expect. Make sure you avoid any careless mistakes by following the directions.

Then begin working through the questions, pacing yourself as you've practiced. If you're not sure on an answer, don't spend too much time on it, and don't let it shake your confidence. Either skip it and come back later, or eliminate as many wrong answers as possible and guess among the remaining ones. Don't dwell on these questions as you continue—put them out of your mind and focus on what lies ahead.

Be sure to read all of the answer choices, even if you're sure the first one is the right answer. Sometimes you'll find a better one if you keep reading. But don't second-guess yourself if you do immediately know the answer. Your gut instinct is usually right. Don't let test anxiety rob you of the information you know.

If you have time at the end of the test (and if the test format allows), go back and review your answers. Be cautious about changing any, since your first instinct tends to be correct, but make sure you didn't misread any of the questions or accidentally mark the wrong answer choice. Look over any you skipped and make an educated guess.

At the end, leave the test feeling confident. You've done your best, so don't waste time worrying about your performance or wishing you could change anything. Instead, celebrate the successful completion of this test. And finally, use this test to learn how to deal with anxiety even better next time.

**Review Video: Test Anxiety**
Visit mometrix.com/academy and enter code: 100340

## Important Qualification

Not all anxiety is created equal. If your test anxiety is causing major issues in your life beyond the classroom or testing center, or if you are experiencing troubling physical symptoms related to your anxiety, it may be a sign of a serious physiological or psychological condition. If this sounds like your situation, we strongly encourage you to seek professional help.

# How to Overcome Your Fear of Math

Not again. You're sitting in math class, look down at your test, and immediately start to panic. Your stomach is in knots, your heart is racing, and you break out in a cold sweat. You're staring at the paper, but everything looks like it's written in a foreign language. Even though you studied, you're blanking out on how to begin solving these problems.

Does this sound familiar? If so, then you're not alone! You may be like millions of other people who experience math anxiety. Anxiety about performing well in math is a common experience for students of all ages. In this article, we'll discuss what math anxiety is, common misconceptions about learning math, and tips and strategies for overcoming math anxiety.

## What Is Math Anxiety?

Psychologist Mark H. Ashcraft explains math anxiety as a feeling of tension, apprehension, or fear that interferes with math performance. Having math anxiety negatively impacts people's beliefs about themselves and what they can achieve. It hinders achievement within the math classroom and affects the successful application of mathematics in the real world.

### Symptoms and Signs of Math Anxiety

To overcome math anxiety, you must recognize its symptoms. Becoming aware of the signs of math anxiety is the first step in addressing and resolving these fears.

#### *Negative Self-Talk*

If you have math anxiety, you've most likely said at least one of these statements to yourself:

- "I hate math."
- "I'm not good at math."
- "I'm not a math person."

The way we speak to ourselves and think about ourselves matters. Our thoughts become our words, our words become our actions, and our actions become our habits. Thinking negatively about math creates a self-fulfilling prophecy. In other words, if you take an idea as a fact, then it will come true because your behaviors will align to match it.

#### *Avoidance*

Some people who are fearful or anxious about math will tend to avoid it altogether. Avoidance can manifest in the following ways:

- Lack of engagement with math content
- Not completing homework and other assignments
- Not asking for help when needed
- Skipping class
- Avoiding math-related courses and activities

Avoidance is one of the most harmful impacts of math anxiety. If you steer clear of math at all costs, then you can't set yourself up for the success you deserve.

### Lack of Motivation

Students with math anxiety may experience a lack of motivation. They may struggle to find the incentive to get engaged with what they view as a frightening subject. These students are often overwhelmed, making it difficult for them to complete or even start math assignments.

### Procrastination

Another symptom of math anxiety is procrastination. Students may voluntarily delay or postpone their classwork and assignments, even if they know there will be a negative consequence for doing so. Additionally, they may choose to wait until the last minute to start projects and homework, even when they know they need more time to put forth their best effort.

### Physiological Reactions

Many people with a fear of math experience physiological side effects. These may include an increase in heart rate, sweatiness, shakiness, nausea, and irregular breathing. These symptoms make it difficult to focus on the math content, causing the student even more stress and fear.

### Strong Emotional Responses

Math anxiety also affects people on an emotional level. Responding to math content with strong emotions such as panic, anger, or despair can be a sign of math anxiety.

### Low Test Scores and Performance

Low achievement can be both a symptom and a cause of math anxiety. When someone does not take the steps needed to perform well on tests and assessments, they are less likely to pass. The more they perform poorly, the more they accept this poor performance as a fact that can't be changed.

### Feeling Alone

People who experience math anxiety feel like they are the only ones struggling, even if the math they are working on is challenging to many people. Feeling isolated in what they perceive as failure can trigger tension or nervousness.

### Feeling of Permanency

Math anxiety can feel very permanent. You may assume that you are naturally bad at math and always will be. Viewing math as a natural ability rather than a skill that can be learned causes people to believe that nothing will help them improve. They take their current math abilities as fact and assume that they can't be changed. As a result, they give up, stop trying to improve, and avoid engaging with math altogether.

### Lack of Confidence

People with low self-confidence in math tend to feel awkward and incompetent when asked to solve a math problem. They don't feel comfortable taking chances or risks when problem-solving because they second-guess themselves and assume they are incorrect. They don't trust in their ability to learn the content and solve problems correctly.

### Panic

A general sense of unexplained panic is also a sign of math anxiety. You may feel a sudden sense of fear that triggers physical reactions, even when there is no apparent reason for such a response.

## Causes Of Math Anxiety

Math anxiety can start at a young age and may have one or more underlying causes. Common causes of math anxiety include the following:

### *The Attitude of Parents or Guardians*

Parents often put pressure on their children to perform well in school. Although their intentions are usually good, this pressure can lead to anxiety, especially if the student is struggling with a subject or class.

Perhaps your parents or others in your life hold negative predispositions about math based on their own experiences. For instance, if your mother once claimed she was not good at math, then you might have incorrectly interpreted this as a predisposed trait that was passed down to you.

### *Teacher Influence*

Students often pick up on their teachers' attitudes about the content being taught. If a teacher is happy and excited about math, students are more likely to mirror these emotions. However, if a teacher lacks enthusiasm or genuine interest, then students are more inclined to disengage.

Teachers have a responsibility to cultivate a welcoming classroom culture that is accepting of mistakes. When teachers blame students for not understanding a concept, they create a hostile classroom environment where mistakes are not tolerated. This tension increases student stress and anxiety, creating conditions that are not conducive to inquiry and learning. Instead, when teachers normalize mistakes as a natural part of the problem-solving process, they give their students the freedom to explore and grapple with the math content. In such an environment, students feel comfortable taking chances because they are not afraid of being wrong.

Students need teachers that can help when they're having problems understanding difficult concepts. In doing so, educators may need to change how they teach the content. Since different people have unique learning styles, it's the job of the teacher to adapt to the needs of each student. Additionally, teachers should encourage students to explore alternate problem-solving strategies, even if it's not the preferred method of the educator.

### *Fear of Being Wrong*

Embarrassing situations can be traumatic, especially for young children and adolescents. These experiences can stay with people through their adult lives. Those with math anxiety may experience a fear of being wrong, especially in front of a group of peers. This fear can be paralyzing, interfering with the student's concentration and ability to focus on the problem at hand.

### *Timed Assessments*

Timed assessments can help improve math fluency, but they often create unnecessary pressure for students to complete an unrealistic number of problems within a specified timeframe. Many studies have shown that timed assessments often result in increased levels of anxiety, reducing a student's overall competence and ability to problem-solve.

## Debunking Math Myths

There are lots of myths about math that are related to the causes and development of math-related anxiety. Although these myths have been proven to be false, many people take them as fact. Let's go over a few of the most common myths about learning math.

### Myth: Men Are Better at Math Than Women

Math has a reputation for being a male-dominant subject, but this doesn't mean that men are inherently better at math than women. Many famous mathematical discoveries have been made by women. Katherine Johnson, Dame Mary Lucy Cartwright, and Marjorie Lee Brown are just a few of the many famous women mathematicians. Expecting to be good or bad at math because of your gender sets you up for stress and confusion. Math is a skill that can be learned, just like cooking or riding a bike.

### Myth: There Is Only One Good Way to Solve Math Problems

There are many ways to get the correct answer when it comes to math. No two people have the same brain, so everyone takes a slightly different approach to problem-solving. Moreover, there isn't one way of problem-solving that's superior to another. Your way of working through a problem might differ from someone else's, and that is okay. Math can be a highly individualized process, so the best method for you should be the one that makes you feel the most comfortable and makes the most sense to you.

### Myth: Math Requires a Good Memory

For many years, mathematics was taught through memorization. However, learning in such a way hinders the development of critical thinking and conceptual understanding. These skill sets are much more valuable than basic memorization. For instance, you might be great at memorizing mathematical formulas, but if you don't understand what they mean, then you can't apply them to different scenarios in the real world. When a student is working from memory, they are limited in the strategies available to them to problem-solve. In other words, they assume there is only one correct way to do the math, which is the method they memorized. Having a variety of problem-solving options can help students figure out which method works best for them. Additionally, it provides students with a better understanding of how and why certain mathematical strategies work. While memorization can be helpful in some instances, it is not an absolute requirement for mathematicians.

### Myth: Math Is Not Creative

Math requires imagination and intuition. Contrary to popular belief, it is a highly creative field. Mathematical creativity can help in developing new ways to think about and solve problems. Many people incorrectly assume that all things are either creative or analytical. However, this black-and-white view is limiting because the field of mathematics involves both creativity and logic.

### Myth: Math Isn't Supposed To Be Fun

Whoever told you that math isn't supposed to be fun is a liar. There are tons of math-based activities and games that foster friendly competition and engagement. Math is often best learned through play, and lots of mobile apps and computer games exemplify this.

Additionally, math can be an exceptionally collaborative and social experience. Studying or working through problems with a friend often makes the process a lot more fun. The excitement and satisfaction of solving a difficult problem with others is quite rewarding. Math can be fun if you look for ways to make it more collaborative and enjoyable.

### Myth: Not Everyone Is Capable of Learning Math

There's no such thing as a "math person." Although many people think that you're either good at math or you're not, this is simply not true. Everyone is capable of learning and applying mathematics. However, not everyone learns the same way. Since each person has a different learning style, the trick is to find the strategies and learning tools that work best for you. Some people learn best through hands-on experiences, and others find success through the use of visual aids. Others are auditory learners and learn best by hearing and listening. When people are overwhelmed or feel that math is too hard, it's often because they haven't found the learning strategy that works best for them.

### Myth: Good Mathematicians Work Quickly and Never Make Mistakes

There is no prize for finishing first in math. It's not a race, and speed isn't a measure of your ability. Good mathematicians take their time to ensure their work is accurate. As you gain more experience and practice, you will naturally become faster and more confident.

Additionally, everyone makes mistakes, including good mathematicians. Mistakes are a normal part of the problem-solving process, and they're not a bad thing. The important thing is that we take the time to learn from our mistakes, understand where our misconceptions are, and move forward.

### Myth: You Don't Need Math in the Real World

Our day-to-day lives are so infused with mathematical concepts that we often don't even realize when we're using math in the real world. In fact, most people tend to underestimate how much we do math in our everyday lives. It's involved in an enormous variety of daily activities such as shopping, baking, finances, and gardening, as well as in many careers, including architecture, nursing, design, and sales.

## Tips and Strategies for Overcoming Math Anxiety

If your anxiety is getting in the way of your level of mathematical engagement, then there are lots of steps you can take. Check out the strategies below to start building confidence in math today.

### Focus on Understanding, Not Memorization

Don't drive yourself crazy trying to memorize every single formula or mathematical process. Instead, shift your attention to understanding concepts. Those who prioritize memorization over conceptual understanding tend to have lower achievement levels in math. Students who memorize may be able to complete some math, but they don't understand the process well enough to apply it to different situations. Memorization comes with time and practice, but it won't help alleviate math anxiety. On the other hand, conceptual understanding will give you the building blocks of knowledge you need to build up your confidence.

### Replace Negative Self-Talk with Positive Self-Talk

Start to notice how you think about yourself. Whenever you catch yourself thinking something negative, try replacing that thought with a positive affirmation. Instead of continuing the negative thought, pause to reframe the situation. For ideas on how to get started, take a look at the table below:

| Instead of thinking... | Try thinking... |
|---|---|
| "I can't do this math."<br>"I'm not a math person." | "I'm up for the challenge, and I'm training my brain in math." |
| "This problem is too hard." | "This problem is hard, so this might take some time and effort. I know I can do this." |
| "I give up." | "What strategies can help me solve this problem?" |
| "I made a mistake, so I'm not good at this." | "Everyone makes mistakes. Mistakes help me to grow and understand." |
| "I'll never be smart enough." | "I can figure this out, and I am smart enough." |

### Practice Mindfulness

Practicing mindfulness and focusing on your breathing can help alleviate some of the physical symptoms of math anxiety. By taking deep breaths, you can remind your nervous system that you are not in immediate danger. Doing so will reduce your heart rate and help with any irregular breathing or shakiness. Taking the edge off of the physiological effects of anxiety will clear your mind, allowing your brain to focus its energy on problem-solving.

### Do Some Math Every Day

Think about learning math as if you were learning a foreign language. If you don't use it, you lose it. If you don't practice your math skills regularly, you'll have a harder time achieving comprehension and fluency. Set some amount of time aside each day, even if it's just for a few minutes, to practice. It might take some discipline to build a habit around this, but doing so will help increase your mathematical self-assurance.

### Use All of Your Resources

Everyone has a different learning style, and there are plenty of resources out there to support all learners. When you get stuck on a math problem, think about the tools you have access to, and use them when applicable. Such resources may include flashcards, graphic organizers, study guides, interactive notebooks, and peer study groups. All of these are great tools to accommodate your individual learning style. Finding the tools and resources that work for your learning style will give you the confidence you need to succeed.

### Realize That You Aren't Alone

Remind yourself that lots of other people struggle with math anxiety, including teachers, nurses, and even successful mathematicians. You aren't the only one who panics when faced with a new or challenging problem. It's probably much more common than you think. Realizing that you aren't alone in your experience can help put some distance between yourself and the emotions you feel about math. It also helps to normalize the anxiety and shift your perspective.

### Ask Questions

If there's a concept you don't understand and you've tried everything you can, then it's okay to ask for help! You can always ask your teacher or professor for help. If you're not learning math in a traditional classroom, you may want to join a study group, work with a tutor, or talk to your friends. More often than not, you aren't the only one of your peers who needs clarity on a mathematical concept. Seeking understanding is a great way to increase self-confidence in math.

### Remember That There's More Than One Way To Solve A Problem

Since everyone learns differently, it's best to focus on understanding a math problem with an approach that makes sense to you. If the way it's being taught is confusing to you, don't give up. Instead, work to understand the problem using a different technique. There's almost always more than one problem-solving method when it comes to math. Don't get stressed if one of them doesn't make sense to you. Instead, shift your focus to what does make sense. Chances are high that you know more than you think you do.

### Visualization

Visualization is the process of creating images in your mind's eye. Picture yourself as a successful, confident mathematician. Think about how you would feel and how you would behave. What would your work area look like? How would you organize your belongings? The more you focus on something, the more likely you are to achieve it. Visualizing teaches your brain that you can achieve whatever it is that you want. Thinking about success in mathematics will lead to acting like a successful mathematician. This, in turn, leads to actual success.

### Focus on the Easiest Problems First

To increase your confidence when working on a math test or assignment, try solving the easiest problems first. Doing so will remind you that you are successful in math and that you do have what it takes. This process will increase your belief in yourself, giving you the confidence you need to tackle more complex problems.

### Find a Support Group

A study buddy, tutor, or peer group can go a long way in decreasing math-related anxiety. Such support systems offer lots of benefits, including a safe place to ask questions, additional practice with mathematical concepts, and an understanding of other problem-solving explanations that may work better for you. Equipping yourself with a support group is one of the fastest ways to eliminate math anxiety.

### Reward Yourself for Working Hard

Recognize the amount of effort you're putting in to overcome your math anxiety. It's not an easy task, so you deserve acknowledgement. Surround yourself with people who will provide you with the positive reinforcement you deserve.

## Remember, You Can Do This!

Conquering a fear of math can be challenging, but there are lots of strategies that can help you out. Your own beliefs about your mathematical capabilities can limit your potential. Working toward a growth mindset can have a tremendous impact on decreasing math-related anxiety and building confidence. By knowing the symptoms of math anxiety and recognizing common misconceptions about learning math, you can develop a plan to address your fear of math. Utilizing the strategies discussed can help you overcome this anxiety and build the confidence you need to succeed.

## Online Resources

Due to our efforts to try to keep this book to a manageable length, we've created a link that will give you access to all of your online resources:

**mometrix.com/resources719/terranextg8math**

# It's Your Moment, Let's Celebrate It!

**Share your story @mometrixtestpreparation**